M000251216

"This is a timely, compelling, well-ar
Christians wondering how to respond t
book astutely dispels, with a deeply per
conceptions, awakens us to see our 'neighbors' differently, and calls us to
our welcoming responsibilities to the immigrant 'other' among us. Highly
recommended!"

—**Ronald T. Michener**, Professor and Chair of Systematic Theology,
Evangelical Theological Faculty, Belgium

"This book is the considered outcome of years of experience of, and reflection on, immigration, from inside and from outside. It is an informed and
informative book about one of the most troubling and unsettling hap-
penings of our time. It is instructive on many levels: the legal, the ethical,
the political, the religious. Yet it never loses touch with the vulnerable
humanity of those caught in the reality and experience of immigration,
forced and unforced. The book is very balanced in taking into account the
many sides of the crucial issues at stake. I found it to be calm, judicious,
wise, compassionate, and Christian in its account and in its judgments.
Warmly recommended."

—**William Desmond**, David Cook Chair in Philosophy, Villanova University

"*Entertaining Angels Unaware* is an informative and compassionately written book, which offers a balanced and thoughtful approach to immigration
through a theological lens. By using a learned but conversational tone, Dr.
Philip Gottschalk helps the reader look beyond themselves to their larger
community. As a book which is both pastoral and reflective, *Entertaining
Angels Unaware* will be a necessary part of a more complete spiritual forma-
tion for today's globally engaged Christian."

—**Cristina Richie**, Lecturer in Philosophy and Ethics of Technology,
Delft University of Technology, Netherlands

"Phil Gottschalk is an American scholar who has spent decades overseas
serving others. In *Entertaining Angels Unaware* he blends stories and insights
from these many years of experience with philosophical and theological reflection in order to produce a book that offers both theoretical and practical
understanding of the attitude that Christians—and by extension people in
general—should have toward immigrants. That attitude is, in a word, 'love.'
This is a timely and needed corrective to the reactionary responses that have
typified American attitudes in recent years."

—**Michael S. Jones**, Professor of Philosophy and Religion, Liberty University,
President, Virginia Philosophical Association, and Executive Editor, *Journal for
the Study of Religions and Ideologies*

Entertaining Angels Unaware

Entertaining Angels Unaware

Welcoming the Immigrant Other

Philip A. Gottschalk

FOREWORD BY
David W. Shenk

CASCADE *Books* • Eugene, Oregon

ENTERTAINING ANGELS UNAWARE
Welcoming the Immigrant Other

Cascade Books
An Imprint of Wipf and Stock Publishers
199 W. 8th Ave., Suite 3
Eugene, OR 97401

www.wipfandstock.com

PAPERBACK ISBN: 978-1-7252-5947-8
HARDCOVER ISBN: 978-1-7252-5948-5
EBOOK ISBN: 978-1-7252-5949-2

Cataloguing-in-Publication data:

Names: Gottschalk, Philip A., author. | Shenk, David W., foreword.

Title: Entertaining angels unaware : welcoming the immigrant other / by Philip A. Gottschalk ; foreword by David W. Shenk.

Description: Eugene, OR: Cascade Books, 2021 | Includes bibliographical references.

Identifiers: ISBN 978-1-7252-5947-8 (paperback) | ISBN 978-1-7252-5948-5 (hardcover) | ISBN 978-1-7252-5949-2 (ebook)

Subjects: LCSH: Emigration and immigration—Religious aspects—Christianity | Emigration and immigration in the Bible

Classification: BR115.E45 G68 2021 (print) | BR115.E45 (ebook)

Dedication

PEOPLE ARE MIGRATING FROM one nation to another in massive numbers in our generation. Many are fleeing violence and war, while others seek a better life for themselves and their families. How do governments respond to these crises in the US and in Europe? What are the laws? How should we look at these events? How can we help?

My family and I have lived through several periods of time which have affected my thinking deeply about migrants and refugees:

First, when my mother and my future mother-in-law helped our church in Pittsburgh to receive and care for a Vietnamese refugee family in the 1970s and by their example taught us to love immigrants.

Second, when I worked with Russian immigrants in Chicago while I was in seminary.

Third, when we as missionaries lived in Serbia, learned Serbian, and taught in a Bible school for Serbo-Croatian speakers in Vienna during the late 1980s and 1990s during the rise of national hostility, the breakup of Yugoslavia, and the war in Bosnia. Many of our brave friends served selflessly during the war.

Fourth, when we lived in Belgium in the late 1990s, where I studied and completed a PhD—a lovely country with its own ethnic divisions and lately many problems with terrorist activity.

Fifth, from 2000 to the present in the Netherlands, where my wife and I teach at Tyndale Theological Seminary in which at any given time twenty or more nationalities are represented in each class, and where I have taught a class on "War, Peace, and Peacemaking" for many years.

Sixth, since 2012 in Ukraine, where I regularly travel to teach at Zaporozhe Bible Seminary—a region deeply affected by war, political aggression, and the suffering of refugees and internally displaced peoples.

Seventh, my brief but (for me) significant time as a volunteer on Lesvos, Greece, in 2017, where I was confronted by the enormity of the need of those seeking refuge there.

In this book, I share my stories and those of my friends and colleagues, try to explain the situation, and suggest what you, the reader, can do. Thank you to all our students in Vienna, in Serbia, in Ukraine, and now in Amsterdam, who have changed our lives forever, giving us hearts of compassion for refugees and IDPs.

I thank all who allowed their stories to be used and especially Sue Kirby, my editor. God has his reasons for the "angels" he sends our way. May we respond in the awareness that, as Jesus said, "whatever you do for the least of these, you do for Me."

Philip A. Gottschalk, PhD

Chair, Division of Theological and Historical Studies
Professor of Philosophy
Tyndale Theological Seminary
Egelantierstraat 1
1171JM Badhoevedorp
The Netherlands
Serving under Eastern Mennonite Mission

Contents

Foreword by David W. Shenk

I WRITE THIS FOREWORD at a time wherein eighty million immigrants encircle the world looking for refuge. These migrants are mostly within the family of Abraham. They are Jewish, Muslim, Christian, and multitudes of the homeless. I write at a time when, in renewed ways, the family of Abraham needs to own commitment to peacemaking. For these children of Abraham were themselves refugees or orphans: we remember that Jesus was an orphan boy, Muhammad was an orphan son, Ishmael was sent away from home, and Moses was a castaway.

That is why I need this book in my commitment to protecting the orphan and the alien. Welcoming the alien not only blesses the alien but also the nations and communities who care.

I need this book to remember that Jesus' friends were killed by terrorists. I need this book to remember that God invites us to protect those who are entwined in terrorist threats. I need this book, for it is grounded in biblical revelation. I need this book, for it reminds me to open my arms and invite the stranger and that neighbor whom I have not yet learned to know. I need this book, for it reminds me to confront the evil doer and to protect the helpless. I need this book, for it commands me to confront the scoundrel while protecting those who maliciously take from the poor. I need this book, for it reminds me to hold our governments responsible to act wisely and in the ways of justice. I need this book, for it reminds me that our lecherous evil doers will destroy the hopes of the poor if they can do so. I need this book, for it describes for me stories of men and women of good will who live within the current global village, who crisscross our tent cities in our modern world, and who do their very best to find the way for the worthy to escape. I need this book, for it reminds me of the hope of Christ who seeks to bind the wounds and bring families to restoration and hope wherever it may be found.

This book through its stories shares of heroic commitment to bring healing to the refugee and those who in Christ's name walk those refugee paths from people to people giving hope. This book reveals that people of goodwill are not alone for Jesus is also there. He is also within the lives of the refugee and orphan.

Preface

WHEN I BEGAN WRITING this book I had hoped to do more than I was able to. I did not want this book to be merely a collection of anecdotes. In fact, I have two main points. The first is that we need to have compassion on refugees and immigrants. The second is that we must be involved in helping refugees, internally displaced people (IDPs), and immigrants.

My concern is that we as individuals may become so overwhelmed by the magnitude of the problem that we "switch off." Even as I researched this book I found myself overwhelmed by the immensity and complexity of this problem of refugees, internally displaced people, and immigrants. Perhaps we all feel this way as we watch the nightly news or follow a news feed: there are millions of refugees, millions of internally displaced people, millions of immigrants . . . ; there are so many different types of refugees, internally displaced people and immigrants . . . ; sects and factions: Sunni, Shi'ia, Sufi, Ahmaddiya Muslims, Yazidis, Marionite Christians, Orthodox Christians, Mar Sargus and Mar Thomas Christians, Falasha Jews, Coptic Christians . . . . Who or what are they all? The list goes on and on.

How can an ordinary person understand all of these distinctions? How can a simple citizen know how and when to engage and with whom?

Of course, any country must be careful about whom it allows to immigrate and to what degree we as citizens personally become involved, but the main question is: Do we care? Do we have compassion on those who have been driven from their homes by war and persecution? Do we want to help?

In one sense the answer is simple: Look around you. See the immigrant, the refugee, the stranger, as a real person. Have compassion and want to help. With the numbers of refugees and immigrants, chances are you will find some very nearby you. Churches and communities are already involved helping these unfortunate people. Usually churches and community organizations are short-handed and need help. Perhaps that is where we might go.

If we wish to look further, governmental and non-governmental agencies have very developed programs in which we can have a part. Usually these agencies are very happy to have volunteers or contributions. Even if we may not be able ourselves to help physically, we might be able to share our means to help. Sometimes just collecting old clothing and furniture and helping immigrants have adequate clothing can help (e.g., the Netherlands is a lot colder than Syria). A couple members of our church here in the Netherlands helped a handicapped immigrant who has no other family to prepare and furnish her apartment with donations. Perhaps we could give a ride to someone, bringing them to church or taking them to the market. We could help an immigrant or immigrant family to understand how bill paying works and how apartment regulations work, for instance when they are allowed use a communal washing machine.

We take many things for granted like knowing the difference between a credit and a debit card. Even help with simple things is welcome.

This book is made up of three sections. The first section is about our fear of immigrants and biblical and practical ways we can engage with immigrants. The second section contains chapters which help explain how one becomes a refugee and an immigrant. The third section tells about my experiences with refugees and immigrants.

Part I: Welcoming Strangers

Chapter 1: **Welcoming Strangers . . . or Terrorists?**

TERRORISM IS DEFINED AS "the unlawful use of violence and intimidation, especially against civilians, in the pursuit of political aims."[1] We have all seen the face of terror on TV. There are constant reminders on the news when those seeking to advance some cause use violence against civilians to achieve their goals.

I had wanted to avoid addressing terrorism, because I do not believe it is really the problem when we discuss immigration of refugees into the US. Legal immigration, becoming a refugee and following the legal path, which amounts to "extreme vetting," does not allow for the immigration of terrorists. However, after thinking about it. I decided that the topic could not be left out. In fact, I realized that I should address this fear first.

A common misconception is that the 9/11 terrorists were immigrants. In fact, none of the 9/11 terrorists were US nationals, neither born in the US or naturalized. They entered the US on business, tourist, or student visas.

There have been some shootings in the US carried out by US citizens, of Muslim descent. For instance, one terrorist attack was that carried out by Syed Farook and Tashfeen Malik on December 5, 2015, in San Bernadino, California.[2] Farook had been born in Illinois. His wife was a permanent legal resident of the US (being married to a US citizen). She held a Pakistani passport. She was not processed on a refugee visa. She was processed as a K-1 fiancé(e) visa, and so was not scrutinized as refugees are.[3] The couple were not part of any terrorist cell. They represent perhaps the worst sort of terrorist, because there was very little, if anything, that anyone could have done to foresee and prevent their actions.

Mustafa Kuko, the director of the Islamic Center of Riverside, where Syed and Tashfeen celebrated their marriage and where they had attended, was shocked by their actions. He said when interviewed:

"He is someone who used to listen to my sermons, my talks here," said Mustafa Kuko, director of the Islamic Center of Riverside. "I sat up last night thinking about him and what's happened." Kuko has trouble understanding how Farook could have betrayed the very principles of his religion. "We're told in Islam if you take one human life, it's as if you've taken all of mankind."[4]

Other Islamic groups condemned the shooting, including the Ahmadiyya Muslim Community. I did not know who the Ahmadiyya Muslims were before I came to the Netherlands. In short, because they believe that Mirza Ghulam Ahmad was the new Prophet, they are rejected by "mainline" Muslims. Ahmad combined the ideas of many of the world's religions, but above all he sought peaceful conversion. (Ahmad was a figure similar to Bahá'u'lláh, the founder of the Bahá'i faith.) I ran into a group of Ahmadiyya Muslims in our local mall.

Our neighborhood is a planned community here in the Netherlands, with a shopping center in the middle of the neighborhood. There are mainly row houses on the one side of the mall and apartment buildings on the other side. Many of those living in the apartment buildings are Muslims: Turks or Moroccans. One day, I saw a man addressing a group of mostly Muslim women and some children in our small shopping mall. I guessed that he was speaking in Arabic or Turkish—it was not Dutch, in any event. As he spoke and I watched, a tall Muslim man in a white caftan with a white cap, like a small fez, came up and listened for a while. The tall fellow then circulated among the women speaking to each one until all the women left. The speaker then went and sat down, and manned his table of literature. I took a brochure and found out that they were representatives of the Ahmaddiyya Community in The Hague, the seat of government of the Netherlands. I will quote from their website to show that their views, at least, are not what we might expect from Muslims. Did you know some Muslims are pacifists?

The Ahmadiyya Muslim Community believes that God sent Ahmad, like Jesus, to end religious wars, condemn bloodshed and reinstitute morality, justice and peace. Ahmad's advent brought about an unprecedented era of Islamic revival. He divested Islam of fanatical beliefs and practices by vigorously championing Islam's true and essential teachings. He also recognized the noble teachings of the great religious founders and saints, including Zoroaster, Abraham, Moses, Jesus, Krishna, Buddha, Confucius, Lao Tzu and Guru Nanak, and explained how such teachings converged into the one true Islam.

The Ahmadiyya Muslim Community is the leading Islamic organization to categorically reject terrorism in any form. Over a century ago, Ahmad emphatically declared that an aggressive "jihad by the sword" has no place in Islam.[5]

So, whatever we might think we know about Muslims, we're probably wrong unless we have studied Islam. While we might argue that the Ahmadiyya Community is a sect and a small one, my point is still the same: Islam is a very large religion with many sects and groupings. We can't simply just lump all Muslims together.

Still, some terrorist acts continue to occur in America and elsewhere and they often result in tragic consequences. Some solutions for the domestic terrorist threat in the US range from the ridiculous to the insane. Some argue for the outlawing of all firearms, except for law enforcement and the military. Those most vociferous about stopping terrorism are probably the least likely to accept such a solution.[6] Some others would argue for the internment and deportation of all Muslims from the USA. To me this is frankly illogical and even dangerous.

How can we decide that because a few people of one faith are extremists that all law-abiding citizens of that faith should be deported? The argument "They weren't born here!" doesn't apply to many of them. They were born here. How could a government carry out such a policy? If it did, on what basis?

George Takei, the well-known actor from the *Star Trek* series on TV, is a Japanese American. He has written an article about how he, his family, and other Japanese Americans were forced into internment camps during World War II.[7] Many of these people had to sell their property at a disadvantage and were never given compensation. There was no legal process. There were no hearings or trials. Rank fear, following the bombing of Pearl Harbor in 1942, and cynicism, drove this policy. It was based on only one presidential Executive Order 9066 by President Franklin Roosevelt, which was challenged in the Supreme Court but was upheld in 1944. I will discuss the *Korematsu* Supreme Court decision further below. German Americans, on the other hand, weren't interned. Neither were Italian Americans—even though both Germany and Italy were Axis powers along with Japan. The three nations were members of the Tripartite Pact and were US enemies during World War II.

On what basis would a government argue that one faith is more dangerous than another? Some have argued that Islam is determined to take over the world. But, so are some Reformed Christians (Theonomists) and some Baptist militia men. In fact, all conservative Christians look forward to the return of Christ and the setting up of his kingdom over all the earth.

But are all Muslims determined to take over the earth? If we mean, do they long for the *Umma* (the kingdom of God on earth) in the way that a Christian longs for Christ's reign, the answer is probably "yes." Desiring the *Umma* and even the institution of Sharia law do not necessarily mean administering terrible punishments in the name of that law. It is true that, for instance, the Al Shabab in Somalia use cross-amputation, the cutting off of one arm and one leg on opposite sides of the body, as a judgment under Sharia law.[8] However, this sort of cruel punishment is by no means universal. Most Muslims long for the brotherhood of mankind under the reign of the one true God.[9] Most Muslim theologians do not argue for violent overthrow of governments which are not Muslim. Many Muslims live happily in Western democracies. I am deeply offended when people, who are not Muslims and do not have a single Muslim friend, tell me that all Muslims are terrorists. This is nonsense, dangerous nonsense; worse, it's propaganda. I will repeat these numbers later, but perhaps they are necessary at this point. There are 1.8 billion Muslims in the world.[10] At the most there are 230,000 Muslim terrorists, armed fighters, according to the most politically conservative analysts.[11] That means that there are only 0.01 percent of all Muslims who are terrorists and most are fighting other Muslims. Most of these fighters are involved in conflicts in Syria and Afghanistan, for instance.

The solution to our problem with terrorism is not to hate or to try to round up and intern all possible terrorists. The solution to our problem is to seek justice: "To act justly, to love mercy and to walk humbly with our God," Micah 6:8.

As I was writing this chapter and as I was writing this book, the US presidential election was underway. The new president, Donald J. Trump, has been in office about three and a half years now. President Trump had campaigned on a platform which included stopping the immigration of Muslims, and perhaps even expelling them from the US, based on a message of fear. This played well in terms of getting votes, and perhaps helped him win the election.

One of President Trump's first actions was to pass a presidential Executive Order 13769: "Protecting the Nation from Foreign Terrorist Entry into the United States" (January 27, 2017).[12] After studying the order, I tried to evaluate it. President Trump spoke vigorously about 9/11. He admitted that visa policies have changed since then, though he found them wanting. He didn't elaborate, though, on how these visa policies were changed. He only asserted they are not sufficient, but gave no evidence. However, nowhere did he consider or speak about who the 9/11 bombers were. Not one of the 9/11 bombers, however, entered the US on an immigration visa. As well, there has not been one deadly terrorist attack carried out in the US by a foreigner entering the US on an immigration visa since the mid-1970s.[13] The 9/11 attack and any terrorist attacks since have been carried out by either US-born citizens or those who entered on business, tourist, student, or K-1 fiancé(e) visas.

President Trump ought to have called for stricter procedures for visas granted to tourists, businessmen, students, and fiancé(e)s, which he has now done. However, when he ordered the "travel ban" (Order 13769), he called for the complete ban of all people from seven specific countries only: Iran, Iraq, Libya, Somalia, Sudan, Syria, and Yemen. None of the 9/11 terrorists who have committed attacks in the US have come from any of those seven countries. Saudi Arabia is one main country from which terrorists who committed the 9/11 bombings came, but Saudi Arabia was not one of the seven countries to be banned.

In any event, President Trump's "ban" should not have focused at all on legal immigrants, who are refugees, who have all been vetted through the earlier special nine-step process which was required of all immigrants who came to the US as refugees whose visas were processed prior to his administration's changes to these steps. Many will be surprised to learn that eight of those steps were carried out outside the US. These steps included biometrical data collection (fingerprints, facial scans, etc.) by the State Department, the FBI ,and Homeland Security, before the potential immigrant was even considered for possible immigration. It is hard to imagine how vetting could have been more thorough or "extreme."

But President Trump took no notice of these categories and called for a ban of anyone entering the US from these seven countries, including those receiving tourist, student, businessman, fiancé(e), or refugee/ immigrant visas. In section 5 (d) of Order 13769 (the "first travel ban") he cancelled the promise of President Obama to allow fifty thousand Syrian refugees to immigrate to the US. There is no evidence to suggest that this would have been indeed "detrimental to the interests of the United States," as he suggested. He gave no evidence at all to support this claim. So far there have been no terrorist acts carried out by Syrians, and certainly not by any Syrian immigrants in the US.

In the week following his issuing Order 13769, the Ninth Federal Circuit Court of Appeals rejected the legality of President Trump's travel ban (Order 13769).[14] The judges noted several things which were questionable in the Presidential Order 13769. Perhaps most important to them, President Trump's Order 13769 seemed be an attempt to establish a religion: Christianity. By making special allowances for the immigration of persecuted Christians from the seven countries under the travel ban, but forbidding

Muslims, the court felt that President Trump's Order 13769 was discrimina-
tory of people of a particular religion: Islam. Whatever benefit President
Trump's anti-Islamic statements were to his election, these sorts of reasons
apparently were not acceptable to US federal courts. The US Constitution
guarantees freedom of religion and a separation of church and state. The
government may not establish any religion, Christian or otherwise.

There were, of course, other things to which the judges objected or by
which they were not convinced. The judges noted that the arbitrary choice
of these particular seven nations had no real supporting evidence or legal
precedent. The court also wondered at the necessity of implementing the
"ban" so quickly, merely ignoring other legal process, which had been in
place when the visas were issued. In addition, the court noted the extreme
inconvenience that resulted from the sudden implementation of the travel
ban with travelers stranded in the thousands.[15]

Whatever the legal merits (or lack of legal merits) of President Trump's
original "travel ban," his orders must offer evidence in their favor. President
Trump referred to the 9/11 bombings in his Order 13769, thereby blurring
the distinctions between the 9/11 terrorists and legal immigrants, i.e., refugees. He said more terrorist acts had been carried out, but failed to say by
whom and under what visas they did so.

President Trump ordered "the Secretary of Homeland Security [to]
expedite the completion and implementation of a biometric entry-exit
tracking system for all travelers to the United States."[16] This was prudent.
There is no reason why anyone who is not intending to carry out any sort of
violence would need to fear such a system. Americans typically find the idea
of having to be fingerprinted and having facial or retinal scans done invasive
of their privacy. I freaked out when I as a resident legal alien in the Netherlands had to go to the immigration office here in Rijswijk to be fingerprinted
and have a facial scan (picture). However, as my Dutch friends pointed out,
any Dutch person who wants a passport submits to the same thing. As well
all foreigners entering the US are required to have at least a one finger/
thumb scan, besides presenting a valid passport. Many passports, like US
and Dutch ones, have an electronic chip with biometrics contained in them.
If Dutch citizens object to this procedure, they don't need to get a passport
or travel abroad. It is a fact that when most of us carry a mobile/cell phone,
and/or have personal data devices (laptops, iPads, etc.), our movements can
be tracked easily. If we use a bank card or a credit card, our movements
can also be easily tracked. Thus, personally, I don't see any objection to any
security measures of this sort to verify our identity, since we can easily be
tracked or identified anyway by our devices and cards.

Another issue to deal with is that, rather than blur two or more categories, it would be more useful and wiser to concentrate on a clear reworking and strengthening of other sorts of visas which have been used by terrorists—student, tourist, business, fiancé(e)—rather than speaking about "immigrants" (which almost always confuses two groups of immigrants: illegal immigrants and legal immigrants) and their perceived danger.

Since there were some changes between the first version of the Presidential Order "Protecting the Nation from Foreign Terrorist Entry into the United States" 13769 and the second version, Executive Order 13780, titled "Protecting the Nation from Foreign Terrorist Entry into the United States," which was issued March 6, 2017,[17] it would be well to note some of these changes, as well as some of the issues and contentions, which remained the same. The first assumption is that the then-current US Refugee Admission Program (USRAP) needed to be improved or could be improved. Some attempted proof of this was given. A robust defense was attempted as to why six of the seven countries in the original Order 13769 were chosen. The basic contention was that Congress had already expressed concern that these countries were considered "state sponsors of terrorism." These countries should be restricted as far as the Visa Waiver Program was concerned. That is, applicants from these countries should be subjected to more scrutiny than in the past, when foreign nationals were allowed to arrive at a US border and get a visa. State sponsors of terrorism were identified as: Iraq, Syria, Iran, and Sudan. Later, Homeland Security added Libya, Somalia, and Yemen as "additional countries of concern for travel purposes."[18]

Reasons for denying a person from one of these countries a visa were said to be: that a person entering could pose a threat to national security; there is an existing terrorist organization in the country of the applicant; or that person's country of origin is a country considered to be a "safe haven for terrorists."[19]

The breakdown in cooperation between these states and the State Department in terms of sharing information was also listed as a reason for concern. For example, the US embassy had closed in that country or the country had expelled US embassy personnel.

President Trump reiterated that his earlier ban for 120 days for refugees without family in the US should stand until the review of the USRAP can be made. He cited possible terrorist infiltrators from the nations he had identified as a reason for this 120-day ban on issuing visas.

The new Order 13780 claimed that the president was not motivated in his previous Order 13769 by ill will towards Islam. This version of the "travel ban" (Order 13780) had also removed any special exemptions for Christians from these countries who might be subjects of persecution. Instead, in other sections of the Order 13780, such broad powers of exception were given to the secretary of state, the secretary of Homeland Security, US consulars, and "consular fellows"—in effect, anyone the president designates could admit anyone he or she chose. These designates of his could allow Christians from Sudan or Syria to get visas to enter the US as refugees or those who should be protected by the Convention Against Torture.

The president made a special case for allowing visas to Iraqis, because Iraq is a friendly government which is cooperating with the US. Though there may be concern about connections between visa applicants and known terror groups, like ISIS, still there should be allowance of visas being granted to Iraqis. Iraqi citizens with visas would be allowed to enter the US, if they are well-screened.

The president cited two examples of immigrants from these countries who had committed "terrorism-related crimes." The first example was two Iraqi men who were caught in an FBI sting in Bowling Green, Kentucky. These two Iraqi men agreed to and took part in supplying funds for aiding terrorists in Iraq, as well as buying rifles, "bomb making materials," and other equipment. However, it was not explained that these two Iraqi men did not, in fact, carry out any attack in the US. They thought that they were supporting terrorists in Iraq. One had, though, made bombs in Iraq, which killed US service people. He was convicted of the bombing in Iraq and the involvement in aiding terrorists in Iraq in the FBI sting.[20] However, these two men did not kill anyone in the US. They did not even plan or attempt to carry out a terrorist act in the US. As we have mentioned, no immigrant, since the mid 1970s, has killed anyone in a terrorist attack in the US. Some analysts go so far as to assert that the withholding of visas to deserving Iraqis, based on this case involving these two men, actually led to the death of friendly Iraqis, who were unable to get US visas.[21] As these two Iraqis were the subjects of a sting by the FBI, they were known, and their actions observed and limited. Thus, they could not have carried out an act of terrorism on US soil. Also, oddly enough, the president exempts Iraq, of all countries, from his Order 13780, and these two were Iraqis.

The second example given of the danger of refugees carrying out terrorist acts, which the Order 13780 cited, was of a Somali young man who attempted to detonate a bomb in Portland, Oregon, on Christmas 2014. This young man was a child when admitted as a refugee, along with his family. He was radicalized later as a teenager. His Somali origin had nothing to do with his crimes. In the end, he was even unable to detonate his "weapon of mass destruction" (homemade bomb), because his own father and Somalis in his community reported him to the authorities! Immigrants actually aided in his capture and foiled his plot.[22]

The revised Order 13870 also asserted that there are "more than 300 persons who entered the United States as refugees, who are currently subjects of counterterrorism investigations" by the FBI. That might be true, but how many will lead to convictions? Are Muslims necessarily guilty unless proven innocent?

We can draw a conclusion from the case of the two Iraqi men mentioned above who were convicted. These two who were involved in "terrorism related crimes" were the only two out of about seventy thousand Iraqis who have been admitted to the US until now. Even if we ignore that they carried out no attack and killed no one, that still only means a failure rate of 1 in 35,000, or 0.00003 percent.

Even including the Somali young man with these two, and the 9/11 bombers, who were not in the US on immigrant visas, the odds of being killed by someone who was admitted into the US as a refugee is 1 in 3.64 million per year. The odds of being murdered by a US-born citizen are much higher at 252.9 percent.[23] In other words, your chances of being murdered in a typical, non-terrorist related murder are more than 250 times higher than the odds that you would be murdered by a terrorist of immigrant origin.

Thus, it seems that the hazards posed by foreign-born terrorists are not large enough to warrant extreme actions like a moratorium on all immigration or tourism. Only "134 foreign-born terrorists entered the United States out of a total of 1.14 billion visas issued in these categories from 1975 through 2015. That means that only 0.00001 percent of all foreigners who entered on these visas were terrorists."[24]

It would be almost impossible to do any better than the US INS has done. If we accept that the rules for visa issuance got stricter after 9/11 (which the president admitted in his first version, Order 13769), the number of potential terrorists, who might enter is astronomically small, too small to be affected by any other cost-effective changes. "The Department of Homeland Security (DHS)" values "each life saved from an act of terrorism at . . . $13 million."[25]

It would be impossible to "vet" refugees, those given an immigrant visa, any more stringently than they are now, and it would be bankrupting to try. The real risk is so small that it would be unrealistic to expect Congress to fund further measures. In short, there is no real risk worth protecting against or possible to fund against.

The real bone of contention for advocates of refugees was section 6 of Order 13769, "Realignment of the U.S. Refugee Admission Program for Fiscal Year 2017." It provoked much reaction to the original Order 13769 and to the second version Order 13780. This section stated that the president, due to his concerns about refugees being terrorists in disguise, would be stopping the US Refugee Admission Program (USRAP). In section 6 (b) of Order 13780, the president again maintained that "the entry of more than 50,000 refugees in fiscal year 2017 would be detrimental to the interests of the United States." The president does have the right to determine the number of refugees who will be allowed into the country, whatever his reasons.[26] This is his prerogative as the president. It is in effect a statement of his desire. President Obama had set a target of 110,000.[27] The main issue, though, is that President Trump really has not presented any evidence that these refugees would be detrimental to the interests of the United States.

On another topic, a later section of the revised Order 13780, section 6 (d), seemed to suggest that, in the past, places receiving new refugees did not know or were intentionally not told that refugees would be coming to their states, regions, or municipalities. This seems quite unlikely, as all refugees must have a sponsoring agency, for instance the Hebrew Immigration Aid Society (HIAS) or Church World Services (CWS) or United States Conference of Catholic Bishops (USCCB).[28] Such sponsoring organizations also work with local synagogues or churches or other citizens' organizations to sponsor individual families and individuals. Each refugee would be enrolled for US social benefits at the Social Security Administration under their domicile in their area. There doesn't seem to be much evidence that refugees enter a community without relevant community and regional authorities being aware of their coming.

There are other issues which Order 13780 dealt with which are beyond the scope of this book: illegal immigration and the related "sanctuary cities," which are meant for illegal immigrants. There is, though, one other issue which bears discussion here: whether local municipalities know about refugees moving into their municipalities. It seems impossible for a *bona fide* refugee / legal immigrant to settle in any neighborhood in the US and to be unknown to the government, both local and state, or even federal. As we noted above, for a refugee / immigrant to enter the US, he or she must have a sponsoring agency. The Hebrew Immigration and Aid Society is such an agency, which brought Russian Jewish refugees from the Soviet Union in the 1970s. Forest Hills Mennonite Church in Leola, Pennsylvania, for instance, has sponsored a Syrian family through the auspices of Church World Services.[29] Every refugee has to have such a sponsor. As a result, it's impossible that local people would not know of a refugee settling in their midst. While there may be concern about illegal immigrants "staying below the radar," refugees who are legal immigrants have been vetted as *extremely* as is humanly possible and are also known and cared for by sponsors.

While the US Supreme Court decided not to rule against President Trump's "second travel ban," Order 13780, on June 26, 2017 (in other words they issued a stay to a previous lower court order, thus allowing President Trump's "ban" to remain in force), they only did so for Constitutional reasons. They did not wish to circumscribe the executive powers of the presidency. They also did not make any comments about the reasons for the "ban" that were given or the motivations for ordering the "ban." What they did do, though, on this first ruling was to leave a "loophole" in the "ban" by not excluding anyone who had a valid visa prior to the giving of the Executive Order 13780. On the first imposition of the "ban" (Order 13769) many people were stranded in airports since no procedure to deal with them had been put in place. Thus, the Supreme Court's decision allowed people from the seven affected countries who had a previously issued visa to enter to the US. Also, the Supreme Court put off making any final decision about the president's "travel ban" for 120 days, which was his own time limit. Perhaps they hoped, it seems, that the 120-day period, which the "travel ban" (Order 13780) envisioned, would pass before they would need to rule about it. In other words, they may have hoped that it would become unnecessary to rule on it.

If the Supreme Court did not rule directly on the president's "travel ban" before Order 13780 itself expired, according to its own wording, they would not be responsible for circumscribing the executive powers of the presidency. Also, in the 120 days originally envisioned in the "ban," President Trump had ordered the Secretary of Homeland Security to investigate the visa entry situation and give suggestions for tightening visa issuance. By not ruling on the case, the Supreme Court allowed the commander-in-chief to order the investigation, allowed the investigators to do their jobs, and yet by their careful response at the same time allowed those with valid visas to enter the US.[30]

In the final battle over the "travel ban(s)" the president ordered a "third travel ban," Presidential Proclamation 9645, "Enhancing Vetting Capabilities and Processes for Detecting Attempted Entry into the United States by Terrorists or Other Public-Safety Threats," issued on September 24, 2017.[31] In each iteration of his "travel ban," President Trump sought to deflect earlier criticism of his previous "ban." Between the first "ban" (Order 13769) and second "ban" (Order 13780) he corrected mistakes which were obvious. I have mentioned before the fact that the origin of the 9/11 bombers was misreported in his first "travel ban." Another error of the first "travel ban" (13769) was not allowing for visas for diplomatic personnel from the seven countries listed or for friendly military personnel (e.g., Iraqi military figures allied to the US). Other misstatements about historical and other factual matters were corrected. The president also tried to avoid showing prejudice or favor towards any particular nation, i.e., to show there was in fact a clear and present danger from people from those countries. The hardest charge which all three of his "travel bans" had to overcome was an apparent bias towards Christians and prejudice towards Muslims. In the first "travel ban" (Order 13769) he allowed Christians from Iraq visas when they were withheld to other Iraqis due to the potential threat of terrorists from Iraq. Iraqi Christians, he felt, should be given visas as they were not a terrorist threat since they were fleeing that (Muslim) terror. In the second "travel ban" (Order 13780) he withdrew exceptions for Christians per se, but gave to his designates such power as to override any other barriers to obtaining a visa.

In the end when the US Supreme Court could not remain outside the debate any longer, they allowed President Trump's administration to request a hearing to overturn the ruling of the Ninth Circuit Appellate Court *Trump v. Hawaii*. They ruled on June 26, 2018. In a 5-to-4 decision the justices ruled in favor of President Trump's "travel ban," which at this point was Proclamation 9645. It was, as decisions in the US Supreme Court go, close. In other words, the justices were very divided. It was a narrow decision. Those justices who ruled in favor of President Trump's "ban" argued that the "ban" did not in fact "establish" any religion, i.e., Christianity, or in other words, discriminate against Muslims.

The First Amendment of the US Constitution bars "establishing" any religion or ruling against any religion. The purpose of the amendment was to prevent a state religion, as in England. Many of the early settlers, the Pilgrim Fathers, and the Quakers and Mennonites of Pennsylvania, for instance, had fled countries where a state religion persecuted them. The text of the First Amendment reads:

> Congress shall make no law respecting an establishment of religion, or prohibiting the free exercise thereof; or abridging the freedom of speech, or of the press; or the right of the people peaceably to assemble, and to petition the Government for a redress of grievances.[32]

Some justices feared that President Trump's "travel ban" was in fact establishing Christianity as the state religion of the US. By allowing Iraqi Christians to enter the US for reasons of persecution, but not allowing, for instance, Yazidis from Syria who were persecuted by their Muslim states to enter, he was *de facto* making Christianity the state religion.

It is interesting to note that the justices who ruled in favor of the President's "travel ban" explicitly rejected this interpretation.

These same justices, the majority, made clear that this "travel ban" was not a case of racial profiling. Justice Sotomayor, however, in her dissent, with which Justice Bader Ginsburg concurred, felt that this "travel ban" was quite similar to the racial profiling that happened in the case of Japanese Americans who were interned during WWII. She referred explicitly to the case known as *Korematsu v. United States*.[33]

Fred Korematsu was a Japanese American who was arrested in 1942 for resisting deportation to secure a military facility pursuant to an Executive Order 9066 by President Franklin Roosevelt. After the bombing of Pearl Harbor in 1942 President Roosevelt felt that Japanese Americans and Japanese nationals in the US posed a threat to the US because of supposed ties to Japan. For this reason, President Roosevelt ordered a whole-scale internment of 110,000 Japanese American and Japanese nationals in the US. Many Japanese Americans were tenant farmers and so lost no property. Others were forced to sell their property quickly and lost a lot of money on the sale of their property to speculators.[34] It took decades before the US government made any efforts to reimburse these Japanese Americans for their losses or even to apologize for the internment and loss. Some analysts and historians have felt that President Roosevelt was just trying to calm the populace. Later in 1983 a legal team found vital evidence which had shown that the FBI and other authorities had repressed or destroyed evidence in 1942 in which government intelligence authorities showed there was no threat from Japanese Americans at that time. A federal judge finally cleared Korematsu in 1983. However, even in 1944 Supreme Court Justice Robert Jackson at the original time of the Supreme Court decision on the *Korematsu* case "called the exclusion order 'the legalization of racism' that violated the Equal Protection Clause of the Fourteenth Amendment."[35]

The majority justices in 2018 forcefully dismissed "Justice Sonia Sotomayor's invocation of *Korematsu* in her dissent."[36] They said that no case like *Korematsu* should ever happen again and that this decision for President Trump's "travel ban" was no *Korematsu*. In fact, in their comments as they gave their rationale for their decision on President Trump's "travel ban," the majority of the court consciously overturned the *Korematsu* decision. The majority Justices wrote:

> The dissent's reference to *Korematsu*, however, affords this Court the opportunity to make express what is already obvious: *Korematsu* was gravely wrong the day it was decided, has been overruled in the court of history, and—to be clear—"has no place in law under the Constitution." 323 U. S., at 248 (Jackson, J., dissenting).[37]

After seventy-four years, not only was Fred Korematsu vindicated, but the *Korematsu* case was overruled. All of the justices agreed: no one should be discriminated against due to race or religion. They disagreed, however, about how that should be worked out in practice. Karen Korematsu, Fred's daughter, however, believed the same mistake which was made in her father's case was being made again in allowing President Trump's "ban" to stand, since it meant allowing a judgment merely upon racial profiling.[38]

The justices considering President Trump's "travel ban" recognized the problems of the establishment of one religion above another or the potential racism (racial profiling) of President Trump's "travel ban" case, but they ruled to allow the executive branch to keep its powers to issue such a ban, i.e., a restriction of travel and other visas, if the president felt there was a real danger. The opposing Justices Sotomayor and Bader Ginsburg, as we saw, were not convinced that there was no animus against Muslims or that the "ban" did not in fact discriminate against Muslims. It was a close vote and a long battle.

However, the conclusion of all the endless arguments and court cases seems rather pointless related to the question of legal immigration through the usual INS procedures, since there is no evidence that anyone entering the US on a regular immigration visa has committed a deadly act of terror since the mid 1970s.[39] Since the 1980 Refugee Act there has been no death due to a refugee. Parse the sentences however one will, there have been no lethal acts of terrorism by refugees / immigrants who went through the regular immigrant visa process. There is, on the other hand, a goodly amount of evidence that some who entered on business, tourist, student, or fiancé(e) K-1 visas have. There is also a problem of radicalization of children brought to the US from abroad by immigrant parents or parents entering on asylum and other visas. It is right to focus on changing these types of visas and the procedures for these types of visas which are connected with proven acts of terror. However, there is no credible evidence to discriminate against immigrants who come through normal immigrant visa channels.

There are surely at least two problems: misuse of business and tourist visas and radicalization of Muslim youth, but shutting our doors to refugees who are vetted through the normal immigrant visa procedure is not one of them.

Has a legal immigrant killed anyone in the US?

Every time I mention that there have been no deadly terrorist attacks carried out by legal immigrants, people give me examples of other incidents involving terrorists who, in fact, were *not* admitted with immigration visas as refugees. For example, the two brothers who bombed the Boston Marathon on April 15, 2013, Dzhokhar and Tamerlan Tsarnaev, entered the US on tourist visas. They came as children with their parents, who were from Chechnya. They entered as tourists and then asked for political asylum.[40] The parents had no intent of ever committing any acts of terror nor have they. They wanted freedom from Russian attacks on their homeland. However, the process of political asylum, which they invoked, is carried out in the US, not abroad. By contrast no immigrant/refugee enters the US until he or she has completed a previous nine-step process, mentioned above. The Tsarnaev family entered at an airport on a normal tourist visa, and then invoked political asylum, a procedure which was carried out after they had entered the US, in contrast to an immigration visa for refugees, which is processed while the candidate is outside the US. This is in effect a completely different procedure than the procedure for refugees. Throughout the whole process, the family and brothers were not subjected to the same process or scrutiny which a refugee is subjected to. As well the older brother seems to have been self-radicalized. The younger brother had even recently become a US citizen, but seems to have followed his older brother into terrorist actions out of admiration for him.[41] The point is that neither the parents or the brothers were processed as refugees from outside the US. They were processed while in the US. Also, the brothers radicalized later. They were not terrorists trying to sneak in.

The point is that this terrorist attack, as with the San Bernadino shooting, was not carried out by people who entered on immigrant/refugee visas. They were not vetted as refugees are in UNHCR camps and US Resettlement Support Centers.

It is wise and right to do our best to prevent potential terrorists from entering our countries. However, there must be demonstrable evidence that the people prevented from entry are, indeed, a threat. There needs to be consideration given to banning people from countries from which attacks have originated, like Saudi Arabia, rather than discriminating arbitrarily against whole people groups.

Immigrants as a group should not be a focus for refusal of visas or discrimination. This is unfair and unfounded. If there is any vetting system which is extreme and effective, it is the system which was already being used to vet refugees/immigrants. Reasonable precautions should be taken, but measures put into place by ungrounded fear cannot be supported logically or financially.

Chapter 2: **Welcoming Strangers . . .**
Who Do You See at Your Door?

Reactions to terrorism
and causes of fear

FOR MANY OF US who have never lived outside our country of birth, it is hard to imagine how an immigrant feels. If we have never experienced war or fled from persecution, it is hard for us to comprehend what immigrants must cope with, having lost home and country. Because some immigrants are easily identified, we find them an easy target for our fear. It's easier to label all Muslims as terrorists than to learn the differences between the world's 1.8 billion Muslims and then to strive to understand them.

"Being a refugee sucks!"

I teach a course called "The Ethics of War, Peace, and Peace-making." In this class, I ask students to consider various views of war: "Just War," "Crusade or Jihad" (a war for religious reasons, for "righteousness'" sake), "Non-violence," and "Pacifism" (or "Pacificism": making peace, not merely inaction or disengagement). I have had several students from East Africa who have suffered in genocide and war in Rwanda or Congo.

One day a student of mine from East Africa gave his presentation, which in his case was in favor of "Just War." I challenged his view. He admitted that he didn't really have a strong case for his view. At the same time, he felt no position on war and peace could give strong evidence for its claims. When I pressed further, he said, "Being a refugee sucks!"

He is a gentle, kind, intelligent person. He is a godly person. I have never heard him swear. However, in light of his experience in a refugee camp, where he was kept on the border of his country, while fighting went on, he concluded that at some times the use of force was necessary to obtain justice.

I doubt that anyone meeting him would know that he had ever been a refugee. Probably most North Americans could not even guess his nationality. Many of us are probably very poorly acquainted with the genocide in Rwanda. It wasn't a big deal in the Western news media, since there were other international problems, like the Bosnian war, going on at that time which filled the news. The point is: would we recognize a refugee if we saw one?

The face of the Other

Emmanuel Levinas was a Jewish philosopher who moved from Eastern Europe to France.[42] Levinas lost many relatives in Auschwitz. He suffered for decades and wrote little philosophy, though he was influenced by and translated the philosophy of some other thinkers into French. After the Second World War, Levinas turned to the Talmud, the Jewish commentary on the Torah, the Five Books of Moses, the Old Testament Law, and Jewish studies and began to write more. He wrote at times as a pure philosopher and at times as a Talmudic scholar.

For the sake of this part of this chapter, I want to use a concept of Levinas's which is very well-known: the face of the Other. Levinas is trying to think about how another person presents himself to someone in consciousness. He designates these beings as the Other, the nonreducible. We are presented with another, an Other, who exceeds our gaze or look, our grasp or definitions of him or her. We cannot fully define or limit the Other. We are not able to fully control or even recognize all the Other is. However, when we are faced with an Other, we have an ethical responsibility for the Other. To see the face of the Other is to become immediately responsible in an ethical way for the Other.[43]

For some thinkers to see or to gaze at something is to define and control that thing. Either we are the one seeing and so defining and controlling, or we are being seen and are so defined and controlled.[44] Our Gaze is insatiable and, in the end, helpless and powerless to attain what it desires. At the same time, our Gaze simply seeks justification for what it wants. It is selfish.[45] If we control the perception of the Other, we control them.

For Levinas, our seeing does indeed define someone. Seeing the face of the Other, to see the Other, defines the one who sees as responsible. When we see an Other in need, we become responsible. Levinas is saying that we cannot come in contact with someone in need and just turn away.

One can see in his philosophy an Old Testament theme: the place of the foreigner or sojourner in the midst of Israel. "Love the sojourner, therefore, for you were sojourners in the land of Egypt" (Deut 10:19). Since the nation of Israel had been "sojourners," i.e., temporary residents and slaves in Egypt, they were to be kind and fair to those who dwell among them as foreigners and sojourners.

This commandment to love the sojourner can be found in the Second Table of the Law, the Ten Commandments, which are commands which relate to other people: honor your father and mother, do not murder, do not commit adultery, do not steal, do not lie, do not covet anything that belongs to your neighbor: not his wife, not his servants, not his things.

What is interesting is that when Jesus was asked, "Which is the greatest commandment (of the Old Testament)?" he didn't recite the Ten Commandments. Jesus in a sense cut to the chase. He cited two other verses of the Old Testament, which summarize the Ten Commandments: "Love the Lord your God with all your heart, with all your soul, with all your strength" and "Love your neighbor as yourself" (Mark 12:30–31).[46]

Jesus doesn't mess around! There are 613 laws in the Old Testament (according to some). If you have ever seen a *tallis*, a Jewish prayer shawl, you might have heard that the 613 fringes, the tassels, stand for the 613 laws. One of these laws is to love the sojourner. It is a very difficult task to keep track of whether you have broken one of these laws. Those who make their lives out of the study of the Talmud can wonder every second whether they have broken a law inadvertently or unknowingly.

If we become embroiled in trying to keep all 613 laws in the Old Testament, we will have a full-time job. In a scene from the movie *Hiding and Seeking*, Akiva Daum says to his father, Rabbi Menachem Daum, "Daddy! You have such great questions! I don't know how you sleep at night. I can't deal with your questions. I am worried about whether I have kept the commandments regarding the Sabbath. I don't hate the *goyim* [the non-Jewish, gentile people]. I don't have time for them."[47] Akiva Daum is expressing the view of some Orthodox Jews, who feel that their greatest concern is to keep (or not break) these 613 laws.

We, as evangelical Christians, often sound similar to Akiva Daum. We are concerned with remaining holy, and especially we are concerned with maintaining or defending true doctrine. We spend a lot of time comparing our doctrinal views with the views of others whom we see as unorthodox or different. We have developed historical statements of faith, which we defend and expound at the least provocation. I do not decry sound doctrine or preserving the truth. I am an ordained Baptist minister with a master of divinity (theology) from a well-known seminary which is a bastion of Evangelical orthodoxy, and I am not unhappy with that connection. I have studied New Testament Greek and Old Testament Hebrew. I have learned the entire gamut of theology in the Evangelical Christian tradition, and even that of Roman Catholic and Eastern Orthodox traditions. I have been a theological educator for more than thirty years. I am all for sound doctrine.

What I am sad to see is that often we, evangelical Christians, are examples of modern-day Pharisees. We are more concerned with sound doctrine than we are with mercy and truth in a broader sense. We are so busy reading our books about doctrinal disputes or reading Christian self-help books that we fail to see the sojourners and the foreigners in our midst.

It is uncomfortable to put down our books or magazines, or turn off the TV, and face the Other. We do not wish to be defined by the Gaze of the Other. We don't want to be responsible for someone else. It's easier for us to remain absorbed in our doctrinal disputes than to turn our eyes to world affairs and the needs of those around us. Frankly, we are either engaged in lesser things or we are afraid to follow Jesus' commands because of what it might cost us.

"Religion that God our Father accepts as pure and faultless is this: to look after orphans and widows in their distress" (Jas 1:27).

I had another student in my classes, an Anglican minister from a war-torn part of his country. After his first year at the seminary, he sent all of us an e-mail saying that he was sorry but he had to go home that summer. Students are not to go home between the first and second years. However, he had received a call from his Bishop to return to his homeland due to a crisis: war had broken out again and there were, as a result, a lot of orphans to care for. To emphasize his point, he included terrible, gory pictures of bodies which had been decapitated and from which the limbs had been hacked with machetes.

Later, I asked if I could help by raising some money from within our church for his orphanage ministry. He was glad for the help. I asked for some pictures of the orphans to show the congregation. He sent me a lot of photos. His region uses French as the language of education. The photos he sent of little children had captions in French. I don't know French really, but I understood enough of the words to get the point: "Orphelin de guerre" (Orphan of war); "Orphelin des la sides" (Orphan of AIDS); "Victime d' Abus" (Victim of Abuse); "Victime de guerre" (Victim of war). There were thirty-nine pictures. They were of thirty-nine orphans. My former student and his wife have taken these orphans in and provide meals, shelter, clothing, and schooling. It is a gargantuan task for them in their setting.

Though I had some knowledge of the situation, I didn't realize the face of the Other, the faces and frail forms of these children, until I saw them.

We see similar images of children on TV ads for Save the Children and other charities, but they are not individuals to us as they are to my former student. I know a missionary in the same country who is a medical doctor who started a medical clinic far up in a less populated area. Twice he and his family have been evacuated and returned. However, for most of us this is just another war-torn area that we might hear about.

In essence the second command which Jesus mentions, "Love your neighbor as yourself," is a very easy sentence to diagram grammatically. But it is a command. The verb is a second person plural verb: "You all love!" The direct object is "your neighbor," that is, the person next to you physically or metaphorically. There is an adverbial phrase to clarify: "as yourself," that is, just as you care for your own body, feeding and bathing it, just as you care for yourself by providing a home for yourself, a roof over your head, etc., so care for your neighbor.

Unfortunately, we are often like the Jewish scribe who asked Jesus which commandment was the greatest. We feel the pinch of the reply: we are to care for our neighbor as we are to care for ourselves. The scribe wasn't able to bear Jesus' words. "But he wanted to justify himself, so he asked Jesus, 'And who is my neighbor?'" (Luke 10:29). (I won't go through an exposition of the good Samaritan passage now. I will refer to it later in the chapter, in which I deal with other specific passages of Scripture which bear on us as we consider refugees and immigrants.)

I want to return to Levinas: we have seen the face of the Other. We have seen it in the refugee, who is on the TV screen. We are faced with a responsibility for the Other.

We may not yet be personally acquainted with an Other. However, all of us have seen the Other. Do we wonder about our responsibility now that we have seen? Or do we pass on our responsibility for the Other?

Which of us has not seen the iconic image of the small Syrian boy dead on the beach in Greece, a small refugee drowned trying to escape a war zone? Which of us has not watched in horror as we saw Aleppo being bombed to rubble, with even hospitals being bombed? We have seen footage of people huddled into shanty towns made of thin tents. We have seen these people shivering from the cold. How can we, if we are Christians, not act compassionately, as Jesus told us to?

The face of the Other and the face of terror

Why do we not act? Often, it is because we are afraid. *Because we are selfish!* We may have watched the Twin Towers fall. We may have watched the bomb explosions in Boston.

We have watched the frenetic activity trying to stop the horrific shooting in San Bernadino. We do not know what to do and we are afraid that terrorists will enter our country and harm us or our loved ones.

Fear is not necessarily a bad thing. We ought to take reasonable precautions to stop terrorism. It is wise to be cautious. However, it is heartless to sit silently and do nothing for victims of war, who own nothing and have nowhere to go.

Will the real Osama bin Laden please stand up?!

I was in the security line in London's Heathrow airport, that endless snake-like set of barriers that winds travelers through a large room before your check-through luggage can be rechecked and you make your way to your connecting flight. The British are very concerned and careful about terrorists and terrorism.

There was another American near me. He cocked an eye at a security guard nearby and said, "They have Muslims as security guards!" I turned and said, "The guard is a Sikh. He is not a Muslim. In fact, he probably doesn't like Muslims. You should be happy he is here. Sikhs have guarded the Royal Family for centuries." I don't remember his reply, but it was probably something mumbled like, "I didn't know that."

We see what we want to see or what we are prepared to see. This traveler saw a turban and a long beard, and concluded the guard was a Muslim. (So what if he had been?) This traveler was wrong due to a lack of knowledge. Given his background, it was an understandable mistake, but it was still a mistake.

Seeing correctly, recognizing the Other as a person, an individual, means attending to what we see, seeing subtle differences. It is a natural part of assessing people from our own countries. An American who speaks with a drawl is likely from the South of the US. A young woman from the UK with a particular accent is likely a "Geordie girl."

To see that the Sikh's turban is wound differently than an Iranian mullah's, and that it is a different color, takes knowledge. To see that the Sikh's beard is gathered in a net, rather than simply flowing and long, takes perception. That kind of perception takes time to develop and time to appreciate. However, our attention span is often no more than ten seconds, the length of a sound bite and one image. We must do better.

Controlled by images

We are an age which is more driven by pictures and images than words. The photographer who photographed the Syrian child, who had drowned in the Aegean Sea off the coast of a Greek island and washed up ashore, knew, I think, that that image would haunt us. And it should. This is the presence of an absence. Here is one who is gone, who is not, yet he is here. The tormented face of the child's father cannot be erased. We see his pain. We cannot help but empathize, but we turn away. Why? Though there may be many reasons, the primary one seems to be fear.

People who are different scare us. We don't understand them. Or maybe we're too lazy to try to understand them. It is easier to accept a stereotype and categorize them, to define them and then to dismiss them as not worthy of further concern, than to learn who they really are.

Too busy about the "Lord's work" to care

The Jews of eastern Europe, the Ashkenazi, are and were very different looking than their Christian neighbors. Since World War II and the Holocaust, we have been presented with many films and images to make us ever aware of our inhumanity towards Jews. The Jews have had a horrific history. Even after a pilgrimage to Poland to Dzialoszyce to see the place where gentiles, Polish Roman Catholics, saved one of their grandfathers and two of their great uncles, one of Menachem Daum's sons, Akiva, says, "I know what you want me to say, Dad. What can I say, 'Yes, there were a couple good *goyim* among the thousands of *goyim* who hate us. The exception makes the rule. The history of our people is that the *goyim* try to exterminate us. That's the way it is.'"[48]

During the Middle Ages, during the time of the pogroms in Russia, and then during the Holocaust, Jews were targeted simply because they were different (and perhaps because they had land and wealth their persecutors wanted to steal). They weren't Christians. They were considered to be "Jesus' murderers." They wore "strange" clothes. They wore long beards. They had side-locks and wore "strange" hats. They carried out "strange" rituals in their synagogues. They kept to themselves.

Now we have Others, who are again different. They wear different clothes. Women wear *hijabs*, head scarves. Men wear long beards, long white robes, and caps. They have other scriptures. They reject Jesus as Redeemer. They have different houses of worship and use another language or languages, which we can't understand. It is easy to stereotype.

To be fair, we have seen images of raving maniacs: Osama bin Laden and others, preachers of hate and violence. We have (perhaps) watched some Muslim terrorists behead people. We have heard of and seen the destruction some have caused with suicide bombs and warfare. We have heard of those who are willing to kidnap all the girls from a whole village and force them into polygamous marriages.

Blessed are the peacemakers

I have a Christian brother and friend, Dr. David W. Shenk, who has stood for peacemaking and reconciliation around the world. I was happy to connect him with a student from eastern Nigeria who wanted to write his thesis about the need to work on peacemaking between Muslims and Christians in his area of Nigeria. His area, Chibok, was where the Boko Haram had taken away many young women.

My friend and my former student went to the region to talk with the Muslim insurgents, the Boko Haram, who had taken the young women. Perhaps my friend and my student were partly successful in their negotiations, as later some of the young women were allowed to return to their home towns.

However, my friend once asked me after meeting them, "What do you say to people who are prepared to kill every man in a village?" I have only one answer to that question: "Jesus died for us all. There is none righteous; no, not one." Jesus was a man of peace, who preached peace and reconciliation. We as Christians must seek to make peace. It is easier to make war than to seek peace, but it is the way of Christ.

Threats real and imagined

We face real threats. The issue for us is: how large are these threats? If we live in eastern Nigeria or southern Sudan, the threat is live and immediate. If we live in North America, the UK, or the Netherlands, it is not so great. However, it is easy for us label all Muslims as terrorists and not consider how few Muslims really are terrorists.

It is difficult to reconcile the images that we have seen on TV with the messages we hear that we are to care for Muslim refugees. Aren't they just terrorists waiting to strike? Or, perhaps even more frightening, aren't they really being silent now, but hope to take over our society and take away our rights later? Such fears become unfalsifiable conspiracy theories: we cannot disprove them and so we believe them.

In all things, it is important to make good distinctions, which we seem unable to do, particularly if we choose to remain ignorant. If fear keeps us from learning to know the Others, we will continue to fear them. It is easier to stereotype than to see the person before you.

We can fix our Gaze upon a refugee, and because we are afraid, we define that refugee as a threat and a potential terrorist. We are taught to do this. Anyone who wishes to defend their war against someone else will have to use propaganda, images, to drive sentiment to their side.

Almost every single night for months I saw the Twin Towers of the World Trade Center in New York City fall. These few seconds of footage are indeed "iconic" in the sense of defining our lives since 9/11. I saw them because on TV, the National Geographic channel had a show called *Evolution of Evil*. In the trailer, which was played every night numerous times, at every commercial break, the Twin Towers fell and Osama bin Laden raved. Saddam Hussein strategized alongside Kim Jong-un pointing a pistol.

We are taught that these Others are wicked and evil. Surely, they are. They are even equated with Hitler, whose picture also appears in the ad. We know evil when we see it! Or do we?

The UN says that about 79.5 million people are at risk due to war and natural disaster, mostly due to war.[49] That's more than five times the population of the Balkans.

War drives people from their homes. It destroys their cities. There is nothing to return to and no life left there to live. They flee because they are driven out and their homes are destroyed. They have nowhere to go.

We see images—images of Others. They are often confused images, which merge together in our minds. We see in one commercial minute, the *Evolution of Evil*, with Osama bin Laden and Saddam Hussein. In the next commercial minute, we see a dead three-year-old child, a refugee on the beach, and a seemingly incessant wave of refugees. Images become blurred. Reality becomes skewed. We confuse Muslim terrorists with Muslim refugees.

If we are to believe some people, anyone who is a Muslim is a terrorist. This is plainly false, but we are not reasoning with people who use logic. We are dealing with people who use images and slogans—to win elections, to control outcomes, or to sell advertising. These violent images sell newspapers and commercials on television, because they capture people's attention. Love might threaten the perception they want to give us. One side of the news media is trying to tear at our heart strings to get us to contribute to a charity to aid refugees. The other side of the news media uses fear to keep us focused on ourselves and to encourage us through self-protection to become isolationist. How can we stay sane in this environment?

First, we must stop being mesmerized by the TV screen or the computer screen. Then, we need to see the face of the Other before us, both metaphorically and physically. We need to deal with flesh and blood people.

How did I learn to see things this way?

We are all born in a particular place. We do not choose our homeland or birthplace. We do not choose our parents, or even, initially, our faith. We come into a place that receives us and shapes us. We are defined by the environment we inhabit. It receives us and we inhabit it.

We are given to, receive, and are giving. We are embraced in a relationship with the world around us. It is not merely a case of us seeing, and determining the world and Others with our Gaze. We are seen and seeing, touched and touching. Our perception about how things are is constructed by our environment.[50]

We see, but do not see. We see what we are accustomed to see. We see what we expect to see and think this perhaps is a terrorist rather than a refugee.

How can I learn to see differently?

Consider how a painter, someone like Paul Cézanne or Claude Monet, sees.[51] It is not a "one way" relationship with the painter determining what he or she paints. It is not merely the painter "reducing" something to canvas. The painter is captured and enchanted by what he or she sees. The mountain is painted by Cézanne, but the mountain also expresses itself through Cézanne. His fingers and hands are captured and serve the Gaze of the mountain, as it expresses itself through him. Cézanne painted Mount St. Victoire many, many times, and each time failed to capture all that he saw. So, he painted it again: on a rainy day, on a sunny day, on a snowy day, at dawn, at dusk, at midday . . . Amazing paintings! Cézanne was struggling to expand his view, his gaze. He was trying to capture all he saw at different times, in different weather.

Monet also painted the same scenes many times, again for similar reasons. Haystack after haystack, water lily after water lily, scenes of the same bridge from the same garden in Les Lauves, France. Why? Because he could not capture the scenes in their fullness; they exceeded his grasp. He was moved and he moved.

So, what does my excursus about painting have to do with terrorism? It's about seeing. Just as the painters had to wrestle with a subject that couldn't be captured in one painting, so we face complex realities that can't be defined with sound bites. We must not reduce to "black and white" what is multifaceted and rich in color.

What do we see when we see a Muslim? A terrorist? A refugee? Someone to be feared? Someone who will threaten my comfortable lifestyle? It is easy to fear what we do not know, and living people will always exceed our definitions and our grasp.

They are not merely terrorists or hungry beggars. They are not just refugees or adherents of another faith. They become real people with names: Ahmed, Afra, Sayyed . . . adults or children, husbands or wives, sons or daughters. In this way they are the same as we are.

Our minds reel and our hearts are torn asunder. How can we deal with all of the hate and terror that we see? The easiest way and quickest way seems to be to stereotype, to label. Refugees are all just terrorists, and therefore we turn away.

However, when we get to know individuals, we cannot maintain these stereotypes. When a dark man, with a long beard, wearing a cap picks up a saxophone, donated to the drop-in center, and begins to play expertly . . . we gasp. Such beauty, such artistry! Him, a terrorist? Impossible!

When we have been invited for dinner to the home of a refugee family, and they serve us exquisitely prepared lamb, lovely salads, and wonderful, delicious desserts, along with strong, sweet tea, can we continue to see them as terrorists? As dangerous? They are people like us. They are Others for whom we bear a responsibility. When they share their lives with us, they become individuals, whom we know and care about.

Some fears may be realistic and unavoidable to a point, and such a simplistic solution as stereotyping may be appealing. However, we are the poorer for such thoughts. By choosing to renege on our responsibility for the Other, we diminish our own lives. When we embrace the Other, we find ourselves expanded and our horizons stretched. When an Other is simply excluded, we are impoverishing ourselves.

Our lives and our countries have been enriched by immigrants. In the US, most of us are the grandchildren or great-grandchildren of immigrants. True, nowadays we need to make a distinction between illegal immigrants and legal immigrants. Governments must debate and decide the fate of both groups. Still, there is no reason to fear legal immigrants. Alex Nowrasteh has shown that there is very little to fear from legal immigrants. "The chance of an American being murdered in a terrorist attack caused by a refugee is 1 in 3.64 billion per year."[52] It is 252.9 times more likely that you would be murdered by a non-immigrant! The odds of being struck by lightning in a given year are 1 in 960,000.[53] So, you are millions of times more likely to be struck by lightning in America than to be killed by a terrorist.

We must master our fear, or risk being impoverished for the rest of our lives. Reasonable precautions have been put into place; at least, precautions have been put in place which do all that one can do. Perhaps vetting of certain types of visas could be improved: student, tourist, business, fiancé(e), but not immigrant—the threshold is already as high as humanly possible.

When we see the face of the Other we cannot simply reply: "I'm changing the channel," or "You're a hidden terrorist!" We need to engage with real people, with individuals, with Others, who exceed, who break our stereotypes and surprise us—by playing a saxophone or baking and sharing some delicious baklava. Rather than being in more danger and having to fear, we will find ourselves . . . loving and being loved, caring and being cared for.

Perhaps you are not convinced. Jesus' commands, those two simple commands, "Love God" and "Love his children," were not necessarily rejected by the Jewish scribe to whom Jesus was speaking, to whom he told the parable of the good Samaritan. In fact, it says that he admitted Jesus was right, and that Jesus' summarizing all of the Old Testament Law into these two simple commands was wise, a good thing. However, perhaps like us, the scribe wanted to justify himself, i.e., avoid his responsibility for the Other.

Jesus chose just about the most disgusting person to a Jew that he could have chosen to be the hero of his story. The "good" Samaritan was a despised person, an outcast, a half-breed, a false religionist. The Samaritans were the result of the Assyrians bringing other nations into Israel, leading to intermarriage, which was a crime against the OT Law. Their children were rejected. The Samaritans had a truncated scripture. They believed in only the Torah, the Five Books of Moses, but not the further writings of the OT, e.g., the Prophets and the historical and poetic books. There was no contact between Jews and Samaritans (isolationism). To touch a Samaritan was to become ritually unclean.[54]

The Jewish priest and the scribe heading to Jerusalem refused to touch the wounded man. The man, having been badly beaten to near-death, was surely bloody, which would have caused ritual defilement for the priest and the scribe and made them ineligible for their duties in Jerusalem. In Jesus' story, it's not the people that we'd expect to help the wounded man, other Jews, the listeners' coreligionists, who do help him—it's the hated foreigner, the despised sojourner. He has nothing to lose, except money and time, but he sacrifices both to help the injured man. The Samaritan even promises to pay further expenses if the injured man needs further help.

Jesus likes to blow up our stereotypical thinking, just as he exploded those of the Jews of his day. He sent twelve men to buy bread, just so that he could talk to what appears to be a Samaritan prostitute (John 4)! Jesus doesn't like stereotypes, since he sees something we don't want to see, or won't or can't see: he sees individuals. He looks past female or Samaritan, just as nowadays he looks past refugee and volunteer. He sees a person behind the appearance, an Other. He calls us to look past prejudice and fear. He calls us to love. And by engagement with the Other, he calls us to see and be seen, to touch and be touched, to love and be loved.

We have seen the enemy and he is . . . Osama bin Laden?

All of my reflections about seeing and art are nice, but is this really the way the world is? I could call to mind other, more disturbing paintings: Chagall's *White Crucifixion*,[55] Kandinsky's *Cannons (Improvisation No. 30)*.[56] Isn't life also war? Isn't life a struggle to survive? Isn't life a Darwinian "survival of the fittest"?

Personally, I find Darwin's idea of the survival of the fittest disingenuous. Our world could not have arisen by chance without direction. There must have been a source—God. Something, the universe, came from somewhere or someone. This Someone, who created the world and directs it, is what Thomas Aquinas calls the Final Cause, the Good, All-knowing, All-powerful, Omnipresent, Creator God.[57] Matter didn't spring up from nowhere. Neither do societies spring up from nowhere. The world is not a happenstance. We are not here without reason. We are not isolated, disconnected atoms.

I also don't find Herbert Spencer any better. Spencer thought that our ethical behavior and our civilization, and the rules by which we live, were a result of evolution. He proposed an evolutionary ethic.[58] However, I find his ideas also quite unconvincing. For instance, his idea that I should sacrifice one of my sons to "protect" my country is the result of evolutionary behavior. Why should I care about my country or its future? Why should I value anyone or anything more than my sons?

If we are to make any sacrifices for the good of anyone else, there must be a greater ground for our ethical behavior than what is good for me and my loved ones in the short term. Jesus has given us a code of ethics, two commandments, that summarize what we are to do: "Love God with all your heart, soul, strength and mind" and "Love your neighbor as yourself."

We are born through no merit of our own into a certain family, place, nation—perhaps even religion. We may "own the covenant" later in life, decide to be Christians or Muslims or Jews, but we have nothing to say about whether we are white or black, North American, African, or Asian.

I cannot hope to deal with why people become terrorists. I don't wish to enter into a long political debate. It is, frankly, fruitless. Ordinary people have little or no influence over large governments.

Whatever we think of the foreign policy of previous or current administrations, one thing is clear to us as Christians: we are to care for the homeless, the rootless, the stateless, the orphans and widows, the hungry, the maimed.

We cannot hide behind the propaganda that labels all Muslims as terrorists. This is far too simplistic. If we simply ignore the problems which exist, and all we do is turn our backs, we are being false.

Bad faith: are we viewing others in a way that allows us to control what is expected of us?

Often, we live as if, once we have defined someone else, for instance labeled them as "terrorists," we have "won our war" with them: we know them, and don't have to deal with them as people, as individuals.

However, we fear being objectified by others. We don't want to be considered "things." We don't want to be stereotyped or labeled. We want to be seen as individuals. When someone catches us doing something we know we shouldn't do or we are found to be lazy and uncaring, we don't want to be categorized as such—as sinful, lazy, or uncaring. Probably, we feel shame. It's easier to label the other person as a terrorist, and thus avoid the feeling of being responsible for a refugee.

Two thinkers have inspired my reflections here. We have considered Emmanuel Levinas above. It's easier for us to look away than to look at the Face of the Other and feel our ethical responsibility for the Other. The other thinker who has provoked me is Jean Paul Sartre. In his massive book *Being and Nothingness* Jean Paul Sartre has a section in which he discusses the Look or the Gaze, in French *le Regard*. I won't do justice to Sartre here, but I wish to consider his ideas of the Look and Bad Faith.[59] Sartre's philosophy sees us as either defining or being defined (labeling or being labeled), either objectifying or being objectified. Either we determine the Other or the Other determines us. It is a battle of the Gazes, a battle of the Looks. If I let someone else objectify me, define me by their Look, I have become a thing, an object. For instance, if I am labeled just another selfish American, I no longer control who I am. However, if I first look at the Other and define the Other, then I objectify the Other and I am in control: I am Master. He becomes a "terrorist" and I can ignore my responsibility for him and perhaps even attack him.

We fear being objectified. We don't want to be defined. We believe in our own free will and don't want anyone to tell us who we are or force us into any role we don't choose. We believe in our own aims and goals and don't want to be told what to do.

In a certain sense almost anyone in the Western world has been influenced by this view of Sartre's even if they have never heard it. Try to tell someone that they cannot achieve some impossible goal that they have set for themselves and they will rebel.

I have had to tell a student upon occasion that he will never go further in his studies, that he just doesn't have the gifts. It's a rare student who can "hear" this judgment and wisely decide about his further future. In our self-actualized world, I become the enemy for defining him as "less than." Our Western culture at its worst insists that we can achieve anything we choose given enough drive and determination. There are no limits!

On the other hand, there is another sort of Bad Faith which often describes many of us. Bad Faith means allowing someone else to objectify you. In Sartre's view Christians falsely believe in God so that they don't have to be brave and make existential choices without guarantees. Sometimes he is not far from wrong. Some Christians prefer a simple explanation and hide behind someone else's determination of things rather than struggling with truth.

We accept someone else's appraisal when he or she objectifies refugees by calling them terrorists. When we do this, it allows us to refuse to help these refugees and to feel justified in not helping them. We win the battle of the Gazes by defining anyone who is Muslim as a terrorist, and this absolves us from responsibility for refugees who are Muslim.

Usually the media, political parties, and politicians do something similar. We choose our political affiliation and then we go "brain dead." We repeat slogans and don't look at the Other who is before us. We see only "Osama." We listen or watch only those sources of media which confirm our already made up minds, or our minds which have already been made up for us by politicians, pundits, propogandists, and journalists. We are guilty of Bad Faith. We allow ourselves to be objectified as "Nationalists," "Patriots," "Populists," but all the while there is a niggling feeling that we are not being honest with ourselves. We are allowing someone else to define us, to objectify us for their own political and financial gain.

Fear may drive us into isolationism to try to avoid encounter with the Other, but we cannot remain long in isolation. We may wish to "cop out" and let someone else set the policy for us. However, we are always in community.

Like it or not we come face to face with the Other. We cannot simply shut out the rest of the world and pretend that we have responded to Christ's command to love our neighbor. We must take responsibility for the Other.

How stereotypes harm us

I grew up in a neighborhood which was almost entirely Roman Catholic. The nearby town had a large Roman Catholic church, the Church of the Assumption. People in our neighborhood were defined by whether they went to "Assumption" (church) or not.

However, we were Lutherans. My father was defined as a non-Roman Catholic. We drove back to my father's home neighborhood of German immigrant stock to go to church—a journey of about ten to fifteen minutes by car. The church I grew up in was defined as the "*not* Roman Catholic" church. "St. Luke" (Evangelical Lutheran Church) and "St. Athanasius" (Roman Catholic church or "St. A's") were enemies. Whatever the one held dear, the other eschewed.

It all sounds rather surreal now. How can Roman Catholics and Lutherans be enemies? Roman Catholics and Lutherans are having dialogues. They hold ecumenical gatherings. I even attended a Roman Catholic university in Leuven (Louvain), Belgium.

However, in old Pittsburgh, ethnic distinctions were important to people. Today it would be offensive even to write out the terms of derision people used of each other. Some, however, crossed "barriers," which wouldn't seem like barriers now. My uncle, a Methodist, who was a mix of Scotch-Irish, English, and Swiss German descent, married a Polish Roman Catholic. His sister, my mother, married a "German" Lutheran.

Isn't it strange how coming to know an individual, Janet or Patty, changes a young man's mind! Or a young woman's mind. We live in societies which change. The world changes. We are in the world, but the world is also receiving us, helping us, changing us.

Where once groups of people were segregated and even despised each other, now we see no boundaries. When we allow fear, hate, or laziness to determine how we define people, we are the poorer for it. If we expand our horizons, we will discover a rich world all around us.

The world is sometimes a fearful place. Television, news, and videos tend to focus on the horrific and sensational, since it mesmerizes us. The news media changes its focus every five minutes. It is interested in keeping us viewing so that it can make money by showing commercials. As a result, it gives us horrific images of heinous crimes carried out by fringe groups. It rarely reports "good" news. Our temptation is to try to isolate ourselves and avoid facing our responsibilities, those which Jesus has given us for those in need.

However, the world around us is rich and it can enrich us. As we share, people share with us. As we care, people care for us. As we reach out, people reach out to us. As we embrace, we are embraced. The way to overcome fear is to come to know those who are different, the Other. The way to come to a richer understanding of the world is to engage with people who are not like us. We will never understand God's love for others if we insist on labeling 1.8 billion Muslims as terrorists on the basis of the anecdotal evidence of sensationalist news media.

If we accept the highest estimate (which is questioned by some) of possible "Salafi-jihadist terrorists" worldwide we get a number between 100,000 and 230,000. This means that at most 0.013 percent of Muslims are terrorists and at least 0.006 percent. We also need to remember that most of these "jihadists" are involved in local fighting and are not a factor in international terrorism.[60] So, even if we assumed the largest number of jihadis and assumed all are trying to carry out terror in the West—the US or Europe—(which is clearly false), we would be talking about no more than 0.013 percent of all Muslims worldwide. This number is so small as to be almost insignificant. We know, though, that it is not insignificant when terrorists succeed. However, all studies show that terrorism in the West is declining, while local conflicts in, for instance, Afghanistan or Syria are where most of these jihadis are fighting.

We should not label over a billion people terrorists because less than 0.01 percent are possible terrorists. We must change our mental picture of Muslims. Even if we accept this inflated number we should keep in mind that most "Salafi-jihadists" hate any other Muslims whom they consider "idolaters," which is most other Muslims, for example the rulers of Saudi Arabia. More Muslims are killed by Muslim terrorists by far than are or have been killed by Muslim terrorists in the West.

The bottom line is that Muslim immigrants to the US especially, but also in general, are not only unlikely to be terrorists, but more likely to be victims themselves of Muslim terrorists. Aside from this fact, we must also remember that the immigrant visa procedure set in place by the US Immigration and Naturalization Service and those procedures of the countries in the EU, like the Netherlands, are extremely effective at screening out any potential terrorists. The Immigration Service of the US has been so successful that there has not be a death attributable to an immigrant terrorist since 1970. We must stop believing propaganda and face the facts. We should receive refugees from terror-stricken countries with open arms. We must see them as the Other whom we must care for.

Further reading

For a better understanding of Islam:

Katerrega, Badru D., and David W. Shenk. *A Muslim and a Christian in Dialogue*. 2nd ed. Harrisonburg, VA: Herald, 2011.
Shenk, David W. *Journeys of the Muslim Nation and the Christian Church: Exploring the Mission of Two Communities*. Harrisonburg, VA: Herald, 2003.

For help on outreach to Muslims:

Shenk, David W. *Christian. Muslim. Friend: Twelve Paths to Real Relationship*. Harrisonburg, VA: Herald, 2014.

Chapter 3: **Welcoming Strangers**
—A Biblical View

WHEN WE CONSIDER WHAT the Bible has to say about loving others, even our enemies, we must ask: How well are we doing at that task? We say that we believe the Bible and want to live by it, but when we are faced with strangers, aliens, immigrants, how consistent are we?

In the summer of 2016, North Way Christian Community in Pittsburgh, Pennsylvania, was preparing to send a short-term team of church members to work in Honduras.[61] Many on the team were teenagers.

However, the team was warned not to come to Honduras, as there was imminent danger due to armed conflict in the region. They decided to look for somewhere else to serve. They were prepared and ready to go. They were fully funded and now without a place to go.

In seeking for an alternative place to serve, they were directed to the possibility of working among refugees, legal immigrants from war-torn countries, who had been settled right in their home town of Pittsburgh, Pennsylvania. The team accepted the challenge and found to their joy that these refugees were extremely open to their help and warmly welcomed them to their community and homes.

As one young person shared her joy at serving the Lord among these people right in her own backyard, she was met with skepticism and harsh words. "They have come to take our jobs!" "They are terrorists! They should be sent back."

This reaction was so common that North Way Christian Community's lead pastor, Scott Stevens, addressed it in a sermon. Pastor Stevens was doing a sermon on Obadiah, which might not seem like a place to start with making a case for accepting immigrants, but he noted that Israel had been instructed to welcome strangers and aliens into their midst. Just as Israel had sojourned in Egypt, so Israel was to help and encourage the aliens and strangers who were living among them.

Pastor Stevens rightly encouraged his congregation that they already had a justified concern and compassion for orphans and widows. North Way's mission strategy has focused on orphans and disadvantaged children for many years. They were "getting that right." However, they failed to follow through on the command to love "orphans, widows, AND strangers." They needed to get God's heart for the aliens, the immigrants, on their doorstep.

Far from taking jobs from people in Pittsburgh, the refugees were doing jobs no one else wanted. These people were not terrorists, but victims of war and violence. They were not warlike, but peace-loving people, warm and open towards others. These immigrants were welcoming the teens from North Way, making and serving meals for them, even in their small apartments and with what little means they had.

God has brought the nations to our doorstep. We have prayed for decades for opportunities to evangelize in closed countries. Now God has sent these people to our neighborhoods, and yet often we only view them with ill will and suspicion. Congratulations to North Way Christian Community of Pittsburgh, Pennsylvania! May we all learn from them!

In this chapter I will survey a few biblical passages that all Christians acknowledge as significant Scriptures which apply to us. My main point will be that the Bible and Jesus require us as Christians to welcome strangers (aliens, foreigners) in our midst.

Remember that you yourselves were strangers

> When a stranger sojourns with you in your land, you shall not do him wrong. You shall treat the stranger who sojourns with you as the native among you, and you shall love him as yourself, for you were strangers in the land of Egypt: I am the LORD your God. (Lev 19:33, 34)

The people of Israel were given many laws by Moses. Moses transmitted the commandments of God to them. Among the 613 commandments was the above law that pertained to foreigners or strangers, aliens: "When a stranger sojourns [stays temporarily] with you in your land, you shall not do him wrong."

I have been on a "temporary sojourn" for many decades in five different countries. I have visited many more. I currently reside in the Netherlands on a "temporary sojourn" visa. I have a limited "resident alien temporary visa."

With the exception of three years, which we have spent in the US on home assignment, we have been resident aliens somewhere in Europe since 1986.

I don't wish to blame anyone, and there are evil and unkind people everywhere, but I understand existentially ("on my own skin," as Yugoslavs say) what it means to be an alien, a stranger. We lived in Yugoslavia from 1986–89 and 1992–94. Often xenophobia is subtle: people don't greet you, or they laugh at you. Other times it is outright meanness: you are cheated or lied to.

Americans like to believe that we never do these sorts of things, but I'm afraid we do. We are people, and all people everywhere at some times succumb to their baser natures. Most often, though, I believe we are just plain afraid. We are told things that are either untrue ("All Muslims are terrorists.") or half true ("These attackers were Muslims," begging the question of whether all Muslims are the same.).

You may not be a "resident alien." You may never have experienced what it is like to be finger-printed (all ten fingers) and photographed by a special camera at the Immigration and Naturalization Department, just because you are a foreigner. You may never have been cheated in an open-air market or by a rapacious landlord. You may not even have had anyone laugh at your stupid language mistakes.

However, you are an alien.

Those of us who know Christ do not dwell "here below." While we are citizens of earthly states, our citizenship ultimately is in heaven.

We are strangers and sojourners on the earth. Though we love our homelands and cultures, we must realize and accept that our homeland is not the new Jerusalem or the new Israel. (Wasn't that what Nazi Germany thought? The Third Reich, the "Third Rome"?)

God is gracious to us. He has given us plenty. He has given us all the goods of the earth and all the treasures of heaven. He has promised to "supply all our needs through his riches in glory in Christ Jesus" (Phil 4:19).

And yet we act as if it is our own labors which have won us profit and wealth. We behave as if our country's history is somehow free from reproach and shame. "Manifest Destiny" (the idea that the US is the best nation on earth and God's kingdom on earth) is not merely an American idea. Many races and nations believe they have been especially picked by God for his blessing and protection.

Nothing that we as Christians have is ours. We have been bought with a price and we are not our own. What God has given us we are to use for the good of others and the advancement of his kingdom. Unfortunately, we become comfortable with our wealth and fail to see the widow and orphan at our door.

All that we have we will one day lose. We will die. What we own will be given to someone else. We can choose to use our wealth to help others (to love others as ourselves) or we can hoard and grasp, and lose what we have struggled for.

Donor fatigue is a real issue. But if nothing is ours, why can't we share?

> Give, and it will be given to you. A good measure, pressed down, shaken together and running over, will be poured into your lap. For with the measure you use, it will be measured to you. (Luke 6:38)

I help to provide professors to teach in a master of theology program at a seminary in Ukraine, a country at war. One of the students in that group wanted to write his MTh thesis about how people in the churches there in Ukraine have reached the point of complaining about not having anything to share.

Actually, I think the Christians in Ukraine have done admirably. They have taken people into their homes. They have shared their meager meals (Potatoes and potatoes and potatoes and . . . well, millet for variety).

Nowadays, our Western lifestyles demand great outlays of cash. I don't begrudge anyone what they feel that they must have to live (for example, two or three cars per family due to living in an area with poor public transport). However, I am amazed at trends that I can't comprehend. I don't say they are sinful, but at best they seem to be confused.

For example, people expect to travel to exotic places for vacation. My grandfather was an electrical lineman. When I was a child we either went to a cabin on Lake Erie (a few hours from our home) or we went to a state park and camped. My grandfather's big splurge was to go to Florida for a week in the winter. He gave liberally to his church from his moderate income. I don't believe he ever flew anywhere.

Times change and costs for flying have gone down. Traveling to a small island in the ocean no longer seems to be such a big deal. However, many of us act as if this life is all we have and so spend selfishly or as if we will die and that is the end.

If we believe in heaven and its glory, why do we spend so much on luxuries that we know won't last into eternity and ignore people who are eternal?

We weren't strangers, pilgrims on the earth. We *are* strangers, pilgrims on the earth. God reminds the Israelites: "You shall love him as yourself." Jesus reiterates: "Love your neighbor as yourself."

"Love your neighbor as yourself!"

Jesus—The Gospel according to Matthew 22:39

Jesus was a radical. He was despised by the religious establishment. He was a renegade. He taught without having been taught or approved by recognized teachers (Matt 21:23, 24; John 7:15).

As Jesus' ministry progressed, his enemies sent people to test him, to see if he would either overtly break some obvious law of the Torah or fall afoul of the Roman overlords. The short command, with which our section began, is a part of Jesus' reply to such enemies.

Jesus was very good at escaping from the dilemmas his enemies put before him. He was able to show how they in fact had missed the point of the Scripture, emphasizing lesser commandments and ignoring more important ones. After all, as we all know, following rules is far easier than letting your heart be changed.

According to Jewish reckoning, there are 613 commandments in the Torah. Perhaps there are 613 commands in the Torah, but Jesus wasn't interested in merely counting them. In some places, he criticized Jewish teachers of the Old Testament Law for focusing on minor issues, and thereby avoiding fulfilling more important laws.

> Woe to you, teachers of the law and Pharisees, you hypocrites! You give a tenth of your spices—mint, dill and cumin. But you have neglected the more important matters of the law—justice, mercy and faithfulness. You should have practiced the latter, without neglecting the former. (Matt 23:23)

Jesus saw that it is easier to focus on small things (in some of today's churches: perhaps the question of whether you watch movies or whether you play cards), than it is to deal with bigger heart issues: justice, mercy, and faithfulness.

After Jesus had escaped the false dilemmas of several teachers of the Jewish Law, one such teacher was very impressed with the young renegade rabbi:

> One of the teachers of the law came and heard them debating. Noticing that Jesus had given them a good answer, he asked him, "Of all the commandments, which is the most important?" (Mark 12:28)

There must have been some question as to the motives of the questioner, since Matthew's Gospel said that the question was posed by Pharisees to trick Jesus. But perhaps, like all encounters, it wasn't one or the other, but both.

Jesus' response was, as always, magnificent. They expected he would be caught on the horns of a dilemma: "Which of 613 commandments would he choose?" Surely then they could attack him and his choice. It was a nearly unwinnable situation. But Jesus answered wisely:

> "The most important one," answered Jesus, "is this: 'Hear, O Israel: The Lord our God, the Lord is one. Love the Lord your God with all your heart and with all your soul and with all your mind and with all your strength.'" (Mark 12:29; cf. Deut 6:4, 5)

His opponent said: "Well said, teacher!"

Jesus refused to descend to the level of minutiae. Instead, he focused on, in effect, the two sides of the Table of the Law, the Ten Commandments. He summarized the Ten Commandments (and the other 603) into two. Though I have already discussed the Two Greatest Commandments above, they bear further discussion.

The commandments in the first Table of the Law concern loving God and obeying God. The second five commandments focus on one's neighbor, others.

Jesus teaches us that the way to obey God is to love him with our entire being. Rather than focus on how much a tithe or tenth of a spice we bought must be given to the temple service, we are to love God so thoroughly that all our actions reflect that love.

Jesus leaves nothing out. The heart represents our will and the seat of our emotions. It represents what we want and will strive to achieve. The soul refers to our eternal being and spiritual being. The mind concerns our intellectual abilities and gifts. Our strength represents our bodily abilities and skills. No less than the whole of our being and person is required. We were created by God as his children and all that we have, even our physical and spiritual being, belongs to him.

If we love God in this way there will be no worrying about fulfilling the lesser laws. Augustine says that it is impossible to force anyone to do anything. We will do what we love. If we say that we love something or someone and ignore them, we are either confused or lying. If we say we don't love something or someone, but it or they occupy all our thoughts and waking moments, we again are either confused or lying (perhaps to ourselves as well as others). We will strive to attain what we love.[62]

It's true that the apostle Paul laments that he chooses that which he does not want (Rom 7:15–20). However, here Paul is pitting his human nature, which is still in the process of being conformed to Christ's image, with the higher desire of his spirit and the Holy Spirit to follow God and keep his laws. In fact, later, in Romans chapter 8, Paul shows how following the promptings of the Holy Spirit overcomes the downward pull of the old human nature.

The book of James also addresses this question. It is true that we all sin and when we sin we actually choose what we want. James says,

> When tempted, no one should say, "God is tempting me." For God cannot be tempted by evil, nor does he tempt anyone, but each person is tempted when they are dragged away by their own evil desire and enticed. Then, after desire has conceived, it gives birth to sin; and sin, when it is full-grown, gives birth to death. (Jas 1:13–15)

The issue is desire: What do we really want? If we are in the process of being conformed to the image of Christ, we will want what Christ wants, and lament when we fail him and fail to fulfill his commands. We will want to do what our Beloved wants of us. Think of a young man who is madly in love with a young woman. He will think about her constantly. He will be obsessed with her. His emotional state will be constantly perturbed. He will devote his soul to her, perhaps writing poetry or songs for her. He will dedicate every waking hour to trying to please her and understand her. He will long to embrace her. He will use all of his energy and ingenuity to earn the money necessary to buy an engagement ring. We might say of such a person that he is besotted. He might be, but he is also in love.

If we really loved God, we would fulfill all his commands. We wouldn't quibble about which are higher or better, and we wouldn't focus on minor ones to avoid weightier ones.

But Jesus doesn't stop with loving God with all one's being. He goes a step further and says:

> "The second is this: 'Love your neighbor as yourself.'" (Mark 12:30; cf. Lev. 19:18)

By truly loving God, we will love what he has created, and that includes humankind, our neighbors. Jesus encapsulates the second half of the Table of the Law by focusing on how to fulfill one's obligation to others.

If one loves one's parents, he or she will honor them. If one loves one's neighbor, he or she will not steal from them or murder them or lie to them. If a man loves his neighbor, he will not have sex with his neighbor's wife. If one loves one's neighbor, one will not desire what his neighbor has.

Jesus' opponents weren't happy with his response. They had been caught out. They had been shown to be petty and mean. On another occasion one of these enemies challenged Jesus again:

> An expert in the law stood up to test Jesus. "Teacher," he asked, "what must I do to inherit eternal life?" "What is written in the

Law?" he replied. "How do you read it?" He answered, "'Love the Lord your God with all your heart and with all your soul and with all your strength and with all your mind'; and, 'Love your neighbor as yourself.'" "You have answered correctly," Jesus replied. "Do this and you will live." But he wanted to justify himself, so he asked Jesus, "And who is my neighbor?" (Luke 10:25-30)

Perhaps this expert in the law had heard Jesus' earlier response, since, when questioned, he repeated Jesus' words. Jesus commends him for his correct answer, but then challenges the questioner to live up to his words. This was not what the expert in the law had expected or wanted. So, to justify himself he asked: "And who is my neighbor?"

The parable or allegorical story that Jesus then told cut through any obfuscation. It is a well-known story, the parable of the good Samaritan, which I mentioned above.

Now, we may understand what it means to be a Good Samaritan and we might even at times act like one, but often we are fooling ourselves when we choose who we want to be our neighbor. It is easy to love those who are like us. We generally aren't afraid of them and we believe that we understand them. Sympathy is easiest when it's directed at people who are like us and whom we think we understand.

Jesus' story cuts through this self-deception of the teachers of the law. As is often the case, Jesus' story is not even a thinly-veiled attack, it is a direct attack. Jesus lays bare the smallness and hard-heartedness as well as the racism of his day.

A Jewish man was traveling and is attacked by robbers. He was badly beaten and left for dead on the road. First, a Jewish priest happened along. He was rushing somewhere (possibly to serve in the temple).

It's helpful to understand something about the Old Testament law to understand this parable. If a Jew touched a dead body, he became ritually unclean, which in the case of a priest would mean not being able to perform his priestly functions. He would need to be, in effect, quarantined until he was declared ritually clean (Lev. 19). If the priest was on his way to some service in the temple and touched a dead body, he would not be able to serve there. Now, the priest could not tell if the man was dead or not. He couldn't risk touching him. So, intent on his religious duties, he passed the bleeding man.

The second person to come along was also a Jew, a Levite. He might have been a priest or he might have been a musician in the temple. Perhaps he, too, was rushing to Jerusalem to serve in the temple. Again, he could not touch a dead man or he would be disqualified from service. So, he too passed by.

The next man who comes along was a Samaritan. Jews despised Samaritans as "half-breeds" and heretics. The Samaritans were a mixed-race people who had originated when Jews left in Palestine after the Assyrians invaded intermarried (a sin according to their law) with non-Jewish peoples, who had been forced into Palestine by the Assyrians. In addition, the Samaritans were also religious heretics. They accepted only the first Five books of Moses, i.e., the Torah, and rejected the rest of the Old Testament. They also worshiped in another place, Mt. Gerizim, rather than in Jerusalem.

This Samaritan person had no reason to worry about a Jew who had been robbed and beaten. Yet, he stopped, filled with compassion, and helped the Jewish man, who as it turned out was not dead but only badly beaten.

The Samaritan took the man to the equivalent of a local motel and told the manager, "Take care of him. Whatever you spend I'll repay when I come back." He also paid the equivalent of two days' wages up front for the care of the beaten man.

Then Jesus asked the "million-dollar question":

> "Which of these three do you think was a neighbor to the man who fell into the hands of robbers?" The expert in the law replied, "The one who had mercy on him." Jesus told him, "Go and do likewise." (Luke 10:36, 37)

The expert in the law, the religious teacher, the seminary professor, and even the ordinary citizen cannot evade Jesus' question. Surely, the teacher was shamed. The point of the story is so self-evident that even a child could not fail to understand.

But Jesus wasn't content to ask him who was the true neighbor to the man. He gave the teacher a command: "Go and do likewise."

I have spent a lot of time on this story, and it's well-known to many of my readers. But I hope the point is clear. We tend to love those like us. When we look like the "Other" we see, we assume we have things in common. We don't tend to fear people like us. If someone who is English-speaking comes to our church here in the Netherlands (our church is an expatriate church of mostly native English-speakers), we welcome them.

However, it's much more difficult to love those with whom we disagree or who look different either by skin color, hair color, or dress. If they practice another religion, which we don't really understand but think we understand, and only understand poorly, we may be very nervous about helping them.

Jesus' point in this story is that it's the foreigner, the despised one, who is actually the good neighbor. He is moved by compassion, not stopping to think of consequences, and even spends his hard-earned money to help this person.

I believe that often our worries about "dangerous" others are more involving our lack of compassion, our lack of love than the real danger of those others. If I grant that we want to follow Christ and love our neighbor, I must still ask: Do we actually love our neighbor in practice?

It won't do to ask as the teacher of the law asked: "Who's my neighbor?" If we have eyes and watch the news, we see who our neighbors are. Our neighbors are now those who have been driven from their homes, who have lost everything and must now begin again as strangers in new countries. We have an opportunity to practice this sort of love of neighbor in a way which is unique in our history as Western nations and Christians in the West.

Perhaps we have "donor fatigue" or we suffer from fear of "terrorists," but if we do not take the time to learn who the "Other" is, we are playing a game.

Compassion moved the Samaritan to give up front two days' wages for the beaten man's keep. Two days' wages . . . Compute it in your own salary. My salary is $2907/month; divided by 23 days is $126/day; $126 times 2 is $252. Would I be willing to spend $252 to help someone who reviled me and considered me a heretic? Would you?

Compassion must move us. However, just contributing once to a fund is not what is needed.

Immigrants are those who have been legally allowed to come into our countries. They need companionship, fellowship, someone to give them a welcome.

They need help adjusting to life in their new countries. The government can only do so much.

It is the duty and job of the church to help those in need. It is not something we may do only when it suits us.

Do not neglect hospitality

> Do not forget to show hospitality to strangers, for by so doing
> some people have shown hospitality to angels without knowing
> it. (Heb 13:2)

I have taken the title of this book from this verse. I admit that to some degree I am "reaching" in my interpretation—the writer of Hebrews is emphasizing the need for Christians to welcome and host other Christians, preachers, evangelists, and missionaries who are traveling to advance the cause of the gospel.

At the same time, the writer of Hebrews is reminding us that in Old Testament times, some people thought that they were just observing typical "Near Eastern" hospitality, when they had in fact entertained "angels" without knowing it. The first example is when Abraham was sitting in the shade of his tent. He noticed some strangers (foreigners, travelers) (Gen 18), who appeared before him in the heat of the day, i.e., the hottest time in Israel. He RAN out to meet these "men" (older Middle Eastern men did not run) and asked them to come into his home. He gave them water to wash. (Water was not running out of the tap. Someone had to fetch it, perhaps from a long distance away.) He ordered his wife to bake bread (not merely to run to the market). He selected a calf from his herd. (I don't know, but I suspect that slaughtering a calf was not a small thing. In Yugoslavia those who kept livestock did so waiting for it to fatten up at the end of the season [fall]. Butchering an animal and giving it to guests was not only a grand gesture, it was giving of one's substance.) He also took curds and milk and SERVED the guests. (Eastern men did not serve. Women served.) He offered them hospitality—not just a meal, but also a place to stay. There was no nearby hotel to send them to.

In fact, only later Abraham learned that one of the men was the LORD, i.e., God in human form. The others were, apparently, angels, or (in the view of some Eastern Orthodox Christians) this was a pre-incarnate appearance of Christ along with the two other members of the Godhead, God the Father and God the Holy Spirit. (See Andrei Rublev's famous icon.)

It's not really even clear whether Abraham realized that the Lord, who promised him a son and warned of Sodom's destruction, was the "LORD," i.e., Yahweh, God himself. There is, though, no question that by extending hospitality to total strangers in a time and place where he and his entire household were very vulnerable, he entertained angels unaware.

In the next chapter (Gen 19), Abraham's nephew, Lot, entertains two of these visitors whom Abraham had entertained. I do not wish to go into the moral nature of Lot's actions beyond offering hospitality and protection. I don't wish either to go into just what sort of danger these "men" (visitors, strangers) were in. The text is clear that there would have been violence and assault involved, if Lot had not protected them.

In fact, Lot's action of welcoming the strangers and helping them resulted in his salvation. The angel visitors had determined what they had come to establish: the awful condition of the cities of Sodom and Gomorrah. For his part in trying to help and protect them, Lot won the lives of himself and his family.

Neither Abraham or Lot knew that the visitors they were feeding, helping, and protecting were angels or even God himself (or maybe even the Trinity). They weren't thinking, "This is the Trinity come to earth!" They hadn't seen Andrei Rublev's icon. They were simply behaving as they knew their culture and God expected them to do.

In contrast to Abraham and Lot, we have something more exalted than common sense, culture, or even Old Testament Law. We have the words of Christ, which compel us to care for strangers. We are without excuse when we ignore the cries for help around us.

I was a stranger and you welcomed me

> Then the King will say to those on his right, "Come, you who are blessed by my Father, inherit the kingdom prepared for you from the foundation of the world. For I was hungry and you gave me food, I was thirsty and you gave me drink, I was a stranger and you welcomed me, I was naked and you clothed me, I was sick and you visited me, I was in prison and you came to me." Then the righteous will answer him, saying, "Lord, when did we see you hungry and feed you, or thirsty and give you drink? And when did we see you a stranger and welcome you, or naked and clothe you? And when did we see you sick or in prison and visit you?" And the King will answer them, "Truly, I say to you, as you did it to one of the least of these my brothers, you did it to me." (Matt 25:34–40)

Because this passage about the final judgment is following two parables, we sometimes consider it a good suggestion, rather than a solemn warning. I know many people who are doing some of these things for refugees and internally displaced people. It doesn't take a deep exegesis to see someone in a flimsy tent for a home to realize that we ought to do something about it.

However, what we need is a heart of compassion. We need to feel a kinship, a oneness with people who are driven from their homes, sometimes only with what's on their backs and a handful of belongings. How would we feel in their place?

The news media keeps us appraised of big humanitarian catastrophes. However, since something new always drives the media, once it moves on to the next catastrophe we quickly forget the people behind the headlines, the tens or hundreds of thousands stuck in detention centers or asylum centers. When the "ceasefire" is signed, we stop paying attention to the undeclared war that continues, when forces wait until dusk to start shelling in a "ceasefire" zone.

We experience donor fatigue. We only have so many dollars or euros. We have bills, and budgets, and commitments.

All of this is true, but we must decide now "how to use worldly wealth to gain friends for yourselves, so that when it is gone, you will be welcomed into eternal dwellings" (Luke 16:9). What we do with the goods, wealth, talents we have in this life determines what rewards we will have in the next life. Some see this idea of rewards as mercenary. However, Jesus promises to reward those who use their worldly wealth to help others.

We become too attached to what money and power can attain. We don't see ourselves as wealthy. Most often, many of us see ourselves as "middle class." Other people are rich, like Warren Buffett.

However, by world standards, people in western Europe, the UK, and the US are among the wealthiest people on earth. We have always been wealthy. By the standards of earlier days, even in the nineteenth century in these same areas and by world standards in most parts of the world, we were wealthy.

We don't haul wood to cook our food or heat our houses. We have central heating. We don't have to pump water from a well in our front yard. We have clean running water and hot water heaters for hot baths and showers. We have electricity and don't have to buy or make candles to have light, or use smelly oil lanterns. Our homes have brick or concrete walls or are insulated and are warm and free of chilly drafts. We have more than enough to eat and throw away billions of dollars of food per year. We can afford the latest fashions—or at least buy what we really want to wear. We have many luxury goods: perfumes, cars, suits, dresses, expensive shoes. This is a far cry from the days of my great grandfather, who had his mining clothes and his one wedding suit.

By sharing our gifts of wealth and prosperity we are not just helping others. We are being asked to put ourselves in the place of Jesus and help those he cares for.

We evangelical Christians say that we are concerned for world evangelism, but when the world is brought to our doorstep, we ignore it and go on with our busy lives. We do not walk our talk.

It was once-upon-a-time argued that evangelical Christians should not engage in "social action," i.e., delivering aid to the poor or helping the downtrodden. The argument advanced was that if we focused on feeding people, but did not share the gospel with them, they would die with full stomachs but go to hell. On the other hand, if we evangelized them first and focused our resources on evangelizing, other more "liberal" groups would feed them anyway.

John Stott, in his book *Christian Mission in the Modern World*, addressed this argument. He said that trying to evangelize a starving person without supplying food was a pointless endeavor because the starving person would not be able to hear the words above the noise of his growling stomach. Stott, in contrast, described his own view of Christian mission as being like the two wings of a dove. One wing of Christian outreach must be caring for people's physical needs. The other wing of Christian outreach must be caring for people's spiritual needs. The dove could not fly with one wing.[63]

This viewpoint seems to me to be both eminently sensible and biblical. Franklin Graham, son of Billy Graham, founded Samaritan's Purse for this reason. While not denigrating his father's efforts in evangelism, Franklin simply began to follow his heart and find help for those in the conditions Jesus describes in Matt 25:34ff. Probably, for most people, the "Shoe Box" campaign, or "Operation Christmas Child," has become the most well-known outreach of Samaritan's Purse.[64]

Many refugees are sitting in asylum or detention centers. They may have a very great amount of freedom, since they have been deemed safe by authorities in the country they seek to immigrate to. These refugees have a lot of time on their hands. They may have lessons in the local language, in our case in the Netherlands Dutch, but they have many hours to kill.

One local church here in the Netherlands near an established asylum center has started opening their church twice a week for the afternoon. People of every walk of life who live in that area have gone there to spend time socializing and getting to know these potential immigrants. Both sets of visitors have been very glad of these attempts to get to know the other side and make friends or to show kindness. It was discovered that both sides had lots to offer.

The life of a refugee is not easy. While they may not be under any obvious physical threat or lack of food, shelter, or clothing in a new country, they enter a no-man's land. They go for months or even longer with no word from authorities. There are many people to process and those who are considered possibly dangerous get more careful scrutiny and quicker processing. Those who are considered safer wait until the authorities can deal with them, which might take many months or longer.

To be left in limbo for many months is very hard. Some of these people have relatives—wives, children, parents—whom they hope to get out of their war-torn countries. These relatives may face immediate dangers. When a Christian reaches out to these people it is a great support. Visiting the drop-in center and having a tea and a chat, or even inviting a refugee home for a meal, is greatly appreciated.

We need to put our money where our mouths are! The apostle John says,

> Do not love this world nor the things it offers you, for when you love the world, you do not have the love of the Father in you. For the world offers only a craving for physical pleasure, a craving

> for everything we see, and pride in our achievements and pos-
> sessions. These are not from the Father, but are from this world.
> And this world is fading away, along with everything that people
> crave. But anyone who does what pleases God will live forever.
> (1 John 1:15–17)

In John's theology, the "world" is the kingdom of Satan, the kingdom of darkness, the system of all that is opposed to God. To love the "world" is to have a set of values contrary to the values of God's Kingdom.

John rejects hedonism, i.e., seeking only pleasures which fill our appetites. When I am in the US at "all you can eat" restaurants, I wonder at our values. Perhaps it might be argued that it's good value ("value for money" as our British friends say), but sometimes it turns into gluttony, and when was gluttony approved of by Christ or in the Bible? Further, a brief glance at many TV shows and movies reveals that we in the West are obsessed with sex and glamor. Since most people in the West have rejected God and the Christian values of their past, we have become hedonists, those who seek pleasure over all. What drives us is the desire to enjoy life now and all it offers without any real thought for the consequences.

John also speaks against desiring everything we see. We are an exceedingly visual culture. With the rise of cinema, TV, and now the Internet, we are bombarded day and night with advertisements and images. In our internet viewing, even on our Facebook pages, our viewings are monitored and ads are tailored for us to fit our earlier "hits." We are pandered to. We are made to believe that if we don't have this new thing we want, our lives will not be rich and full. We have houses filled with gadgets which we don't use and toys we've outgrown. We watch, with glee, shows about hoarders, and don't consider that we hoard more than generations before us could ever have dreamed of. "From everyone who has been given much, much will be demanded; and from the one who has been entrusted with much, much more will be asked" (Luke 12:48).

We work hard for many things. Some strive for academic praise. Degrees on the walls show that we are "worthwhile." As one who has several degrees on my walls, I am proud of my achievements, but I regularly joke that these diplomas and $3.95 will get me a cup of coffee at Starbucks. Academic achievements are meaningful when they serve humanity and the kingdom of Christ. However, we must ask ourselves: Do we use our talents and skills to help others? The "shine" on that diploma, even a doctoral diploma, lasts about a month, and then "normal" life goes on; believe me, I know! Diplomas open doors for work or service, but they don't determine our worth. Christ determines our worth by dying for us. It's not what you know, but Whom you know, and whether you keep his commands.

Love your enemies

But, perhaps we believe these strangers, the foreigners, are our enemies— what then?

> But to you who are listening I say: Love your enemies, do good to those who hate you, bless those who curse you, pray for those who mistreat you. If someone slaps you on one cheek, turn to them the other also. If someone takes your coat, do not withhold your shirt from them. Give to everyone who asks you, and if anyone takes what belongs to you, do not demand it back. Do to others as you would have them do to you. If you love those who love you, what credit is that to you? Even sinners love those who love them. And if you do good to those who are good to you, what credit is that to you? Even sinners do that. And if you lend to those from whom you expect repayment, what credit is that to you? Even sinners lend to sinners, expecting to be repaid in full. But love your enemies, do good to them, and lend to them without expecting to get anything back. Then your reward will be great, and you will be children of the Most High, because he is kind to the ungrateful and wicked. Be merciful, just as your Father is merciful. (Luke 6:27–35)

Many times these are difficult words for us to hear. They are so difficult to hear and accept that we often interpret them away. "This is only 'personal' ethics. This isn't expected of us as nations," say some interpreters.

We call ourselves a "Christian" nation, but then we explain away what Christ expects of us by calling it "personal ethics."[65]

How should we treat an enemy? Do good to them. Pray for them. When punched, don't punch back. When someone robs you of your coat, give him your shirt (thus, leaving yourself without any outer protection against the cold). When an enemy asks for something, give it to him.

Why should we do this? Because this is how God has and does treat us! When we were enemies of God's, he sent his Son to die for us. "While we were yet sinners, Christ died for us" (Rom 5:8). We, too, are to imitate God in his graciousness and mercy.

Miroslav Volf is a theologian at Yale Divinity School. He was raised in the former Yugoslavia. He was studying in California at Fuller Seminary during the time of the "Bosnian" War. However, he was provoked by the war and spent much time reflecting on it.

In his book _Exclusion and Embrace_, Volf uses the parable, the story, of the prodigal son to illustrate how we should treat our "enemy," even if he's our own brother, which was the case for many Yugoslavs during the Bosnian war.[66] It's a very familiar story from the Gospels. Jesus tells of two sons and their aged father. The younger son asks for his inheritance (at that time, saying this to one's father was basically like saying, "I wish you were dead!"). Then, he goes away and wastes his inheritance.

Eventually this younger son realizes that he is starving and it would be better to "eat crow" or "eat humble pie" at home than to starve. So, he returns to his father to ask to be taken in, even if only as a hired hand.

The father, however, has never stopped waiting and expecting the return of the younger son. The father is watching the horizon from his house. He sees the younger son returning. (No father could miss the silhouette and stride of his son.) The father (an older Middle Eastern man) runs out to the son and embraces him. The younger son can't even get out his rehearsed speech begging his father's forgiveness. The father calls for servants to bring a robe and a ring (signs of being a son) and tells them to prepare a banquet.

Meanwhile the older brother is out in the field. When he learns that the younger son has returned, the older brother is not happy. He doesn't rejoice at the safe return of his brother. He thinks only of his inheritance. The older brother remains outside and will not go in to the meal. Finally, true to form, the father goes out to the older brother to beg him to come in.

The older brother says,

> "Look! All these years I've been slaving for you and never disobeyed your orders. Yet you never gave me even a young goat so I could celebrate with my friends. But when this _son of yours_ who has squandered your property with prostitutes comes home, you kill the fattened calf for him!" "Look, dear son, you have always stayed by me, and everything I have is yours. We had to celebrate this happy day. For your brother was dead and has come back to life! He was lost, but now he is found." (Luke 15:29–32, NLT)

We are often like the older brother. We have all that the Father owns. We are princes and princesses of the King of Kings. All he has given us now, and all he will give us in heaven, is a gift, undeserved, unearned. Yet, we withhold what we have and refuse to share liberally.

Volf, also alluding to the philosophy of Emmanuel Levinas, describes our encounter with the "Other." When we are afraid of someone, we are defined by them. Our fear characterizes us.

In war, it is easy for propaganda to demonize, to bestialize others. We stop seeing people as people and see them as "terrorists" or "war-mongers." We see some Muslims behead a journalist, and the easiest thing to do is simply paint them and all Muslims with the same brush and declare all Muslims terrorists. It sells books and gets hits on YouTube to make sweeping statements about others.

Volf, as a Yugoslav in the face of the destruction of his own homeland, recognized that those "enemies" were his brothers. I might try to deny that that person is my brother or sister, but we are "family," we have one Creator. In former Yugoslavia, it was literally true that your own blood brother may have turned against you and gone to war with you.

How should we respond to our "brother" or "sister," another human being, becoming our enemy?

First, we must admit that we are not without fault. Usually the propaganda of the news media and/or our governments deny that we have any fault.

We of the West have a lot of soul searching to do and a lot of questions to ask of ourselves. When we are afraid, we do what we would otherwise consider unacceptable.

According to Jesus, those whom we kill when we bomb are our brothers and sisters, our fathers and mothers. How would we feel if our home town was bombed to kill one or two terrorists and many other innocent people died?

Secondly, we have to drop our defenses. At first, this sounds insane. However, this is what Volf advises. If we wish our brother, from whom we are estranged, to lay down his weapon, we must first lay down ours. This again seems crazy. Won't he shoot me? He might.

But as Volf continues, you cannot embrace when you are holding a gun. You must take the first step and lay down your weapon and open your arms signaling that you want to embrace; you want peace.

Most of us will likely NOT come face to face with an actual terrorist. However, we will come face to face with Muslim immigrants, at least if we are in a major metropolitan area. Probably we can avoid immigrants if we live in more rural areas. If we live in wealthier suburbs, we probably won't encounter refugees. We might even live in a gated community.

But Jesus is asking us to do more than to simply avoid strangers; we are to love them. We are to give to them without expectation of return. We are to do this because this is how God loves us and them. Now, we may find these commands nonsensical. We are used to expecting some sort of return on our investment, even if it is a thank you card. God, however, has given us salvation and all the blessings of this life because he wished to, when it did nothing for him. He even gave his only Son to die for us without assurance that we would respond.

Family feuds are miserable. Even if we act as if "strangers" are not brothers and sisters, we deny that we are all God's children. To be sure we are estranged from some of those children. We may disagree over many things: their religion, customs, clothes, food, even their politics.

However, all people are God's children and deserve our respect and care. If we only love those who love us, what benefit is that?

> If you love those who love you, what credit is that to you? Even sinners love those who love them. And if you do good to those who are good to you, what credit is that to you? (Luke 6:32, 33)

Too often, we hide from ourselves and blame someone else. It is quite common for right-wing political parties and groups, for instance in the Netherlands, Belgium, Germany, Hungary, and Poland, even in the UK and US, to blame foreigners or "illegal" immigrants for a rise in crime. It's easy to pick on someone who is obviously different. It's easy for us to categorize people. Obvious differences are most easily targeted. However, we are called to love all of God's children, whether they are lovable or not, no matter what race, creed, or color. God is "color blind." As the old song says,

> Jesus loves the little children,
> all the children of the world!
> Red and yellow, black and white,
> they are precious in his sight!
> Jesus loves the little children of the world!

Further reading

On biblical support for helping refugees:

Bauman, Stephan, et al. *Seeking Refuge: On the Shores of the Global Refugee Crisis* Chicago: Moody, 2016.

Carroll R., M. Daniel. *Christians at the Border: Immigration, the Church, and the Bible.* 2nd ed. Grand Rapids: Brazos, 2013.

Chapter 4: **Welcoming Strangers**
—A Practical View

THERE ARE MANY WAYS we can help refugees who are entering our countries. These efforts can be on a national level, a regional or denominational level, a city-wide level, and on a personal level. All of us can take some part in these efforts.

Help with efforts organized by the government

While we might not have jobs with government agencies, we can be aware of what our governments are doing with regards to refugees. Often we are woefully and culpably ignorant.

The Internet is like the net which Jesus mentions, which fisherman cast into the sea, bringing forth both good and bad things that then have to be separated. Too often we go to "safe" sites, which say what we have predetermined we want to hear. If a site or news source is considered "liberal," or "right-wing," we might avoid it.

We must not rest content with the seven o'clock news or our favorite news source. We must do more research to find trustworthy sources of information.

The UNHCR gives information which, while we may still wish to critique it, tells us what this large world body is doing. We can at least learn raw data—how many refugees and internally displaced people there are. We can learn what efforts are going on. We can learn the scope of their efforts.

We can also turn to national agencies that deal with immigrants. We can learn the procedures which such agencies use in screening refugees and immigrants. These agencies have a serious mandate to protect and serve all citizens. They are not merely or primarily carrying out the political agenda of one party or another.

Some people have asserted that government agencies are involved in a cover-up, silencing opposition and refusing to report, for instance, the crimes of immigrants. An example of such a theory concerns sexual assaults in Germany. The term translated "sexual assault" (*Sexualdelikten*) is more correctly translated "sexual misconduct." When the legal terms are translated into English as "assaults," we think of outright rapes. It would be more correct to translate the term as "sexual harassment."

An example of this kind of misconduct is represented by the convictions for "sexual assault" of two young refugee men in Germany. In the one case of "assault" the immigrant who was convicted had forced a young woman to kiss him and then licked her face. In the other case of the immigrant convicted of "assault," there was no physical contact at all. The refugee had said, "Give me the girls! Give me the girls! Or death!" This is unacceptable and criminal. The two who were convicted were given a year of probation.[67]

While not diminishing the need to deal with such inappropriate and frightening behavior, the German Interior Minister answered broader concerns. Many right-wing groups fear disruption to the status quo. Amongst other things, they feel that refugees will take jobs from nationals.[68] However, the chief of the German Federal Office for Migration and Refugees noted the negative birthrate in Germany. Germany needs immigrants, he said. If no immigrants were allowed to come into Germany, the German economy and social welfare system and national health care would fail. Immigrants are needed, not to take jobs from nationals, but to take jobs nationals will not take.[69]

When we lived in Vienna in the mid 1980s and early 1990s there was a very influential right-wing politician named Jörg Haider. There were signs up around the capital saying, "Vienna for the Viennese!" (in English and German).[70] They begged the question: "Just who are the Viennese?" Are not all citizens of Austria dwelling in Vienna Viennese, whether of Czech, Slovak, Serb, Croat, Hungarian, Romanian, or any other ethnic descent?

We claim that we are democratic countries, but tend to act as if, since we have been born somewhere, we have exclusive right to that country. How many of us Americans can trace our lineage back further than a few generations? My "ancestors" came to the US in the mid-nineteenth century. Probably many of us are similar. How can we, who are the grandchildren or great-grandchildren of immigrants, deny other people the right to immigrate?

In the US we have wide, rich lands. We have great wealth. We have freedom undreamed of in many places. Surely, God is not exclusive. Surely he is watching to see how generous we will be. Has God given us these things only for our benefit?

Our immigration policy is not simply "Democratic" or "Republican." This policy has developed over the span of and within many administrations.

In any event, our governments are very careful about who gets into our countries and how. I do not argue for illegal immigration or "open borders." However, I am arguing that we as Christians can trust our governments, and those we have elected, to make wise decisions. I am asking that we behave as good citizens, but also as children of God, helping new immigrants, rather than simply giving way to knee-jerk reactions based on fear.

We are rightly concerned about how people enter our countries. Terrorist attacks in Paris and Brussels, and previously the 9/11 attack, have frightened us and raised our level of scrutiny of visas to foreigners—and justly so. However, we also labor under some misconceptions.

Before researching this issue, I thought, wrongly, that the 9/11 attackers were on student visas. Actually, only one was on a student visa, and he had never reported for class. The rest were on tourist visas or business visas. I will quote below from a website which corrects this misconception. I do this for the sake of showing how our misunderstandings can lead us to make wrong assumptions.

> **National Commission on Terrorist Attacks upon the United States, Aug. 21, 2004:** All but one of the hijackers presented visitor visas that immigration inspectors used to decide whether to admit them as tourists or on business. All but two of the nonpilots were admitted as tourists and were granted automatic six-month stays. This allowed them to maintain a legal immigration status through the end of the operation. One of the two nonpilots admitted on business was granted a one-month stay; he, along with another of the nonpilot operatives, was in violation of immigration law for months before the attack.
>
> The one pilot who came in on a student visa never showed up for school, thereby violating the terms of his U.S. visa. Another of the pilots came in on a tourist visa yet began flight school immediately, also violating the terms of his U.S. visa. This pilot came in a total of seven times on a tourist visa while in school. In both cases, the pilots violated the law after their entry into the United States.[71]

From this information, we see that student visas would have been the easiest to control and check, by comparison with tourist or business visas. However, in no case in this incident was one of these persons an immigrant who came through the proper procedure used for refugees who are immigrating.

I worked for a time (about a decade actually) as the director of admissions at Tyndale Theological Seminary. Tyndale is a private foundation in the Netherlands, and so we are foreigners ourselves. We admit men and women from many nations as students. However, there are strict rules about who can be a student in the Netherlands and we have always followed the rules as far as we are aware.

In my role as Director of Admissions at Tyndale Seminary I sometimes dealt with questions about the status of prospective students. In earlier days, before 9/11, I knew a Dutch foreign policeman who would not give me specific information but was glad to talk to me if I had a question about a potential matriculant (a candidate desiring admission). Once, I was concerned about a prospective student who said he could not provide me with any transcripts or even a passport or residence visa. He would only say that he was a legal immigrant, a refugee, and that the Dutch Immigration service would vouch for him. I was concerned, I thought reasonably, as he was from a country with a sizeable Muslim population, and where a war was going on at the time, and so I checked with my acquaintance at the foreign police. He thanked me for checking, and affirmed that the potential matriculant was telling the truth. However, the potential student could not produce documents or diplomas because if he divulged his whereabouts to those in his home country the student would have been killed. I mention this story to point out that I would wager all of us who have had such gate-keeping positions are very, very, very careful. It is no joke. We understand the consequences of making a wrong determination.

Since 9/11, the process has changed and we at Tyndale are no longer allowed any influence into the visa process other than to provide passport details and other information. The Dutch government wants to be sure no one is trying to abuse the system. We have had students and even potential faculty turned down by the Dutch Immigration service. I, for one, am happy that they are so careful.

Because the Dutch government is so careful about student visas, I feel quite safe as to their determinations of refugees and potential immigrants. The Dutch governmental bodies are extremely careful.

I had a visit recently from a former student. He, his friend, and I shared a meal in Schiphol Airport at a restaurant there. I noticed many "parking attendants" in yellow safety vests and personnel in the uniform of the Marechaussee (Royal Military Police) with rifles, patrolling the airport. I am not bothered by such sights because I understand why they are there. The warning level for a terrorist attack must have been on high alert that day. I had to drive around a few times until I could find one of the parking garages I could enter. The entry was monitored by a security camera, which takes a picture of your license plate. I am grateful for these precautionary measures.

There have been very few times that I have felt any moments of tension in living in a Dutch neighborhood with many Muslim neighbors. One was just after 9/11, when the US president at that time, George W. Bush, said that Americans ought to hang out a US flag at half-mast to honor those killed. I felt deeply sad, so I put up our US flag at half-mast in front of the door of our house, forgetting that many young men, mainly of Muslim background, deliver free flyers and local free newspapers in our neighborhood.

As I was washing dishes, I looked out the window to see a teenager, whom I took to be a Muslim, fingering the end of our flag. I stopped my chore and went out to talk to him. He looked at me questioningly. I asked him if he could speak English. He said that he knew some. He asked, "Why?" and pointed to the flag. I said, "Our president asked us to hang the flag like this to show that we were mourning those who died." He looked at me and shook his head. "OK," he said, and left. In retrospect, hanging the flag could have could have been very stupid on my part. The short conversation with the young paper carrier made me realize that. However, despite my hanging a US flag outside my house just after 9/11, I have never had any problems with my Muslim neighbors!

Later, in 2004, after the murder of the Dutch filmmaker Theo van Gogh, there was more concern by many.[72] Van Gogh had made a film in which he interviewed Muslim women who had been abused or beaten by male relatives. For this reason, some extreme Muslim clerics had given him a *fatwa* (a death sentence). Van Gogh was brutally murdered on the street in Amsterdam. The government, even educational agencies, as a result, turned up the scrutiny on "foreigners." In the Netherlands, Roman Catholic, Protestant, and secular schools receive state funding. The Dutch also give funding to some Muslim schools. In light of the murder, government educational representatives took away funding from those Muslim schools they felt were preaching hate.[73] However, despite concern in the wider society about possible unrest or violence in the aftermath of Van Gogh's murder, we experienced none.

I am only a temporary resident of the Netherlands. I have only ever been a "guest," with a five-year visa which is renewable. Since we arrived here in 2000, the visa process keeps getting more and more complicated. One recent event was particularly upsetting to me: I had to be fingerprinted, all ten fingers, and photographed by a special camera. It freaked me out! As an American, I tend to feel that such a demand means that I am suspected of some wrong-doing. I hadn't committed any crime! All the same, I was required to submit to these requirements. Even though it was difficult for me, I remind myself that I have nothing to fear from such a requirement, and those who are trying to hide something will be exposed.

In summary, our governments deserve our prayers and our help, whether in taxes or personal involvement in helping with refugees. Nevertheless, we are aliens and strangers on the earth.

Help with efforts organized by larger church bodies & community efforts

Our larger church bodies, denominations, fellowships, dioceses, community groups, etc. usually have plans in place to help refugees. Those whom we have elected to church offices or who have risen to positions of authority have been called by God to help us make wise decisions and at times goad us into action when we resist.

Sometimes, perhaps often, we are afraid. Strangers are, well, strange. They may look different. They may smell different. They may speak a strange language. We may feel intimidated or fearful when people speak their own language and we can't understand it. "Are they talking about us?" Possibly. So what?

We must get past these fears. One Mennonite church in Pennsylvania—Forest Hills Church in Leola, Pennsylvania—took in a Syrian refugee family.[74] They had help from Christine Baer, a Church World Service congregational resource developer. She described, when interviewed by Mennonite World Review, the process of matching a refugee family to a church:

> After the welcome team decides to commit to the project, Baer matches the team with a refugee family in the process of government screening. **"Refugees are the most screened people who come to the United States,"**[75] Baer said. The Forest Hills team had previously been expecting another family from Syria who gave birth to a baby during the screening process. The baby had to be screened as well, and during that period the other family members' documents expired, setting back their entire process.[76]

Having a baby set back the process of immigrating even though the rest of the family was already approved and had immigrant visas. My point is that Baer's comments clearly show that the US government is not easily allowing refugees into the US. This church had committed to the family, but even the birth of a child restarted the waiting process, i.e., time to screen a new family member.

There is a misconception that the US government easily allows refugees to immigrate. Nothing is further from the truth. Pastor Jon Carlson of Forest Hills Church says:

> The idea that Forest Hills members might have misgivings about their undertaking in light of the Paris terrorist attacks is one Carlson can only laugh at. "This family is resettling in the U.S. through a long-established program with a near-impeccable record of safety," he said.
>
> Carlson considers anti-refugee rhetoric "crazy" and "not at all rooted in fact." "The fear is based on images we're seeing from Europe of border crossings overrun with people, and that's not what this program is," he said. . . . This is such a safe and rigorous process; there's nothing to be afraid of.
>
> "The family we're connected with fled before the rise of ISIS. Their village was destroyed by their own government. When people say, 'Why can't they just go home?'—well, there's no home there; that government is still in power."[77]

I cited this article at length because it shows how one church has helped one family. It also shows there is no danger from refugees / immigrants.

Help with efforts organized by schools

Many schools organize help for refugee children to integrate into our schools. Indeed, our own children have benefited from such programs when we moved to Belgium. When we moved to Leuven, Belgium, where I did my master's in philosophy and my doctoral studies from 1995–2000, our children were put into a special program to learn Flemish (a dialect of Dutch). They had half days at their regular schools and half a day at another school where they focused on learning Flemish. I remember walking our two older children from their "regular" elementary schools in the afternoon to the school which had the special language program.

For our younger son, John, who was four when he entered pre-school in Belgium, it was easier. He learned to read in Flemish before learning to read in English. A little later when we were visiting friends in the Pennsylvania, John fell out of a tree. He was not hurt, but was a little shaken up and needed to rest quietly to recover, so I took him aside up to the boys' bedroom to read him some Dr. Seuss books. About half way through the second book, he said, "I can read that." "Oh?" I asked. He proceeded to sound out words and read. Once in a while his words were a bit "Flenglish" (a combination of English and Flemish-sounding!) but he'd hear what word he was looking for and then switch to perfect English pronunciation (well, I should say, a Pittsburgh American-English pronunciation, haha).

For our older children the language learning was harder, but the special program which the Belgian government had put into place for foreigners and immigrants helped them to learn Flemish quickly and do well in school. They did suffer some rejection by nationalists who disliked them even as Americans. Since kids are kids everywhere, some Flemish kids teased and goaded the "foreign kids," who couldn't speak their language. However, the school system program helped them tremendously and they were accepted and befriended by most.

From this I can see that there are ways we as individuals and groups can help schools. Our home church in the US, North Way Christian Community in Wexford, Pennsylvania, has been involved in a program called LAMP, in which volunteer mentors are matched with students. Mentors help individual students manage their assignments, do their homework, encourage them to finish school and more:

> LAMP, the Learning and Mentoring Partnership, is a collaboration among the Pittsburgh Public Schools, Family Guidance Inc., and area churches—including North Way Christian Community—to impact the City of Pittsburgh, ONE student at a time.[78]

While this program is a specific effort of Pittsburgh educators and churches, similar efforts are being made to help refugee and immigrant children. Anyone who can read and write can help. Elsewhere, people are trying similar initiatives. Sil Ganzo began OurBRIDGE in Charlotte, North Carolina, to help immigrant and refugee children.[79] She has been frustrated in her efforts to help these children and their parents.

But in order to grow, she has to first get Charlotte's residents and politicians to understand that these kids add value, not problems, to the community.[80]

This is just the kind of fear which many countries and communities show. It is really an unnecessary fear when we judge by history. Just as children of immigrants in the past have helped to make America and other countries strong, so they will now. Sil Ganzo noted a similar feeling:

> People need to educate themselves, she adds, about how rigorous and lengthy the refugee-vetting process is, and how unlikely it is for refugees to the US to pose a terror threat.[81]

Help personally

We can all help with volunteer efforts in our own communities. Simply having a cup of coffee or tea and conversing with someone for a half an hour is one more half an hour of practice learning English (or Dutch, Flemish, French, German—any language the new arrival is trying to learn). Helping one immigrant child to learn to read or to do their homework is one less bored and potentially problematic or isolated child.

"But what do they want ME to DO about it?" My wife has heard me say this many, many times. The Dutch may be "going secular" at what, to most Christians, is an alarming rate, but their Christian background can still be seen in their concept of everybody helping by taking part in "*goede doelen*" ("good deeds"—charitable and humanitarian activities). Doing good is somehow deeply imbedded in their souls (I hope, despite their rejection of their traditional Christian faith, their commitment to doing "*goede doelen*" continues!). People are expected to volunteer with some group or for some cause. Individuals circulate through neighborhoods, going door to door with canisters, collecting change for the Kidney Fund, the Heart Fund, the Brain Fund, the Diabetes Fund . . . . My children were required to go out of their school each year on "Horsepower Action Day" (a day to do projects in the community) and do some good deed: stand in front of the supermarket with a canister and collect change for some "good cause," for instance. As part of their school science program, they also went on nature projects to cut brush and rushes at a national park—both educational and helpful to the environment. Also in the US, of course, and in many other nations, many groups like the Scouts of America and others do "good deeds." It's considered, even in our secularized age, a good thing to do, to help others.

Whatever our feelings about government spending, we can all help on a small scale.

The church we belong to in the Netherlands is an example of helping on a small scale, and hopefully might give some ideas for others in other groups. It is an expatriate church, i.e., a church of mostly temporary dwellers in the Netherlands. Being a church in the Diocese of Europe of the Church of England, there is direct help and encouragement from the diocesan office. Aside from that, we are also tied into local organizations and other church groups. Most of us are here in the Netherlands for employment, because we work for a corporation or organization in the Netherlands, e.g., KLM, the Dutch airline; or Unilever, a large multinational firm which does many things, e.g., Kraft foods, Shell Oil, the European Space Agency, the European Patent Office, and so on.

Some of our church members are Dutch. Through our Dutch members, particularly, we have contact with local interchurch groups. One Dutch member of our church council is our "point person" for our involvement with refugees and immigrants. This person meets with other Dutch churches about what the larger Christian community is doing to help refugees and immigrants.

Just to give some background about what our "point person" can and cannot do, the government of the Netherlands does not want any undue influence on the immigration process. For this reason, the organization COA (*Centraal Orgaan opvang Asielzoekers* or "Central Agency for the Reception of Asylum Seekers") was chosen to coordinate all volunteering to help refugees and immigrants.[82] According to the COA, there was a peak of asylum seekers (refugees) desiring to enter and remain in the Netherlands of more than 70,000 in 2016. As of March 2012, it had reported 15,600 asylum seekers.[83] However, another organization, the Asylum International Database (AIDA), a European-wide database, says that there were 20,700 new asylum seekers in 2016.[84] Of these 2,158 were Syrians, 1,497 were Eritreans, and 1026 were Afghani. Of these, 33.1 percent were accepted as refugees and 28.2 percent were rejected. The other 38.7 percent were given sanctuary on other grounds. All efforts are coordinated by COA.

Our Dutch "point person" understands these constraints and others' efforts to help and keeps us appraised of any efforts we can do individually with others, so that word soon gets around about local initiatives. These can be monitored so that there aren't, for instance, too many bicycles donated! Targeted help can then be offered to support individual families such as the provision of curtains, painting, meals, equipment, etc. Our "point person" is also aware of what other churches and civic groups are doing and can coordinate or link in our efforts with theirs.

We also have one friend who, moved by compassion, just set out and started with neighbors to work with a local refugee asylum center that had been operating for many years prior to the current "surge" of refugees. She collected things in her garage and took them to the center. She circulated a newsletter via e-mail and encouraged people to get involved. It was a small effort in the scheme of things, but a very meaningful one.

Personally, I often ask myself, "What can a guy with a PhD in philosophy do to help refugees? Surely teaching philosophy is not helpful to immigrants?" One small answer came when my wife was having a look at Facebook one evening, and saw that someone was asking for a Bible study for refugees in a detention center here in Leiden. I looked into the person asking and it checked out. It seemed amazing that people from a Muslim nation would want a Bible study, but some apparently were Christians already.

We went ahead and met with these refugees in their center. In the end we only held the Bible study six or so times, as some of the refugees soon were processed and left Leiden, or left and returned home, or left for other places in Europe where they had relatives. However, we got to know a few of these folks and eventually were able to host some of them in our home for a meal. We hope that we have made some friends and helped them a little with what we could do for them. Hopefully the Bible studies were also meaningful to them. Our lives are richer for that brief involvement.

I am sure that many US denominations and churches have similar agencies which coordinate their outreach to immigrants and refugees. You can also find opportunities yourself just by paying attention and being open. Many local churches as well have individual outreach to refugees and immigrants. There are opportunities out there, but we have to be open to seeing them!

Further reading

On how to get involved:

Bauman, Stephan, et al. *Seeking Refuge: On the Shores of the Global Refugee Crisis.* Chicago: Moody, 2016.

Part II: **Making Careful Distinctions**

Chapter 5: **Making Careful Distinctions —Whose Job Is Whose?**

IN THE FIRST PART of this chapter I will make an attempt to explain in part how immigration policies and procedures work. I cannot hope to be comprehensive. I can only hope to be adequate enough to illustrate my points above: that while the problems are huge, we must have compassion on refugees, internally displaced people, and immigrants, and secondly, we must become personally involved. Jesus told us to love the stranger and to care for the least of these. He also commands us to love our enemies in very practical ways. We cannot close our eyes and our hearts to these people without sacrificing something of our true humanity and calling in Christ.

Immigration procedures

Did you know that refugees, immigrants, and internally displaced people are not all the same? Governmental agencies have a role to determine who is a refugee (and thus a potential immigrant) and who is not. But all of us need to have some basic understanding of the categories which are used to identify refugees, internally displaced people, immigrants, and others. When we fail to make proper distinctions we "broad-brush" (put in the same category) many people who don't necessarily belong together.

In this section I will focus on how two non-governmental organizations (NGOs) work: the United Nations High Commission for Refugees (UNHCR) and the Mennonite Central Committee (MCC). The first is widely known. The second is less well-known but has a significant role in many parts of the world, as well as being an example of what a smaller Christian organization can accomplish in helping refugees.

It is important to distinguish between refugees, migrants, and internally displaced persons. The United Nations High Commission for Refugees (UNHCR) defines refugees by citing the 1951 Refugee Convention; a refugee is someone who,

> owing to a well-founded fear of being persecuted for reasons of race, religion, nationality, membership of a particular social group or political opinion, is outside the country of his nationality, and is unable to, or owing to such fear, is unwilling to avail himself of the protection of that country.[85]

In June 2019, the UNHCR said that there were 25.9 million refugees world-wide.[86] "They all await one of three possible solutions: repatriation, local integration or resettlement."[87]

At the same time, not all people on the move are refugees. Refugees should not be confused with migrants (economic immigrants or temporary dwellers working in a foreign country) or internally displaced persons [IDPs]. There were 41.3 million IDPs world-wide at the end of 2018, according to the UNHCR.[88]

The UNHCR defines internally displaced people this way:

> Internally displaced persons, or IDPs, are among the world's most vulnerable people. Unlike refugees, IDPs have not crossed an international border to find sanctuary but have remained inside their home countries. Even if they have fled for similar reasons as refugees (armed conflict, generalized violence, human rights violations), IDPs legally remain under the protection of their own government—even though that government might be the cause of their flight. As citizens, they retain all of their rights and protection under both human rights and international humanitarian law.[89]

Surprisingly, internally displaced people can be worse off than those who have actually fled their home countries. For example, Syrian IDPs who are in camps within the borders of their country are worse off than Syrian refugees in the Netherlands. If internally displaced people flee due to persecution by their own government or war inside their countries, they cannot get the same sort of help which can be given to those who manage to cross their own country's boundaries and seek refuge elsewhere. For example, if their own governments object to them being given aid or help, the UNHCR and other international non-governmental organizations (NGOs) are powerless to help them. They are at the mercy of political forces in their own country.

One example is the group of seventy thousand Kurds driven from their homes in 2007 by Saddam Hussein's forces and other Sunni Arab forces in Iraq.[90] Another example is the Yazidi people, a Kurdish-speaking monotheistic community who had been driven from their homeland in Iraq to Mount Sinjar to die:

> The Yazidis drew international attention in August [2014] when Islamic State in Iraq and the Levant (ISIL) fighters trapped them on Mount Sinjar, threatening to massacre thousands of people because of their beliefs. More than 200,000 Yazidis fled their villages, walking through the mountains without food or water, watching the weakest die. . . . The U.N. has described the ISIL assault as attempted genocide.
>
> [As of 2014] Iraq's evacuated Yazidis [were] an internally displaced people, filling the streets, schools, churches and unfinished buildings of northern Iraq's Kurdistan. Half a million displaced Yazidis are in the Dohuk governorate with insufficient food, water and winter supplies.[91]

Another example of IDPs who were unreachable by help from international aid organizations was when Myanmar's military junta refused to accept aid for cyclone victims from the international agencies on the ground. They claimed that the help being offered was actually international interference in their internal affairs and insisted that they could manage the crisis without it:

> International aid for cyclone victims in Burma [in 2009] was deliberately blocked by the military regime, the first independent report into the disaster has found.
>
> The junta's willful disregard for the welfare of the 3.4 million survivors of cyclone Nargis—which struck the Irrawaddy delta last May, killing 140,000 people—and a host of other abuses detailed by the research may amount to crimes against humanity under international law.[92]

Not only did the military junta refuse to let in initial emergency aid, it used the displaced populace as forced labor on reconstruction projects for the military. Even when they eventually allowed foreign aid in, those same goods were found for sale in the open-air market, which means that they were not helping the people who needed them:

> Supplies of overseas relief materials that were eventually allowed into Burma were confiscated by the military and sold in markets, the packaging easily identifiable.

"I went to some of the markets run by the military and authorities and saw supplies that had been donated being sold there," a former Burmese soldier who fled to Mae Sot across the border in Thailand told the researchers. "The materials were supposed to go to the victims. I could recognize them in the market."[93]

Unfortunately, this is not an isolated incident. If a government doesn't care about its people or is actively persecuting some groups, e.g., the Christian Chin people in Mynamar, international agencies are unable to help.

The UNHCR is often thought of first as responding to urgent crises around the world. However, this is not all that they do.[94] The UNHCR gives a brief description of its mandate as follows:

> UNHCR's primary purpose is to safeguard the rights and well-being of refugees. In its efforts to achieve this objective, the Office strives to ensure that everyone can exercise the right to seek asylum and find safe refuge in another State, [or] to return home voluntarily.[95]

The UNHCR has at least three clear aims: 1. get immediate aid to those at risk, 2. help refugees find temporary or permanent residence in another country, and 3. help refugees return to their home countries, if they must or desire to do so.

The main limitations of the UNHCR are the limitations placed on it by individual states or governments, which, as we have seen, can consider UNHCR work to be an intervention in the sovereign government of their states. The UNHCR has only the influence of persuasion and the weight of other member states in the United Nations. As such, only those states belonging to the UN will be concerned about the UN's statements and desires. Even some member states of the UN will consider UNHCR work as interference in their internal affairs. Some states consider the UNHCR's statements to be a criticism of how those states treat ethnic minorities, for example. Such states consider these sorts of actions to be beyond the jurisdiction of the UN.

The UNHCR is also limited insofar as it cannot force any country to accept refugees. It has only the power of persuasion and its offers of help.

The UNHCR had an annual budget of $8.2 billion in 2018.[96] It has more than 16,672 staff with 90 percent of them in the field, that is, those not working in Geneva in the office.[97]

Despite the huge budget and many staff, the UNHCR can only scratch the surface of the problem of refugees and internally displaced people. There are other groups, called non-governmental organizations (NGOs), which help in many circumstances around the world, as well as some governmental agencies within host countries.

Sometimes the UNHCR will partner with one of these smaller agencies on specific projects. One such specific project involved the Southern Baptist International Mission Board USA in Serbia. Dr. William Steele of the Southern Baptist International Mission Board USA, whom we knew in Belgrade, partnered with the UNHCR to provide school supplies to 125,000 Serbian children in Serbia.

Of course, there are many other excellent agencies, like Doctors without Borders, and the International Justice Mission. Another such organization is the Mennonite Central Committee (MCC).

The Mennonite Central Committee is an organization started by Mennonite immigrants in the United States. Mennonites, a peaceful Anabaptist denomination, were persecuted in Germany, Switzerland, and the Netherlands in earlier centuries, and many fled.[98] Some fled to the US and others to Russia, notably the region which is now Ukraine.[99]

While Mennonites are, by tradition, pacifists, they prefer to see themselves as active peacemakers. They are not mere pacifists, quietists that sit and do nothing. Rather they actively engage with hostile sides to make peace. Nigel Dower, though not a Mennonite, has addressed this misperception of pacifists by coining a new word "pacificist" (from the Latin words *pax* and *ficit*—to make peace). A "pacificist" is not one who *only* does no violence. Instead, he or she is one who sets out actively to do good, to make peace, to nurture and preserve peace, as well as to help restore peace.[100] The Mennonite Central Committee is committed to peacemaking. On their website they give the following definition of themselves.

> As an Anabaptist organization, we strive to **make peace a part of everything we do**. When responding to disasters we work with local groups to distribute resources in ways that minimize conflict. In our development work we plan with community and church groups to make sure the projects meet their needs. And we advocate for policies that will lead to a more peaceful world.[101]

I've been privileged to know a number of Mennonites. In my experience, Mennonite workers are quiet people who enter very tense settings and work for the alleviation of those who are suffering from the effects of war or violence and those persecuted. They do much more than this.

The MCC states its mandate as follows:

> Mennonite Central Committee (MCC), a worldwide ministry of Anabaptist churches, shares God's love and compassion for all in the name of Christ by responding to basic human needs

and working for peace and justice. MCC envisions communities worldwide in right relationship with God, one another and creation.[102]

The MCC says that its areas of focus are:

1. Caring for the lives and futures of uprooted and other vulnerable people.

2. Providing water, food and shelter first in times of hunger, disaster and conflict, then education and ways to earn income.

3. Working with churches and communities to prevent violence and promote peace and justice.

4. Investing in opportunities for young people to serve in Canada, the U.S. and around the world.

5. Serving with humility and in partnership to meet local needs with local solutions.

Those who are peacemakers will plant seeds of peace . . . —James 3:18 (NLT)[103]

The MCC celebrates its centennial in 2020.[104] At present, the MCC has offices in more than fifty countries and relief, development, or peacebuilding work in at least ten more.[105]

In their 2019 Annual Report the MCC showed its expenses on worldwide projects as 68.6 million USD.[106] This is a far cry from the budgets of other larger international organizations, but their activities show the far-reaching impact they have. Since the MCC is largely made up of volunteers, numbering their personnel is difficult.

I came to know the MCC indirectly when I lived in Novi Sad, Serbia, during the period of the "Bosnian" War. In brief, they came and cared for refugees or "internally displaced people" depending on whose definition of which country they belonged to; they were in fact stateless. They did this despite difficulties and criticism. It's helpful for us to look at the MCC's involvement in the former Yugoslavia, during the war and after, as an example of their assistance in such situations. My experience with them personally was limited but my purpose in discussing them is to show how a "smaller" relief organization can make a big difference.

One well-known Mennonite worker and scholar is Dr. N. Gerald Shenk, who has written widely about the former Yugoslavia and the conflict there. Shenk, a US citizen, was working and teaching at the Evangelical Theological Faculty in Osijek, Croatia, at the time of the hostilities in former

Yugoslavia.[107] Previously he had worked with the Protestant Theological Faculty in Zagreb, Croatia. Since Shenk was in Croatia, the MCC knew of and aided Croatian Internally Displaced People (IDPs) from Bosnia, before beginning to aid IDPs in Serbia.

Though Shenk was in Osijek, Croatia, he was aware of what happened to Serbian refugees. He was able then to explain to the MCC why it was necessary to send aid for refugees into Serbia.

Though the Mennonite Central Committee was heavily involved in the CIS (Commonwealth of Independent States; a loose federation of former Soviet republics and satellite states) and other places of conflict and need, nevertheless, they donated a lot of aid to the former Yugoslavia. As the MCC reported:

> In partnership with the Yugoslav department of Trans-World Radio, MCC, along with several local churches, has sent several truckloads of emergency aid (food, medicine, clothes) to help with the needs among the many war refugees.[108]

Emily Will, also an MCC worker from the US, visited Osijek in 1991 and documented that 2.2 million Yugoslavs had been displaced, with 600,000 Croats displaced into Croatia. Osijek alone had received 21,000 IDPs as of August 12, 1992. The problems were of gargantuan proportions. Whole villages had been razed to the ground. The IDPs had nowhere to live, no means of finding shelter or food, no hopes of jobs or a warm reception. Will noted then that

> MCC Europe director Hansulrich Gerber and Jacques Baumann, chairperson of the Swiss Mennonite Organization, will visit Croatia August 21 to 25 to ascertain further response.
> MCC has designated $50,000 U.S. for Croatia relief, and European Mennonites hope to raise an equivalent amount.[109]

The MCC "1992 Workbook" under "Statistics—Food Purchase" show $16,600 going to Croatia that year. While this might not seem like a lot of money when compared to larger organizations, this represents the giving of a small community of descendants of immigrants. At the time in January of 1992 the annual income in Croatia dropped to 13 Croatian Kuna.[110] At that time the Croatian Kuna had an exchange rate of 3.8 HRK to one USD.[111] $16,600 would have been equivalent to 63,080 HRK or 4852 annual salaries! Even relatively small amounts, therefore, can make a significant difference in the lives of people in affected areas.

The MCC continued its commitment to help by providing physical care and following its commitment to teaching peace, beginning in Zagreb, Croatia:

> A new graduate program started in fall in Zagreb, under leadership of MCC workers and consultants. Contacts were made and efforts begun for relief in Bosnia, reconstruction in Osijek, and peace education/conciliation projects in the former Yugoslavia. MCC provided various materials, operation tables, specialized equipment and food. MCC is one small one of a host of organizations, official and private, big and tiny, to provide assistance. MCC's longstanding contacts in Serbia, Croatia and Bosnia-Herzegovina are an important asset in working with the conflict.[112]

In addition, many Mennonites are good with practical skills. There was a lot of help particularly to the city of Osijek, Croatia, in 1993. This help included things like: replacing windows at the hospital, funding, finding, and installing an incubator for the pediatric ward of the hospital, obtaining musical instruments for orphans in Osijek, and providing financial support for orphans. In the same report, mention is made of an exploration of working with a local Christian organization, Bread of Life, in Belgrade, Serbia, and providing some help for Serbian IDPs in Vojvodina (northern Serbia).[113] In 1993, MCC records $63,000 of aid to Yugoslavia (former), which included, e.g., eleven metric tons (24,251 pounds) of canned meat, as well as six hundred emergency health kits. The MCC 1993 Workbook notes:

> While our presence with theological education and Christian Information Services in Croatia was interrupted for health reasons, new workers were replaced in Belgrade, Serbia, to work with local church agencies in emergency assistance and other ministries. Bread of Life, a joint organization of Baptists and Pentecostals, has grown into a major agency within a few months.[114]

As noted above, the MCC had become aware of the work of a grass roots Christian organization called Bread of Life. Bread of Life was started by Beba Varga and Jasmina Tošić. Jasmina was our personal friend. We had first met and then gotten to know her as fellow members of the First Baptist Church of Belgrade in the years 1986–89, when we lived in Belgrade and learned the Serbo-Croatian language. We were all part of the First Baptist Church's "youth" group then. (Linda, my wife, and I were twenty-seven years old at the time.)

Bread of Life achieved astonishing results for a small organization. Jasmina, in an interview with the Mennonite Central Committee Peace Office, in their newsletter in the April–June 1996 edition, recalled:

> Our first relief food shipments came from German Mennonites through a Serbian Christian organization, then through a Swedish organization. In the first half year we served 200 families with supplies from Sweden and a Southern Baptist group. We fed 1500 families regularly for a year. In October 1995 that doubled. We served 3000 families for six months, about 14,000 people. Now we are starting with a new group of 3000 families. That is about 20,000 people. That is our limit.[115]

On the website of Bread of Life, they list some remarkable achievements:

> During its first 12 years of "Bread of Life" 90% of the regular humanitarian aid provided was for refugees and displaced persons from Kosovo and 10% of the aid provided was for local families. ... During this period, the following **results** were achieved:
>
> - Imported and distributed about 1200 trucks with 20 tons of humanitarian aid;
>
> - Provided regular monthly financial assistance to some 40,000 refugees and internally displaced persons;
>
> - Distributed humanitarian aid to about 500,000 people in cooperation with social and medical institutions and other organizations;
>
> - Through self-support programs assistance was provided to approximately 700 refugee and displaced families [donations of livestock or tools];
>
> - After the NATO bombing in 1999, Bread of Life ... provided psycho-social support to children and the elderly. . . to overcome . . . trauma. . . . This included over **1300 children**;
>
> - Since **1994 over 500,000 Christmas presents**, provided by children from the UK and Germany were distributed for children in Serbia.[116]

Bread of Life did and continues to do an amazing job of working together with their foreign donors and partners, including such groups as: Mennonite Central Committee, German Baptist Aid, Slavic Gospel Association (SGA), Brot des Lebens, Samaritan's Purse, and Heart to Heart International.[117]

Jasmina reported further to the MCC about Bread of Life's work in Serbia and the situation there. She wrote, "A kilo of meat costs a month's wages or three months' pension, so even people living here cannot afford meat. For refugees who come with only the clothes on their backs it is simply out of reach."[118]

The 1994 MCC Workbook notes: "Additionally, MCC has a shipment of blankets and soap valued at $94,000 US/$127,458 CAD ready for shipment to refugees in Belgrade." Working together with German Mennonites the MCC reported: "Since last October, German Mennonites have sent more than 30 truckloads of food and supplies to this area and have also trucked food purchased by MCC to Belgrade, Serbia . . ."[119] The MCC spent $105,000 in Serbia in 1994 and $25,000 in Bosnia.[120]

One Mennonite couple, Mark and Alice Jantzen, came to serve in Serbia for three years during these difficult times. They worked alongside Beba Varga and Jasmina Tošić with Bread of Life and were involved in distributing aid to refugees.[121] I was deeply impressed with the Jantzens and other MCC workers I met in Serbia during this time. They epitomized to my mind what Mennonite workers were. They were quiet, self-effacing, and efficient. They learned the language well. They did what was needed without fanfare or needing attention. They were, in short, just the sort of people needed in a crisis: level-headed and efficient. [122]

Mark and Alice were in their second term of service with MCC when they went to Belgrade in 1993. Jasmina Tošić had asked the MCC for help. MCC sent the Jantzens. Mark recalls that they lived in the Pentecostal church on Simina Street, the "Hram Sv. Troica" ("Temple of the Holy Spirit" church), where they lived on the top floor. The Yugoslav Red Cross was located across the street. Refugees lined up there on the street in front of the Red Cross in large numbers. They just kept showing up, crowding the street. Mark and his wife could barely open the front door of the church!

About 250,000 refugees (as they are called in Serbia) or internally displaced peopled (IDPs as they were considered by NGOs) came into Serbia in 1993. At first, help was ad hoc. What later became Bread of Life started as such an ad hoc group. Churches just began by starting to help people, without organization or accounting. As Mark says, "It was pretty much Matthew 25, 'Did you do it to the least of these?'"[123] Churches started reaching out. The Pentecostal church "Hram Sv. Troica" and the so-called "First" Baptist church on Slobodanka Danke Savić were inundated with refugees. Then, as awareness grew, the Southern Baptist Convention (through its International Mission Board), the MCC US, German Mennonites, Swedish Baptists, and Pentecostals all came together, to help these refugees and to work with Bread of Life.

In 1995 there was a second wave of immigrants into Serbia from the Lika/Knin region of Croatia. About 200,000 "refugees" (IDPs really) arrived then. For three days in August, the entire block around the Pentecostal church "Hram Sv. Troica" was standing room only. The refugees had nowhere to go. Mark says that it was amazing to see how local evangelical churches lived out the gospel. They saw the influx of refugees as an opportunity.

Jasmina would ask, "Which of us is a Christian?" She felt that a Christian's needs are already met in Christ. Therefore, a Christian always has something to share. Jasmina and Beba developed and ran Bread of Life, an agency which gave physical and spiritual aid to the refugees. Though church leaders supported Jasmina and Beba, they were engaged in keeping the churches running, leading services, preparing sermons, etc. The pastors and churches per se did not do refugee work.

Jasmina and Beba were simply two women who acted. It was great to see the individual believers, Baptists and Pentecostals, working together. A Bread of Life Board was established.

Jasmina and Beba also had help from other people. For instance, Beba's cousin was a truck driver, who helped with moving things. The refugees themselves also helped the two women.

Bread of Life used volunteers who were ethnic Hungarians, Croats from Bosnia, Serbs from all three entities (Bosnia and Herzegovina, Serbia proper, and the Republika Srpska [the Serbian part of Bosnia]), Bosnian Muslims (who called themselves Bošnjaks), and even one person from Kosovo (a Kosovar), all working together in harmony.

Mark mainly did administration. He was a sort of "public relations and development officer." He did whatever Jasmina needed to be done. As Jasmina knew English, she tended to be the spokesperson to English speakers. However, Mark wrote reports in English and German. Mark also basically wrote grants for Bread of Life as an NGO. Jasmina and Beba had no experience with that.

An example of the ad hoc nature of the outreach is that the Jantzens' computer was probably the first computer Bread of Life had. Also, since the banks weren't working due to the war, someone had to change the funds received in German Marks into Yugoslav dinar. This had to be done on the street with money changers.

In general, in Yugoslav culture, you give money to someone you trust and no receipts or records are kept. Jasmina and Beba had to be educated about the sorts of records that Western donors would ask for.

For instance, MCC sent $50,000 to Bread of Life. A receipt was needed and records needed to be kept of what the money was spent on. Other US supporters wanted receipts and records/reports.

Yugoslavs would ask, "Don't you trust me?" It was hard for them to understand the Western need for receipts and records. This is partly a legacy of Communism where you didn't keep records, which could be used against you. Christians had to act clandestinely then.

Refugees came to the churches. Each church was a distribution point. At the beginning the basements of the churches were used for storage. Eventually, a warehouse was rented.

Mark kept track of food distributions. There were two churches, which distributed food two nights a week. That meant eight distributions for each church each month. That's how they were able serve so many families.

Bread of Life served 50 families in sixteen days each month. So, they served 800 families per month. In six months, they would have served 4800 families.

Bread of Life didn't let people come continuously. They were allowed to come only for six months. In this way Bread of Life helped tens of thousands of people in the course of twelve years.

They enlisted assistants and trained them to process people. They and their assistants listened to thousands of stories of rape, of being held in concentration camps, of torture, etc.

One impressive thing about Beba and Jasmina was that they just listened to the refugees. They made tea and served cookies and refreshments to the refugees. They would interact with them and pray with them. They gave a short devotional. They created all of this on their own.

Bread of Life did screening of refugees (who really was a refugee, who needed help and how much). Beba and Jasmina didn't do this to get rich and certainly didn't.

As Mark recalls, the most impressive thing was seeing the gospel lived out. It was a gospel for all nations. There was a clear realization that the church was not national, but international. It was amazing to see people who had every reason to kill each other working together and loving one another.[124]

In conclusion, while big aid organizations can do a lot, smaller groups and even individuals can accomplish significant things which will improve the lives of people suffering from war, displacement, and other hardships. Surely if we were in these terrible situations, we would be grateful for the help of others. Hopefully, this discussion of the Mennonites Central Committee and Bread of Life in Serbia has shown the impact that small organizations and even individuals can have in crisis situations and in the lives of refugees and displaced people. Small organizations can make a big difference when the people involved in them are not interested in glory or headlines but are focused on their work and their Savior. Though amounts of money or goods given and numbers of workers may seem insignificant when compared to larger organizations, these smaller organizations can make a difference when conditions are dismal and the situation tense. Could you see yourself in this picture? Perhaps you could volunteer for a few weeks or a year or two to help in a migrant detention center. Maybe you would be able to give technical aid to a national effort by using your skills as a bookkeeper or a secretary. You could come alongside an NGO to help in some emergency situation, for instance, distributing aid to people caught in a natural disaster.

Further reading

Regarding refugees and work with refugees
in the former Yugoslavia:

Kuranji, Vera, and Daniel Kuranji. *"New Life" in Serbia . . . The Novi Sad Christian Fellowship Story*. Rev. ed. Novi Sad, Serbia: N.P., January 2011.

Chapter 6: **Making Careful Distinctions —What Governments Do**

THE POLICIES OF THE federal government obviously affect the policies of regional government. In the United States, there is one federal immigration policy for all fifty United States. The European Union, on the other hand, is not a federal body like the United States. The EU is a confederation of many sovereign states, who yield some of their autonomy for economic advantages and other benefits.

Determining EU policy on refugees and immigrants has been a laborious process. This has been due to the fact that there is no federal government to force member states to comply with legislation passed by a federal assembly, e.g., a house of representatives or a senate. While the EU has a parliament, it is not a legislative body as such, in so far as the agreements made are often non-binding. Some member states may refuse to cooperate with decisions agreed to by the EU Parliament. One example of this difficulty is that the member states have never ratified the EU Constitution. Though the EU Constitution has been forwarded to the populace of all EU countries, many EU countries have not approved it. Even member states like the Netherlands, which was one of the founders of the EU and framers of the EU Constitution, could not get its citizens to vote in favor of the EU Constitution.[125] This makes passing legislation almost impossible.

EU member states are often jealous of their autonomy and fearful of a "foreign" body forcing its will upon them. Many fear the loss of their national languages but also that they as individual countries will lose control over EU decisions. The end of "Euro-Socialism" is not going down well with trade unions and others, who have lost or will lose benefits and guarantees.[126]

The immigration policy of the EU is also beset with similar problems. Even after the EU Parliament passes resolutions about how many immigrants each member state will accept, politicians must return to their home countries and convince local assemblies, e.g., the Parliament of the Nether-lands, to accept these resolutions.

Obviously, in the current influx of refugees, some member states are harder hit. Potential immigrants arrive by the boatload on the shores of Ita-ly, Spain, and Greece. Land routes through Turkey, Macedonia, Serbia, and Croatia have angered member states such as Hungary and Austria, which border the route followed by refugees. Migrants and refugees arrive on shore in Spain, Italy, or Greece and then hope to continue their journeys on through Macedonia, Serbia, Hungary, and Austria into Germany or Scan-danavia. Understandably, border states are most hard-hit with handling the crisis. As a result, the land route through Macedonia and Serbia to Hungary and the EU has been closed.[127]

With the economies of many of these states in bad shape, they are not happy about hosting so many refugees. Greece is, for instance, suf-fering severe austerity measures to remain in the EU and to have their loans refinanced.[128] To also be saddled with many immigrants is a strain. The different countries compete with one another for public spending to support the refugees. Some, like the Greek Army, have been accused of mismanagement of funds.

Other countries are more stable economically but the refugee flood still poses a problem. Hungary, for instance, has been stable enough, but is rather right wing politically and thus not very open to waves of immigration. Tens of thousands of refugees flooding from Serbia into Hungary resulted in a fence being put up on the Hungarian border.[129] While neighboring Austria has always had centers for asylum seekers, the numbers of refugees in the last several years have been overwhelming.[130]

Many of the current immigrants stream into and through Turkey. When some EU member states wanted relief from the intense influx of immigrants, they proposed setting up temporary shelters in Turkey to keep some refugees, particularly Syrians, closer to home, with the hope of repatriation once hos-tilities ceased. Turkey is not an EU member state, though it would like to be one. However, Turkey's record of treatment of ethnic minorities has not been good, e.g., their treatment of their ethnic minority Kurds. The Kurds are a large minority in Turkey and Syria who would like their own homeland. The Turkish government has fought them militarily. Attempts to get Turkey to agree to better treatment for Kurds, while trying to get them to house refu-gees, even with large cash incentives, has not gone well.[131]

All of this skirts the issue that some of these immigrants, e.g., the Yazidis, have nowhere to return. They were persecuted before the al-Qae-da-inspired Islamic State (IS or ISIL) came. They suffered under Saddam Hussein and Sunni Arab fighters. Since the Yazidi, whose religion is a kind of combination of Christian and Muslim teachings, and who revere angelic beings who cause both good and evil, are considered heretic "devil worshipers," they will never be accepted back into strongly Muslim Syria, Iraq, or Iran, the places from which they fled. Those like the Dutch, who stand for freedom of worship and have a long history of helping people persecuted for religious reasons, have a difficult time saying "Go home!" to those who have experienced such intense persecution for many decades; however, this is changing.[132]

Migration has increased rapidly into EU countries. The EU website's page "Irregular Migration and Return" notes that "in 2014, 276,113 migrants entered the EU irregularly, which represents an increase of 138% compared to the same period in 2013."[133] Then, in 2015, the number of migrants rose to 1,321,600. However, by April 2016, fewer than 300,000 had entered the EU.[134] "In 2017, there was a decrease in the number of refugees and other vulnerable persons assisted under the auspices of IOM for resettlement, relocation and humanitarian admissions; 204,937 individuals in 2016 and 137,839 in 2017."[135] In 2018 by contrast only 26,852 refugees were resettled. "In 2018, UNHCR submitted 81,300 refugees for resettlement and recorded 92,400 admissions for resettlement. 664,700 and 593,800 refugees returned to their countries of origin in 2017 and 2018 respectively."[136] This was due mainly to restrictions of many entry points, leaving certain Greek islands and the south of Italy as the only possibilities for entry.

A number like 137,830 "migrants" is still a very large number. However, this is not a monolithic group. The migrants can be divided into three categories. Some are economic "migrants," i.e., people who want a better life and jobs. Some are "refugees": people fleeing violence in their own countries; e.g., people fleeing war in Syria or Libya. Some earlier migrants, unfortunately, were actual criminals, using the flood of refugees as a means to "blend in" and get through EU borders. EU member states note that there are criminal networks operating businesses to get people into the EU. However, since the new regulations and procedures no one leaves their country of entry until fully processed. One possible scenario is repatriation, i.e., being sent back to the country you came from, ideally your home country.

Who has the right to become an officially accepted immigrant? In other words, which of these refugees and economic migrants may be officially regarded as entering a country with the intent of staying there? This is the key question for the governments involved. All EU states (and most of their citizens) would likely agree that those who suffer persecution and violence should be allowed to emigrate. Where they immigrate is another question.

Actually, all EU member states desire suitable immigrants. This may seem startling, but with low birth rates and increasing numbers of elderly people dependent on the social welfare system, EU states need younger citizens to take over jobs and to pay taxes. The negative birth rate in most EU countries means that EU governments actively seek qualified and zealous immigrants, and this has included some refugees. The German interior minister, Thomas de Maizière, appeared on EuroNews, the EU news channel, and pointed out that the negative birth rate in Germany means Germany needs immigrants.[137] Germany needs more skilled laborers and tax payers. He notes that it is obvious those refugees who require help (in other words, those in real danger) should in fact be helped. Others, who are not in danger, should be returned home. Distinguishing who is who is not an easy task.[138]

De Maizière says: "We have a high share of foreigners in Germany, . . . I do not see a big problem in the acceptance of foreigners who work here, who pay taxes, who behave legally, who respect German laws."[139] Actually, Minister de Maiziere's terms for inclusion in the German state don't sound much different than those in the US which require immigrants to follow similar laws and, as in Germany, to learn the national language.

The difficulties are when immigrants don't "melt" into the "melting pot." When it remains a "stew," there can be problems. Almost all EU states are happy to allow intelligent, hardworking foreigners to immigrate. However, this contributes to the so-called "brain drain": the loss of intelligent and well-educated people from one country to another to the detriment of the first. The Migration Data Portal notes that "the competition for talent has become global. In this context, Europe is working on a number of initiatives to attract more highly skilled migrants."[140] The "brain drain" is a real problem for the nations of the so-called "two-thirds world." In many countries, as many as 60 percent of all graduate students who study abroad in Western countries never return home.[141] This enriches the labor pool in the countries where these graduate students studied but impoverishes their home countries.[142] I know from personal experience in teaching in the Netherlands at Tyndale Theological Seminary that students who complete one of our degree programs are much more likely to be allowed to remain in the Netherlands, and even attain citizenship, than others who have not completed a degree. This is actually not surprising. If you had a choice of allowing two foreign nationals to immigrate, and one has a graduate degree and the other is an unskilled laborer, perhaps an agricultural laborer, which would you choose? Which would you expect both to have greater earning power, and thus tax-paying power, and which is better educated and likely to find a job? It is obvious that governments would like to have highly-qualified and hardworking immigrants.

In short, governments must investigate the migrants seeking to enter and determine who may stay in their countries. On the one hand, all EU states require that their immigration policies and procedures be honored. This is reasonable. However, on the other hand, the humanitarian disaster caused by war (including EU and NATO bombing) requires a compassionate response.

EU member states have a Common European Asylum System. Asylum seekers, as we will see, are a different group than immigrants per se. Immigrants are not necessarily in any danger and may come from a variety of categories: foreign students, migrant workers, economic immigration, etc. However, asylum seekers are people whose lives would be in danger if they returned home. They are similar to but not exactly the same as refugees. Refugees are fleeing violence and are on the move; asylum seekers would be in danger if they returned home and are thus seeking a new home country.

The Directorate General for Migration and Home Affairs gives the following definition of asylum:

> Asylum is granted to people fleeing persecution or serious harm in their own country and therefore in need of international protection. Asylum is a fundamental right; granting it is an international obligation, first recognised in the 1951 Geneva Convention on the protection of refugee.[143]

They note that the number of asylum seekers varies and the member states which must deal with numbers of asylum seekers varies.

As we have noted, by 2015 the number of migrants had risen to 1,321,600. Consider that until April 2016 alone just under 300,000 had entered the EU.[144] However, as we have seen above the number of migrants is shrinking each year: 137,839 in 2017 and 81,300 in 2018 respectively. This means that, while the wave of migration was huge, it is now declining. While it is obvious that a unified EU policy is necessary and desirable, it is less obvious that the countries of the EU are acting in accordance with the policy that has been agreed upon.

The EU notes the difficulties of getting cooperation between member states and neighboring countries. They have been working hard on this.

In general, there is a sustained attempt to get a common approach to these issues. EU countries work very hard to make clear what their policies and guidelines are for immigration of any sort. On the EU Migration and Home Affairs site there is an abundance of materials available for anyone wishing to immigrate.[145]

Since I have lived most of my adult life in Europe, I wanted to begin by showing how the above distinctions are made by EU governments. I now want to turn to US policies, and I have three goals in this section. First, I want to show that US policy is not much different, that is it is in line with the policies of its allies in Europe. Second, I want to demonstrate that US policy on immigration is not the result of any one president's policy or even of the Obama administration per se. US policies have developed over at least the last century and comply with all reasonable and international standards. Third, I wish to show that US immigration policies are as strict as is humanly possible and even as safe and secure as any of the latest technology can make possible. No "vetting" of refugees/immigrants could be more "extreme" than what now, in fact, is taking place in the US.

The United States has a federal policy on immigration. All states of the US subscribe to this policy. As in Europe, not all US citizens agree with the declared legal immigration policy. In the United States, some citizens are concerned that "illegal" immigrants flout the laws, entering the US illegally, and then collect rights and privileges; for example, collecting welfare and free health care. At the same time, some feel that those who have entered "illegally," who are migrant workers, are not being paid fair wages, are kept in squalid conditions, and are overworked. Their employers avoid paying Social Security taxes for these "illegals."

The US has a very large and porous border with Mexico. There is no question that this border has been violated many times. Texas and other states near the border absorb large numbers of immigrants. Many people from Central and South America seeking better lives try to enter through this border.

Such immigration is illegal. There are government, federal, state, and local law enforcement agencies who patrol this border and are tasked to deal with these illegal immigrants.

I cannot hope to deal with both the situation of legal immigrants and illegal immigrants through such a porous border. My first goal is to show that legal immigration is safe and that Christians should be willing to help those who have immigrated legally. As well I wish to show that those who have immigrated legally are worthy of compassion, because they have followed all of the required steps to immigrate. They are not terrorists or illegals. Some politicians and pundits, wishing to confuse the public or drive public opinion, intentionally blur these distinctions to gain support for their views. Ignorance is not bliss. It is unwise and unkind to fail to help someone in need due to confusing them with those whom we see as illegal. Those who go through the steps to legal immigration are legal, and so should be welcomed.

It is not my purpose to debate illegal immigration or the merits of arguments for the rights of such immigrants. The only similarity to the situation in Europe is that in Europe many refugees and immigrants from the affected war zones earlier came into Europe via a land route through Turkey, especially refugees from Syria, or via a sea route to Italy and Greece, i.e., illegally entering through a border, and then by train or bus or foot made their way to Germany, Denmark, and even Sweden. This has now been stopped by the closing of various borders: Hungary, Denmark, etc. Also, this has been nearly stopped by new EU policy, which is reducing migrant numbers by restricting migrants to possible residence visas to the countries that they enter. In words, if you enter Greece as a migrant, a potential immigrant, you can only hope to get a visa to stay in Greece and not move to another EU country. As well, the EU has funded Turkey to keep migrants of Syrian origin within Turkey, as mentioned above.

The US Citizenship and Immigration Services identifies three levels of importance and priority when processing refugee requests. The priorities currently in use are:

- **Priority 1:** Cases that are identified and referred to the program by the United Nations High Commissioner for Refugees (UNHCR), a United States Embassy, or a designated non-governmental organization (NGO).[146]

These would be people who are refugees in a UNHCR camp: for example, people driven by war from their bombed-out homes into a refugee center. They are processed first by the UN and then referred to US agencies. Those might be one of other non-governmental organizations, such as the Red Cross/Red Crescent.[147]

- **Priority 2:** Groups of special humanitarian concern identified by the US refugee program.[148]

President Trump, in his second revision of his "travel ban," for instance, identified Syrian Christians as individuals needing asylum due to being under attack in their homeland.[149]

- **Priority 3:** Family reunification cases (spouses, unmarried children under twenty-one, and parents of persons lawfully admitted to the United States as refugees or asylees or permanent residents [green card holders] or US citizens who previously had refugee or asylum status). For information on the current nationalities eligible for Priority 3 processing, see the "US Citizenship and Immigration Services" page.[150]

This could be a person who was allowed to immigrate without his or her family but who later would seek their immigration. For instance, a Russian young woman comes as a foreign student to the US. She marries an American man. She naturalizes. Then she seeks to bring her mother and siblings to the US.

In addition, it is important to note that refugees must generally be outside their country of origin to apply for refugee status, but some individuals can be processed in their home countries if authorized by the president.[151]

As far as US immigration procedure for refugees is concerned, the procedure is very clear and thorough: [152]

- First, refugees who are potential immigrants are recommended by groups like the UNHCR to a Resettlement Support Center (RSC). There are seven such centers around the world. (If a potential immigrant already has family in the US they may be accepted without UNHCR recommendation.)[153]

- Second, "the RSCs collect biographic and other information from the applicants to prepare for the adjudication interview and for security screening."[154] (This screening is carried out by the State Department and Homeland Security, as well as other government security agencies.)

- Third, "officers from the Department of Homeland Security's U.S. Citizenship and Immigration Services (USCIS) review all the information that the RSC has collected and also conduct an in-person interview with each refugee applicant before deciding whether to approve him or her for resettlement in the United States."[155]

- Fourth, all potential immigrants undergo a health check to prevent those with contagious diseases entering the US.

- Fifth, "the RSC requests a 'sponsorship assurance' from a U.S.-based resettlement agency that is experienced in providing assistance to newly arrived refugees."[156] (For instance, I know in the past, Russian Jewish immigrants, who had been processed in Vienna and Rome, were allowed to move to Chicago [and other cities] under the auspices of HIAS [the Hebrew Immigration and Aid Society].)

- Sixth, many immigrants receive some acculturation training at the RSC before going to the US.

- Finally, "though Congress mandated the program, it is local communities that have ensured the success of the resettlement program by welcoming and helping refugees from around the world."[157] (In other words, churches, civic groups, and others help the refugees/immigrants to settle in the US. This is vital to their success and this is what "ordinary" citizens can do to help. This is where you, the reader, can fit into this process, if you want to do so. You can make a tremendous difference in their lives; you can help them to feel welcome.)[158]

We can see, therefore, that the US has a very strict policy about processing refugees/immigrants which consists of many steps. It is important to note that most of these steps are done outside the US. Security agencies are involved and they are diligent in terms of preventing subversive or terrorist elements from immigrating.

Since processing centers (RSCs) are outside of the US, no one enters the US until all of the appropriate background checks, interviews, and health screenings are done.

There is no need for worry that terrorists or other enemies of the US will enter as immigrants. Actually, no immigrant to the US has killed a US citizen since the mid-1970s.[159] Aside from these careful checks, most refugees are already clearly identified as suffering persecution or fleeing violence in their home countries. Sometimes they are religious minorities who are being persecuted, for example, Yazidis fleeing IS and ISIL in Syria. These are not people who are or would become radicalized Muslim terrorists. Because they have fled totalitarian Islamic regimes which were oppressive, refugees from these countries are more likely to cherish and have cherished citizenship in a democratic country.

At this point, I will begin to discuss immigration as it relates to the Netherlands. It is interesting to compare and contrast what the Netherlands is doing in this matter, so that those from other countries can gain a slightly different vantage point to their own situation. We have lived in the Netherlands for almost twenty years. The Netherlands has almost always been a country which has been open to other groups, especially refugees. Throughout history, the Netherlands was often tolerant of others and allowed them to immigrate, such as persecuted Jews fleeing Iberia in the fifteenth and sixteenth centuries. In the sixteenth and seventeenth centuries, the Netherlands was open to others of Reformed faith who were being persecuted in the UK, Germany, or France.

The Netherlands is now a very tolerant country, which had until recently a very open immigration policy. Unfortunately, recent huge influxes of immigrants have dampened the spirit of open immigration. There are so many immigrants. Many of them acculturate well but others are not acculturating. Some are not learning Dutch (which is the part of immigration policy) and because many keep to their old customs and religion some Dutch people fear Islamic immigrants. Some ethnically Dutch citizens fear the loss of their own heritage, language, and culture.

The Dutch government's positions are in agreement with the larger EU positions. It posts its main objective with regards to immigration of refugees: "Asylum seekers may be given asylum in the Netherlands if they need protection from persecution in their own country on religious or ethnic grounds, for instance."[160] In their section on Asylum Policy, the Dutch Immigration Service says: "Since the summer of 2015 the number of refugees entering the European Union (EU) has doubled."[161]

The Dutch had initially agreed to take 2,000 refugees. With the recent influx of refugees the Dutch have committed to taking another 7,000 of the 120,000 refugees who flooded Europe in 2016 alone.[162] The Dutch are cooperating with the other EU states to deal with this crisis. EU member states have been asked to accept a reasonable number of refugees based on the number of inhabitants in that country, the average national income, the number of asylum applications already under consideration, and unemployment figures for that country.

The Dutch, being quintessentially forthright and well organized, give a clear and helpful diagram of the steps asylum seekers go through:[163]

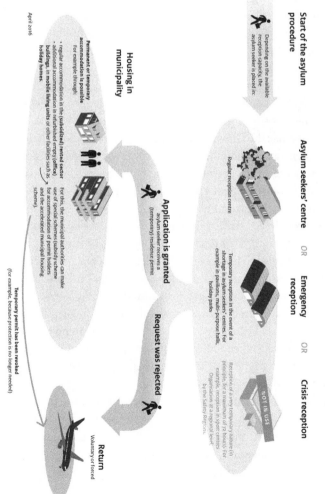

Reception of asylum seekers in the Netherlands

Ministry of Security and Justice

Start of the asylum procedure
Depending on the available reception capacity, the asylum seeker is placed in:

Asylum seekers' centre
Regular reception centre

OR

Emergency reception
Temporary reception in the event of a shortage in asylum seekers' centres, for example in pavilions, multi-purpose halls, holiday parks

OR

Crisis reception
Reception of a very temporary nature (in principle, for a maximum of 72 hours). For example, reception in sport centres. Organisation at a regional level by the Safety Regions.

NOT IN USE

Housing in municipality
Permanent or temporary accommodation is possible. For example through:
• regular accommodation in the (subsidized) rented sector
• additional accommodation in refurbished empty (office) buildings, in mobile living units or other facilities such as holiday homes.

Application is granted
asylum seeker receives a (temporary) residence permit

For this, the municipal authorities can make use of special schemes (subsidy scheme for accommodation of permit holders and the accelerated municipal housing scheme).

Request was rejected

Temporary permit has been revoked
(for example, because protection is no longer needed)

Return
Voluntary or forced

April 2016

Actually, the procedure for seeking asylum can start in one of several ways. First the person may arrive at the Immigration and Naturalization Service (IND) in Ter Apel, a town in the north of the Netherlands, and they will be directed to an asylum center. Alternatively, a person might enter at Schiphol Airport (Amsterdam, the capital), but would have to remain at the application center there until the appeal is dealt with. Then the person is given six days to rest. The second step is that they are then given information about the asylum procedure, can meet with a lawyer, and get a medical declaration. If a person comes from a "safe country," a country the Dutch deem safe, the potential immigrant will be repatriated, sent back to their own country of origin.

Third, there is a second interview with the IND for the asylum seeker to explain why they are in danger. An interpreter is provided. A lawyer can also be provided on request. The IND will also ask critical questions. A transcript is provided to the asylum seeker and their lawyer. Fourth, the IND will assess the asylum seeker's information and the security situation in the asylum seeker's home country.

Finally, if the IND decides in favor of the asylum request, a residence permit is issued. If not, the asylum seeker is repatriated.[164] One Iraqi Christian family, for instance, has been processed and given a decision that they must return to Iraq, because the Dutch government does not consider them to be in danger in their home country. In other words, the Dutch do not believe that Christians are in danger in Iraq simply for being Christians. I know of this family because someone asked us to house them since the family could no longer stay in government housing because they were "out processed" and were required to return to Iraq. They were staying without government help and appealing their decision.

We live in the beautiful and historic city of Leiden, south of Amsterdam and north of The Hague. Aside from larger national strategies, Leiden seems to have a good mix of common sense, a practical attitude, and human standards. The mayor of Leiden has said that Leiden should be a city dedicated to helping immigrants. After all, Leiden has rich history of helping immigrants into the society. The Pilgrim Fathers, in the early seventeenth century, first came from England to Amsterdam, and then to Leiden for twelve years before leaving on the Mayflower to head for the New World.[165] Huguenots (French Calvinist Protestants) fled persecution in France at the time of the Counter Reformation and came to Leiden.[166] There is still a remnant of Huguenot culture in Leiden. For example, there is still an operating French-speaking church, the Waalse Kerk (Walloon Church) in Leiden.[167] Some people still have French Huguenot last names, e.g., Laporte.

Before that, in 1492, Leiden (and Amsterdam) also received many Sephardic Jews from Spain and Portugal when Queen Isabella and King Ferdinand expelled both Jews and Moriscos (Moors or Muslim converts) from their kingdom. Some Sephardic Jews had fled Spain earlier and had already established a community in Amsterdam. Those fleeing later joined them. Later Ashkenazi Jews fled eastern Europe—Russia (and what is now Poland and Ukraine). You can still visit the fascinating Jewish Historical Museum in Amsterdam, which is made up of what were three synagogues, one of which was Ashkenazi, which were recently connected into the one building of the museum. Also, the nearby Sephardic synagogue (the Portuguese Synagogue) is still a working house of worship, despite Nazi efforts to eliminate all Jews from the Netherlands.[168] They got close. Of 150,000 Jews before WWII, only 10,000 survived. Today Leiden also has a small synagogue, which continues to be an active house of worship.[169] So, you can see that both Leiden and Amsterdam have a long tradition of toleration of different religious groups of various nationalities.

In the 1960s, Turks and Moroccans were invited to come to the Netherlands to work in factories and then stayed.[170] They brought their families, as was in accordance with Dutch and now EU law.[171] Eventually, many obtained citizenship. In recent years, Leiden and other cities in the Netherlands have had an influx of Muslim immigrants and refugees from other countries: Iran, Syria, and other nations.

Leiden can be for us a small case study of how Muslims have been helped and accommodated in a small city. I have mentioned elsewhere that I live in a neighborhood with many Moroccan and Turkish Muslims. We have three mosques in Leiden: a newer, larger Moroccan mosque, called "Imam Malik"[172] in the Merenwijk neighborhood, another new mosque, "Al Hijra"[173] on the Haagweg road, and an older, smaller Turkish mosque, "Mimar Sinan"[174] on the Sumatrastraat.

I have watched what has been happening here in Leiden since before 9/11. We arrived in 2000, so we have seen the "before" and "after," both around 9/11 and around another pivotal crisis: the murder of Theo van Gogh, the Dutch filmmaker who was murdered in 2004 on the streets of Amsterdam.[175] As far as I can see, the Leiden City Council has been proactive, working along with the *Contactorgaan Moslims en Overheid* (CMO) ["Contact Organization of Muslims and the Government"] that forms a connectivity between Muslims and the Dutch government. Both government and this organization work very closely on integration and social issues. CMO was immediately activated after 9/11. It also plays a major role in managing Muslim extremism.[176]

The Muslim community in our neighborhood in fact spans two neighborhoods: the Slaagwijk of the Merenwijk, north of Willem de Zwijgerlaan (a four-lane, very busy main artery into the city from the east) and the Kooi, south of the Willem de Zwijgerlaan. There was one tunnel beneath the street for bicycles and pedestrians. However, it was a long way 'round to get from one side of the neighborhood to the other. There was also only one street light, with a pedestrian and bicycle crossing.

After 9/11, renovation of the neighborhood, which had previously been planned, took place. Building of new housing was justified by the fact that the old housing in this neighborhood was substandard. It benefited low-income Muslim inhabitants, since the new housing was subsidized.[177] This was all a result of what the Dutch call the "polder model."[178] The "polder model" is a way that the Dutch have been reclaiming land from the sea and then settling it with affordable housing and planned communities. The government spent forty-four million Euros [about fifty million dollars] renovating the neighborhood, but financing also came from the province and the central government. So, this is a tripartite finance construction: provincial government, central government, and private contractors.[179] They built two bridges across the Willem de Zwijgerlaan. They are pedestrian and bicycle bridges, not open to automotive traffic, which is helpful in this country where so many people travel daily by bike to work or school. They are strategically positioned to allow the two sides of the neighborhoods to cross and connect easily.

Besides the building, the city made big efforts to enhance the socioeconomic position of the inhabitants. This plan included: growth of entrepreneurship, decrease of unemployment, emphasis on education, fostering of neighborhood committees and connectivity, co-designing the neighborhood in close collaboration with the inhabitants, increasing diversity by including housing for the wealthier population, and neighborhood development.[180]

Besides building these bridges, the city planners have demolished older apartment buildings, which were built just after WWII and were no longer up to safety "code." These apartment buildings had previously housed many Muslim immigrants and citizens. As these building have been demolished, the city has given permission to a non-profit housing foundation to build subsidized housing in the form of apartment complexes and housing estates. They have built new high rises and townhouses on both sides of the main street. They also demolished 600 old units and, in their place, have rebuilt 2,100 new ones. One such old facility, which was demolished, was the *Groennoordhallen*, where in years gone by cattle was bought and sold wholesale. With the more modern, highly automated processes of these industries (for example, the *Floriade* in Almere), so much space was no longer necessary. Thus, many new housing units have been built there, but of a more expensive type.

Perhaps not all of this housing has gone to Muslim immigrants or citizens, but it shows that city planners are actively listening to their people, whatever their ethnic or religious origins. As well, as I mentioned a newer mosque, the Moroccan mosque (the Islamic Center Imam Malik) has been built.[181] It faces the main street and is at one end of one of the bridges which had been built. Thus, it stands out. Personally, I like the clean-lined architecture of the mosque. Some do not; perhaps some find it threatening. Everyone is entitled to their opinion, just as every religious community is entitled to build a house of worship. Interestingly, there is a view from the bridge at the mosque into town to the Marekerk, a historic church building downtown and the first church built to serve as a Protestant church in Leiden in the seventeenth century.[182] The Marekerk's rounded, eight-sided form is built on the idea that everyone should assemble around the word of God, the Bible—around the sermon (or pulpit), rather than an altar. In the minds of seventeenth-century Dutch Protestants, a cross-shaped church (like the medieval cathedrals) was no longer suitable, since a cross-shaped church would resemble a Roman Catholic church where the altar and mass (or sacrifice of Christ) would be the focal point.[183]

The Netherlands has a clear and strict separation between state government and church. Alongside this principle there is also a very clear set of laws and regulations that rule the land use. If the people want to build a church, a mosque, or even a bicycle shed, all depends on the rules. This means that if the plans fit the rules, the province or municipality cannot resist mosques being built or any other building that fits the rules. In general, since many people are secular, they are fine with houses of worship being built, as long as these institutions do not interfere with their lives. So, as an example, there is no call to prayer by the *muezzin* from the minaret of the local mosques. In addition, liberty of religion has always been of major importance in the Netherlands. This also means that just as Christians are protected by this law, they also understand and apply this principle to other religions. Therefore, one finds that fundamentalist Protestant groups and Christian political parties stand up for the freedom of Muslim groups. This is not seen, however, as an example of tolerance towards other religions, but as part of protecting the laws that shield all religious groups from the influence of secularization.[184]

The Dutch approach seems to me very wise. Leiden sees itself as a city of refuge and has continued to care for both immigrants and refugees. The Dutch say that they believe in freedom of religion and they demonstrate it. They say that they are multicultural and they provide for multicultural expression. Many cities could take a page out of their book.

In contrast with the Netherlands, where terrorist violence has been almost nonexistent, neighboring country Belgium has been hard-hit recently with terrorist attacks. Probably more troubling is the accusation that their borders are too "porous" and that by turning a blind eye Belgian authorities have made it easy for terrorists to go in and out of the EU from Belgium. Some Belgian towns have become, at times, a haven for terrorists, as happened with the town of Verviers, south of Liege.[185]

In some respects, criticisms that there is not enough monitoring of possible terrorists or *jihadis* is somewhat unjust because of EU rules on freedom of movement of citizens. A Belgian citizen of Syrian origin, for instance, has the right to travel abroad, if their travel documents are in order. No citizen of an EU country is likely to be stopped, unless there is some "flag" placed on their passport number. Also complicating this situation is the "Schengen zone," a subset of the EU countries in which free travel is possible. Several EU countries have no borders between them: the Netherlands, Belgium, Germany, France, Italy, Poland, Romania, Spain, Portugal, Greece, Hungary, and Austria. As a result, once a person is in the EU Schengen zone he or she can travel freely across these national borders.

Below I will explain the Belgian government's immigration policy. However, it's insightful first to consider how Belgium came to exist and its history of immigration.

Belgium as such has not existed very long. The nation of Belgium dates only from 1830. The Allied Powers after the Napoleonic Wars gave the "southern Netherlands" and Luxembourg to the "northern Netherlands" or the Kingdom of the Netherlands under King Willem I or William of Orange in 1813.[186]

However, the Belgians wanted independence and won it again by the intervention of the Allied Powers (France and Britain). Belgium had not been an independent territory before then. It wasn't and isn't a homogenous country. It had been dominated so long by the Spanish and the Habsburg empire that Roman Catholicism was the main "glue" of the country. The southern area of Belgium, Wallonia, is French-speaking and reflects French culture, given the time it was dominated by France. The northern region of Belgium, Flanders, is Dutch-speaking and is somewhat more similar in culture to the southern regions of the present-day Netherlands. As I mentioned the common factor in Belgium has been Roman Catholicism.

The first wave of immigration into Belgium was from Spain and Italy in the late 1940s and 1950s. Most of these immigrants came to work in the mining industry.[187] They were predominantly Roman Catholics. They worshiped in the same churches as their Walloon and Flemish neighbors did. They buried their dead in the same graveyards and their sons and daughters intermarried with the locals. They were "different," but they were the same.

So even though Belgium is made up of the Dutch-speaking Flemish and the French-speaking Walloons, further cultural or racial diversity in the country has come only recently. A friend tells of how she grew up in Aalst, twenty miles (thirty-one km) northwest of Brussels. At that time, Aalst was a small town. My friend recounts not knowing anyone who was not white, not even anyone who was not Flemish. She had never seen a black person as a child.

When Honda opened an auto plant in Aalst some Japanese families came to the town. Some of their children attended local schools. The Flemish of Aalst called these children "Chinese." Such was the dearth of intercultural awareness. These Flemish people did not mean to be unkind, but they were parochial.[188]

The immigration of Spaniards and Italians in the late fifties was not difficult. However, the immigration of people from Morocco, Turkey, Tunisia, Algeria, and the former Yugoslavia in later years presented a bigger problem. These immigrants were not Roman Catholics. They were Muslims, or in the case of Serbs, Eastern Orthodox Christians. In any event, they were "not like us."

These immigrants complicated their immigration by being unwilling to give up their religion and join the prevailing faith. They kept their children at home until it was legally required to send them to school. At this point, the children were still unable to speak French or Flemish and not ready to start school.

We lived in Belgium when our youngest son was a preschooler. Belgian schools have, at least in Flemish-speaking larger cities, a *peuterschool* (toddlers' school), a *kleuterschool* (kindergarten), and then elementary schools. Children begin with school at age three and go half days. For foreign children, such as our son, it is a good chance to learn Flemish. By the time children enter the first grade, they will have had two and half years of schooling. They will have learned the alphabet and to read basic words. By the time our youngest son was four he could read in Flemish (and English, even without having been formally taught the latter. We did speak English at home, and he had been read to in English.).

However, since these new immigrants did not send their children to preschools, their children were behind and generally remained behind.

Unfortunately, many local, Roman Catholic parochial schools were unwilling and unequipped to deal with the cultural divide which they were faced with.

The Belgians began trying to close the doors for immigration in 1974.[189] However, they had already developed extensive measures to allow reunification of families, which kept these doors open.

Despite this history and these difficulties, Belgium does have an official policy of how to handle refugees and immigrants. Below I will lay out how this process works.

The Belgian government has an extensively developed website explaining "Asylum and Migration" into Belgium.[190] As with most governments, Belgian policy is organized in conjunction with "the Convention relating to the Status of Refugees . . . , signed in Geneva on 28 July 1951." In other words, the Geneva Convention.[191] Someone seeking asylum starts by filing an application for asylum. Such an application can be "done either on arrival at the border or within eight working days after arriving in Belgium, at the OE's [Immigration Department's] office, in a closed centre or in prison."[192]

Secondly, a questionnaire is filled out by an agent of the "Office for Foreigners." The goal of the questionnaire is to establish the seeker's status and why they need asylum.

Thirdly, the Commissioner General for Refugees and Stateless Persons (CGRS), which "is an independent authority and the central asylum authority in Belgium," determines all cases regarding asylum.[193] If someone fits the categories of refugee, they are granted said status. If they do not, but there is overweening reason to believe the applicant would be in danger if he or she returned to their native land, he or she could also be granted asylum on the basis of this present danger. If an applicant for asylum is not happy with a negative decision from the CGRS, they can appeal to the Council of Alien Law Litigation (CCE). The CCE cannot investigate, but only adjudicates these disputes.

In regards to asylum, the Belgian government site on asylum uses the following definition of refugee:

> Any person who, owing to a well-founded fear of being persecuted for reasons of race, religion, nationality, membership of a particular social group or political opinion, is outside the country of his nationality and is unable or, owing to such fear, is unwilling to avail himself of the protection of that country.[194]

This definition comes from the earlier mentioned Geneva Convention.

A technical second category is not a refugee per se, but someone facing potential harm if they returned to their home state. This category is called "subsidiary protection status" and is defined as follows:

> Subsidiary protection status is granted to any foreigner who does not qualify as a refugee but in respect of whom substantial grounds have been shown for believing that the person concerned, if returned to his or her country of origin, or in the case of a stateless person, to his or her country of former habitual residence, would face a real risk of suffering serious harm . . . , and is unable, or, owing to such risk, unwilling to avail himself or herself of the protection of that country.[195]

Again, there are very specific reasons for granting this status, which is in fact rare, since in general, Belgian granting of refugee status is fairly broad. Serious harm consists of:

- death penalty or execution;
- torture or inhuman or degrading treatment or punishment of an applicant in the country of origin;
- serious and individual threat to a civilian's life or person by reason of indiscriminate violence in situations of international or internal armed conflict.[196]

In any event, it is clear from this material that Belgium has a very carefully thought-out asylum policy and a very detailed procedure of application, investigation, and even appeal. It is not done quickly or without due process.

Like all European states, Belgium recognizes the difference between asylum and migration. Belgium also has rules and laws about illegal and legal immigration. The categories are separate from asylum, with their own procedures and processes.

Belgian official immigration practices

Legal immigration can be temporary or long term. I was myself a temporary resident/immigrant in Belgium.

The Belgian website on migration says: "Legal immigration concerns several areas such as employment, education, family reunifications, etc."[197] I was an immigrant for purposes of education (pursuing a master's degree and a PhD). My family emigrated from the US and immigrated to Belgium while I studied in Belgium.

The procedure for obtaining a student visa was fairly complicated. I had to get a letter from the department of the university I was to attend, proving that I was admitted. Then, I had to go to the police department in my home town in the US to get a police report to show that I had not been previously arrested in the US. I had to have a very extensive medical evaluation and even take some tests, which were not necessarily pertinent to me, for example, Tuberculosis titers and a Psittacosis test, which one might get from handling pigeon feces!

Before my family could be granted entrance visas to join me, I had to go to the city hall and be inscribed in the city registry. I had to show my passport and my student card. I also had to show my rental agreement for the house my family would live in. As well, I had to show proof of employment and financial soundness that I could provide for my family during our stay in Belgium. It took more than three months for me as an American to complete all the paperwork. It took even longer for my non-American classmates.

To cite one example, one friend there had to flee his homeland upon fear of assassination. He was not a student at first, but a refugee. His family was not with him, but he applied for them to join him. He finished studies for a master's degree while in Belgium waiting. It took seven long years before his family joined him, as there was nothing hurried about the process. The Belgian government was very careful about admitting anyone.

One factor which makes governments both welcoming and cautious, as we mentioned earlier, is that the birth rate among the indigenous nationals is very low or even negative. For this reason, Belgium, like Germany and the Netherlands, needs immigrants. The Belgian website makes this clear:

> The Minister for Immigration and Asylum Policies advocates developing a legal (or economic) immigration system, particularly in order to mitigate the effects of the decrease in the working population, which is forecast to shrink by 23% in Belgium by the year 2050.[198]

Belgium needs more people and with one eye on the future is seeking qualified immigrants. This may seem like social programming but shows that making space for refugees can benefit both sides.

While official treatment of asylum seekers and migrants is clearly and legally prescribed, the unofficial treatment of immigrants is not always so kind. Perhaps this is out of prejudice or fear. Some Belgians, e.g., the *Vlaams Blok* (Flemish Block) or its successor, the *Vlaams Belang* (Flemish Concern), which was a right wing nationalistic political party, at its height when we lived in Belgium in the 1990s, did not like immigrants. As with racial intolerance anywhere in the world, those who look different are easily targeted and therefore suffer. The recent gains by the *Vlaams Belang* in the Belgian Parliament show that nationalism is still quite strong in Flanders.[199]

In the past, Jews in Europe and elsewhere in the world suffered due to their distinctive dress and features. Today, Muslims often suffer because of their distinctive dress and features. When we lived in Belgium, we lived just outside the city center. Most university students lived inside the "Ring" road which is around Leuven. However, we were a family and needed more space. We regularly saw pamphlets blaming crime on those of non-white backgrounds. The *Vlaams Blok* shoved propaganda through our letter box illustrating that crime was increasing due to more "Ahmeds." This offensive propaganda showed the percentage increase in crime by showing an exponential growth of swarthy figures with hooked noses. Thankfully, the *Vlaams Blok* was disbanded. However, its successor the *Vlaams Belang* is once again growing in influence.[200] There are still nationalists in all countries who dislike foreigners and of course there are still such people in Belgium.

One person I know, who is a person of color, was stopped one night and asked for his ID card. He had forgotten to bring it. He should have had twenty-four hours to produce it. Instead he was beaten for his "insolence" and jailed overnight. In the morning he was told to leave the jail. No report was filed and none of the officers in question would reply to his request for justice.

Such behavior on the part of law enforcement must not be tolerated. Though this incident happened more than a decade ago, a Belgian friend wrote to say that, sadly, this sort of treatment of ethnic minorities continues. My friend wrote:

> As far as the racist behavior of the police is concerned, I have the impression that little progress has been made. The Antwerp police corps is regularly attacked in the press and in Parliament for its racist behavior and also Comité P issued a damning report earlier this year. Lack of ethnic diversity in the police corps is a big issue.[201]

Recent news reports also confirm that such things and worse still occur.[202]

We cannot address all of the issues, but as I lived in Leuven, Belgium, for five years and now live "next door," in the neighboring Netherlands, I think I have some insight into the situation. Leuven, where I studied, is a very Flemish city, an old city. At the same time, Leuven is an international city with students from all over the world. The Catholic University in Leuven was founded there in 1425 by Pope Martin V.[203]

Now called KULeuven, the Katholieke Universiteit Leuven, the university is integrally connected and involved with the EU. KUL has been training people from all over Europe in EU law, political theory, even banking and designing currency.[204] Many professors at the KUL are trying to shape the leaders of the EU from Portugal to Lithuania.[205] I studied for and hold a master's degree and a doctoral degree from KULeuven.

Belgium followed a policy in handling immigrants that is quite complex, as is Belgium itself. As I noted above, Belgium is composed of two large groups: the Flemish, i.e., the "Dutch" or Flemish speaking—the majority—and the Walloons, who are French speaking. From the Flemish perspective, the Walloons have too much influence in the Belgian government. Additionally, Brussels is a separate governance from the other provinces. With the headquarters of the European Union in Brussels, Brussels also has special security needs and special circumstances.

Muslims (mostly French speaking) have tended to settle in neighborhoods in or around Brussels, like the now infamous Molenbeek. Molenbeek has continued to be breeding ground or hiding place for terrorists despite raids and arrests.[206] However, violence and crime have driven some immigrants to seek to live in smaller Flemish towns surrounding Brussels, such as Vilvoorde or Baardegem.

From some Muslims' viewpoints, the lack of coordination of the various parts of the Belgian government has resulted in an apparent lack of concern or action. There is freedom, but no real impetus to seek education, or language training, or jobs. There is simply no future for many Muslim young men. As a result, many young Muslim immigrants are ripe for radicalization. While there have always been government programs for helping immigrants get education, language training, and even job skills, Belgium hasn't been the best at achieving these goals. The country itself even went without a government for 589 days in 2010–2011, since the Flemish and Walloons could not reach a satisfactory coalition government. As one newspaper reported, "The maintenance of services in Belgium was partly due to its extremely federalized and decentralized nature, with many tasks carried out by regions, provinces, and cities."[207] The genius of the Belgian system of governance, which allowed this protracted period of existing without a central government, also had the downside of a lack of coordination and consistency in handling immigrants.

Belgian officials are quick to defend themselves, and Molenbeek has been a hotbed for radicalization. Some young Muslim men particularly feel that they have been largely ignored or discouraged from pursuing programs for integrating immigrants.

I have watched interviews of young Muslim men who are trying to protect Muslim young people from radicalization, broadcast on television here in the Netherlands. Radicalization is a common problem to all areas where Muslim immigrants are found. Language learning and cultural acquisition are necessary for immigrants to assimilate. But too often assimilation means secularization in the eyes of many young Muslims. While it's easy to say that all Muslims are terrorists and that a country ought to close its borders, this ignores obvious truths: many/most Muslims are not terrorists, many European countries need immigration, and in Western countries freedom of religion is a guaranteed constitutional right.

When EU countries find it hard to unite and easy to divide over their own national histories and customs, it is no surprise that immigrants find assimilation difficult. Merely "outlawing" expression of religion, as secularists might like to do in the name of law and order, doesn't work. There must be mutual respect and toleration, i.e., accepting that those who are different have a right to their religious beliefs and practices.

However, the religious expression of individuals or groups must not break laws or attempt to overthrow the government. There are laws, such as: if anyone goes to fight with IS or the Taliban, he loses his citizenship. Fighting for a foreign power is called treason. If someone does so, they forfeit their rights. There is no debate.

At the same time, there must be give and take. Cultural mores differ. For emancipated Dutch women, for example, wearing miniskirts is a constitutionally-guaranteed right. However (and I know this might be very controversial of me to say), it's unkind to go to a conservative Muslim neighborhood and taunt the local imam and community with one's freedom by wearing revealing clothing. As well, Muslim young men (or any men) must not heckle, harass, or assault young German (or any) women. At the same time, freedom must allow Muslim women to dress more conservatively, if they wish to do so, without assuming that they need to be "liberated." Space must be given in any multicultural and multiethnic society. Give and take is a part of life.

In the US, we certainly don't want "turf" wars between gangs of people from different ethnic groups, but is it not true that there are some black neighborhoods in Chicago where a white person isn't welcome or vice versa? We don't live in paradise, but we must make room for those who are different.

It wasn't so long ago that Italians in Pittsburgh, my home town, were referred to (please excuse the expression) as "Wops." Roman Catholics were discriminated against in the US in the twentieth century. We must be careful not to boast of our achievements when we are still fighting our own battles at home.

Speaking to you, the reader, I can attempt only to offer some grassroots solutions.

First, as citizens, we must understand who is an immigrant or asylum seeker and why they desire to immigrate to our county. We should be aware of the very specific procedures and processes our countries use to determine who is a refugee and who is not. In most cases, refugees don't enter a country by chance or illegally. No refugee or legal immigrant to the US enters illegally. There is a great difference between illegal immigrants and legal refugees and immigrants.

Secondly, we simply must not stereotype people. Different skin color, hair color, or features do not mean someone is dangerous. Similarly, not knowing the national language doesn't mean a person is a threat, though immigrants should learn the national language for the sake of others and themselves. Some people, when they hear another person speaking a different language, assume that the person is speaking about them. It might be the case, but it is probably not. As wise person used to say to me, "Why do you think you're so important that they would be talking about you?" Paranoia is irrational and unjustified. Most people speaking their mother tongue with their family or friends are talking about the same sorts of things you would when talking with your family or friends—what is going on at work or home, how they feel today, what their favorite sports team is doing, how their children are doing in school.

Thirdly, we need to be compassionate towards people who are under threat of execution or persecution if they return to their homelands. We also ought to have pity for people who have lost all that they have through war and being driven out of their homes and off their land.

Finally, we should follow the Golden Rule: "Do unto others as you would have them do unto you" (as Jesus says in Matt 7:12). Non-Christian people can adopt this same principle. The great "sage of Koenigsburg," the German philosopher Immanuel Kant, formulated the same rule, apart from religion and even from within the phenomenal consciousness (i.e., it doesn't require a command and is autonomously produced within the individual self-consciousness). "Act in accordance with a maxim that can at the same time make itself a universal law."[208] Simply put, he meant, "Act in the way you would like others to treat you." If Kant is right, it doesn't matter if we are Christians, Jews, Muslims, Buddhists, or secularists, everyone knows inside him- or herself what is right to do. It is what we would like ourselves. Discrimination and turning one's back on a person in need are criminal acts, not by definition or perhaps by law, but by the light of conscience, which every human being has.

Chapter 7: **Making Careful Distinctions —Who Is an Immigrant?**

When a foreigner resides among you in your land, do not mistreat them. The foreigner residing among you must be treated as your native-born. Love them as yourself, for you were foreigners in Egypt. I am the Lord your God.

—Leviticus 19:33, 34

WHO IS AN IMMIGRANT? Not all immigrants are the same. This might seem obvious, but it is often ignored or glossed over. There are various types of people who are normally confused together: refugees, internally displaced people (IDPs), economic immigrants and others who immigrate through other means than refugee status. While we may not be familiar with these distinctions, they drive public policy and popular misconceptions. The first distinction I'd like to address is the distinction between refugees and internally displaced people.

According to the UNHCR, a refugee is someone who flees their homeland for some reason which makes it impossible to return. The reason might be war, but it might also be, for example, religious persecution.

Many people fleeing Syria are refugees due to war. They have been driven from their homes by ISIL troops. It's even possible that their villages have been bombed by Allied, NATO, or Russian forces while trying to dislodge or destroy ISIL. Bombing campaigns can unfortunately drive a civilian population out of their territory and homes. It's false to suppose that everyone in a village bombed by Allied forces supports ISIL. Groups like ISIL are made up of individuals who hide among civilian populations. These groups have weapons, like Kalashnikov semi-automatic rifles, hand grenades, rocket launchers, etc. The civilians in these towns have little say about what happens to them.

Aside from people who are driven out of their home by war and bomb-ing, there are people who are driven out of their homes by religious persecu-tion. This persecution may have been going on for some time, but war or attacks by extremists may make the situation worse until they feel that they have to leave to survive.

In another section of the book I mentioned the Yazidi I met. It may be instructive here to look at their story in more detail. They are consid-ered devil worshipers by many Muslims and some Christians. The Yazidis have a syncretistic religion. They are an ethnic minority who speak Kurd-ish but are not ethnically Kurds. They are an endogamous group, which means that they marry only within their own people and their own castes. They have three castes and marry strictly within those castes. The Yazidis claim that their scriptures date back seven thousand years. They claim that their original scriptures were written in cuneiform, an ancient script like Bablyonian or Sumerian.

The Yazidis believe that God created seven archangels. One of them was the "Peacock Angel," also called Melek Taus. God told Melek Taus not to bow down to anyone. Yet, later, God created Adam and told all the arch-angels to bow down to him. Melek Taus refused. According to the Yazidi, this was a correct thing for him to do, since God had told him not to bow down to anyone. As a result, Melek Taus became a benefactor to mankind. He cried seven thousand years and put out the fires of hell. He is considered by some to be an emanation of God.[209]

The reason this story is important is that it is misinterpreted by many Muslims, or at least they interpret it according to their own views, rather than according to the Yazidi view. In the Qur'an (Koran), God ordered all the angels to bow to Adam. Iblis, Satan, or the Devil, would not bow down to Adam and was cast from heaven and is now the source of evil in the world (Qur'an, Surat l-baqarah [The Cow] 2:34).[210]

A Western scholar might find this an interesting transmission of an early Arab mythology or perhaps an even earlier Mesopotamian myth. The Muslim interpretation of Yazidi beliefs, however, due to its similarity with the Muslim story of Iblis, has resulted in the Muslims labelling Yazidis heretical Muslims.[211]

Whatever we might personally make of this dispute, one thing is clear: Yazidis have often suffered persecution to the point of death. They were driven only a couple years ago from their homes in Syria by ISIL, a self-proclaimed Muslim terrorist group, and left to die on a mountain side.[212] And yet if you had met a Yazidi as I have, you wouldn't be able to tell a Yazidi from any other Syrian . . . and I wouldn't have a few months ago. We must open our hearts and our ears to hear the cries of pain that many suffer. Not all immigrants are "economic" migrants or people who merely seek a better life. Some flee certain death. Consider how Mormons were once driven on pain of death from state to state in the US until they settled in Utah, which at the time was not a state. Sometimes people have fled religious persecution even in the US.[213]

In various parts of this book, I have already or will describe internally displaced people, but for the sake of completeness I will also include them here. When news media, NGOs, and the UNHCR talk about how many refugees there are, we need to be able to understand just what that means.

The UNHCR makes a distinction between refugees and internally displaced people.[214] A refugee is someone who has fled their homeland to a neighboring country to escape war or persecution. We usually have more sympathy for refugees, since we understand that their lives have been in danger and that there may be no place for them to return to.

Internally displaced persons or internally displaced people means people who have fled their homes and perhaps villages, but remain within the boundaries of their own home countries. This distinction is important for international organizations, since it determines the jurisdiction of national governments and what is the jurisdiction and responsibility of the international community.

It is not merely a question of who houses and feeds people, though that is part of the issue. International organizations have no right to intervene in the affairs of a national government. For instance, in 2011, Somalia's Al Shabaab Muslim militia revoked "permission for UNHCR and other UN aid organizations to work in areas controlled by the group." This is the sort of restriction that the UNHCR and other aid agencies cannot overcome without outside political pressure or dialogue with those who have set the restriction.[215]

In the former Yugoslavia, during the "Bosnian" War, Serbs fleeing from areas of present-day Croatia and Bosnia were not considered refugees. They were internally displaced people because Yugoslavia was still one country. Responsibility for them fell upon the government of "rump" Yugoslavia, i.e., what was left of Yugoslavia after all but Serbia and Montenegro had seceded, which had little to give. People were suffering and in need. I was asked a couple of times by Serbs living abroad to carry money to relatives in Serbia. Once, when I was traveling by train, there was a discussion of international aid. One fellow quipped, "That's what *we* are!" In other words, those of us carrying money to folks in Serbia were the only international aid arriving. Fortunately for these folks, the Mennonite Central Committee stepped in and helped the Serbs who were "internally displaced people." Popular media coverage in the West had so demonized the Serbs that even the MCC was criticized for helping people who had no other help coming.

In present day Ukraine, a shadow war continues in the eastern region of the country. Many Ukrainians consider themselves to be ethnically Russian. They tend to speak Russian rather than Ukrainian (although they know Ukrainian). Other Ukrainians would not consider themselves Russian at all and do not wish to speak Russian. Despite a ceasefire agreement which has mandated the end of hostilities and shelling, the shelling begins again every day at 6:30 PM. Many people have fled to other parts of Ukraine or neighboring countries to escape the situation. Some ethnically Russian people believed they would be safer in Russia and fled there, to major cities in Novosibirsk or Irkutsk in Siberia or to Chelyabinsk in the Ural Mountains and Vladivostok in the Russian Far East (Pacific coast).[216] Very few were allowed to go to Moscow or St. Petersburg.[217]

These people are considered "refugees" because they left their home country, Ukraine, and fled into a neighboring country. Again, according to Western news sources, some 814,000 refugees have fled from Ukraine into neighboring Russian, Belarus, Poland, Moldova, and other countries.[218] These neighboring countries will receive help from international organizations for these refugees.

However, there are also some 514,000 internally displaced persons in Ukraine.[219] These are people who have had to flee their homes and regions due to fighting, bombing, and accompanying danger. If the government will allow agencies like the UNHCR to work in their country, IDPs in that country can receive some help.[220] Ukraine has allowed aid agencies to work there, but still Ukraine itself must somehow deal with these IDPs. IDPs must be housed as well as fed and clothed. In Ukraine they are usually taken into the homes of friends and relatives and helped by local churches and some NGOs.

The distinction between a refugee and an internally displaced person may seem unimportant, but for a person who bears one of these labels it can be supremely significant. One designation may mean a ticket out of a war zone, while the other may doom them to a very meager existence in one's home country with little hope for the future.

Generally, many people seem unable to distinguish between types of "immigrants." Often all immigrants are seen as economic migrants, i.e., just people seeking work or a better life. For example, in the US, Mexicans and people from Central American nations who cross the US border illegally, to find work and perhaps eventually citizenship, are considered illegitimate immigrants because they have not entered the US legally and they are not fleeing persecution or war. Similarly, some western Europeans view those Syrians, Iranians, other Muslims from North Africa, and other Africans who enter illegally by boat from Turkey or North Africa to

Greece, Spain, or Italy as merely economic migrants. In many cases, it is true that these people seek a better life.

Of course, in the case of illegal entry, the situation is both easy and hard. When Mexicans and Central Americans enter the US illegally, they break laws. It is clear that they have entered illegally and as such they have earned a particular legal sanction. The situation can be, though, complicated. Think of industries which rely on migrant workers, e.g., fruit picking. This industry relies on people to come into the US to do these jobs and has done so for decades. Employers skirt employment laws which are meant to protect workers. The employers also avoid paying US Social Security and wage taxes. In fact, these employers take advantage of people who have no one to defend their rights as laborers and steal from the government by not paying taxes. According to many, these migrant laborers do not deserve the same rights as legal laborers because they enter(ed) the US illegally. However, the situation is complicated, because employers do use these people and because no one else, no citizen, wants to do the job.[221]

In the case of Turks, Poles, and eastern Europeans moving across to western European countries, these workers have entered legally. As Poles and Romanians are EU citizens, they have the right to migrate and find employment wherever they can within the EU. However, many European countries also need more immigrants from non-EU countries.

Most western European countries need immigrants. The reasons are varied: for instance, they need immigrants who will do menial jobs, which many western Europeans with higher education won't do. Western Europe has a negative birth rate, which means the population of ethnically Dutch, German, or French people is declining. At the same time, the need for health care for elderly people is increasing. The post-World War II "baby boom" has resulted in a record number of retirees. Many of them need medical care, if only attendants to help with bathing and using the washroom. Economic immigrants, in this case, if they work in this sector, provide both services and taxes, which enter the system. If there were no immigration, these social welfare systems would likely end.

Right-wing nationalist parties complain vociferously, for instance, in the Netherlands, Belgium, Germany, and France about immigration. Often, workers' unions or nationalist parties claim that foreigners, meaning immigrants, are taking jobs away from nationals of the countries in question. If the German Interior Minister's comments are to be believed, this is a false statement.[222] What actually seems to fuel this hatred of foreigners is that many traditional industries have been hard-hit by new EU policies aimed at making Europe globally competitive. Western European trade unions were used to preferential treatment by police and politicians. Now, due to attempts to make European businesses competitive in the world market, trade unions have lost a lot of power. Workers are not as protected as they once were. They cannot demand high wages and long and frequent vacations or may not even be able to count on having jobs at all without competition. Often, immigrants are willing to work for less, simply because they are used to working for less. They are happy to be in a western European country and not to be facing persecution, war, or economic hardship in their nations of origin. What would seem a meager wage to a person born in western Europe seems quite luxurious to an eastern European.

Some immigrants, though, are just trying to survive or have a future. If you had come from Serbia, you might want to immigrate to a western European country, since nearly twenty years after the war the economy is still shattered. It is part of human nature to want a better life and people all over the world of every shape, size, and color chase this dream.

When we lived in Serbia, there was a popular television show/soap called *Bolji život* ("A Better Life"). It expressed what many people want. People who come from countries where the standard of living is lower than in western Europe or the US often want to emigrate and seek what they think will be a higher standard of living.

As with the Serbs, many Ukrainians today want to leave Ukraine. Ukraine is suffering from a catastrophic economic crisis. The "shadow war" going on in east Ukraine (a "war" which, technically, doesn't exist) has ruined the economy. Russia is punishing Ukraine by denying natural gas and oil and not making payments for use of Ukrainian pipelines.

The Ukrainian currency, the *Hryvnia* (UHR), has lost more than 2 ½ times its value since I first started to travel to Ukraine in 2012. I used to get 10 UHR for 1 US Dollar. Now I get 28.28 UHR for 1 US Dollar. Imagine what this means even for someone who has a job. Your salary stays the same, but its value drops by 2 ½ times.

I have had many students from Ukraine, some from east Ukraine. Many continue to serve as teachers and pastors in central Ukraine. When I went to teach at a seminary in Ukraine recently, I noticed that the midday cooked meal at the seminary was mostly starch: potatoes or millet or buckwheat or oatmeal with fine shreds of meat or only bits of fat or drippings (lard) to flavor it. There were no fresh vegetables, at least in winter. There was only pickle: pickled cucumbers, pickled cabbage, pickled carrots, pickled onions, etc. I asked one of the graduates of our seminary here in the Netherlands, who is a pastor there, "How often do you eat meat?" He thought a moment and answered, "Maybe once a month."

Could any of us in the US be content with this sort of meager existence? You must sell your car to pay bills and then spend hours getting to work on the terrible, slow public transit. You have to rely on your relatives in the villages to share anything they have with you: vegetables, eggs, chickens, pigs, goats, milk, etc.

Compared to any place in western Europe, Ukraine, while perhaps not a Third World country, is at least a Second World country. However, it has awful roads full of potholes. This has not changed since 1996, when I first went there. My friend, who lived there in 1996, said it was better to hire a driver (chauffeur) than to drive your own car, since the driver knew where the potholes were. These are, though, not the potholes I remember from Pittsburgh when I was a kid, which opened up under the roads from the hilly terrain and water springs and were constantly being repaired. These are very large and never get fixed.

So, if you were from a country at war or a country suffering following a war, would you not want to leave? Wouldn't you want to do anything to help your children? And I haven't even talked about the wars in the Middle East. The situation in Ukraine is grim, but it is not nearly as bad for the inhabitants as the total bombing out of cities in Syria like Aleppo which was bombed for fifty-five days from April to July 2016.[223]

I have no answer to the question of economic migrants. It is a compli-cated, messy, enormous issue for governments and the EU Parliament as well as other governments and their legislative bodies. I agree that laws should and must be applied. However, clearly for Christians, there is no exception to the law of love. No matter who my neighbors are—Turks, Mexicans, Africans, whites—I am called to love them as Christ loves them.

Christ has given us a command: "Love your neighbor as yourself." Even at the time that he gave this command, someone asked him, "Who is my neighbor?" Jesus' answer was to tell a story, a parable about the good Samaritan. We Christians have tended to reduce this story to doing good deeds. There is a group of folks who camp in various camp grounds around the US who called themselves "the Good Sam Club." They are kind folks, who have first aid kits, extra supplies, etc. for other campers who have for-gotten something. I don't want to demean them, but Jesus' call is a lot more radical. Jesus used the most despised person he could to make his point. If Jesus were telling his tale today in Iraq or Iran, he would say that the "good Samaritan," the one who stopped to help the man who had been beaten and robbed, was a Yazidi. The Samaritan of Jesus' parable was ethnically despised, a half-breed. He was also a heretic, a person who had mixed the true religion of Israel with pagan ideas. The Samaritans were so despised that Jews did not even speak to them.

We as Christians are called to show love and to do good even to those who are despised by others, and in fact we are called to do good even to our enemies. Whether or not governments can resolve the problems of immigration and economic migration, we as Christians are called to help the least fortunate.

We have earlier discussed the phenomenon known around the world called the "brain drain." We have all heard of it and we all likely think we know what it means. In fact, I doubt many of us really understand.

What it means in simple terms is that we in the West encourage the best students from all nations to come to the US or EU and stay. We even give them scholarships. We pay them to study. When they graduate, we allow them to find work in our countries. Perhaps they fall in love with a "local" girl or boy and get married. Then, though it might be complicated, if they are bright, educated, and well-mannered, we allow them to stay in our countries.

This may sound very harsh, but I have seen this practice (while perhaps not an official policy) at work for more than thirty years. One of the reasons Tyndale, the seminary where I work near Amsterdam, was started in the Netherlands, rather than in the US, was to keep students "nearer" to home and perhaps to encourage graduates to go home after completing their studies. In the US somewhere between 45 and 70 percent of all foreign students remain in the US after graduation.[224] This is also true of theological schools.

Thus, it was felt that Tyndale could help the "brain drain," at least in our field of theological education, because the vision of the school is to enrich the churches of our students' home countries through our returning graduates. Our rate of graduate return is more like 72 percent.[225] However, we have no way to force people to return to their home countries. Many of our students have received scholarships; they know that they are expected to return to their home countries by the school and most do. However, we too have those who stay, in the Netherlands or in the West somewhere else. We have no legal way to stop them staying.

At the same time, it is duplicitous of governments to "cherry pick" the best minds from less fortunate nations and then complain about immigrants. All nations want certain types of immigrants—for instance, highly educated ones, yes, but unskilled or semi-skilled laborers, probably no. An interesting question is: how many of us, who are Americans, would be Americans if these sorts of strictures on immigration had been in place when our ancestors entered the US by way of Ellis Island?

When we complain about economic migrants, we should ask ourselves whether we would be willing to go and live in the countries we expect "economic" migrants to remain in. You might consider this a false dilemma.

You were born Dutch or German or American or English, etc., You have no reason to go to Serbia or Ukraine or Sierra Leone.

Actually, if you are a Christian, you do. Jesus told us, "Go and make disciples of all nations." While you may not be "called" (that is, you might not have had a special subjective experience of God speaking to you), you have been commanded by Jesus when he gave his Great Commission, "Go, therefore, and make disciples of all nations." I recall John Stott once preaching about the Great Commission and saying that it wasn't a question of whether you OUGHT to go, it was a question of why you ought NOT to go.[226]

Whatever our viewpoint about "economic" migrants (or any sort of people), they are people for whom Christ died, and thus people we can befriend, care for, and evangelize without crossing any political borders. Perhaps it is God's intention that the world is coming to the West, with many people coming come from places where evangelizing is illegal and conversion a death sentence. How will we be able to answer our Savior when he asks: "Why didn't you evangelize the people I sent to you? They were right in front of your door!"

Many people fleeing a country at war do not flee for economic advantages. Usually they have lost all that they had. Such flight is rarely carefully organized. People flee fighting in one area and end up in another area. Sometimes even "friendly" forces abuse people fleeing.

When we lived in Novi Sad we worked with many people who had fled fighting in various parts of the former Yugoslavia. They weren't "refugees," since they were in their "own" country. The situation was very complicated. There were, for instance, Serbs who fled fighting in Croatia between "Serb" (I believe mercenaries, even if they were ethnically Serbian) and "Croatian" forces (they may or may not have been official Croatian forces; they may have been nationalist militias). When they entered Serbia, they were no longer citizens of any country. They were required, if they had them, to hand over their Yugoslav passport and get a "rump" Yugoslavia ("Serb") passport. The privileges of this new passport were far fewer than those they had received with the old Yugoslav passport.[227] Many people were the proverbial "man without a country." They received help from churches and the Red Cross, but there was no other level of help because they weren't citizens of the country they were in.

Can you imagine yourself in this position? What if you were from Pittsburgh and troops from Cleveland attacked. Where would you go? You might flee to West Virginia, but you are not a resident there. In this scenario none of your identity documents would be recognized: suddenly you have no driver's license, no voting record, no health insurance records, no Social

Security, etc. How could you see a doctor, apply for benefits, seek work? It would be as if you didn't exist.

Those of us from North America can't begin to understand the sort of circumstances these refugees have faced. Sadly, too often it seems we are simply unwilling to try.

"There's nowhere to return to." We often seem to assume that there is a reasonable choice, that people can return to the country they fled from. Perhaps they could eventually. However, sometimes they have nothing to return to. Their homes have been bombed. Their villages have been destroyed. The economy is shattered.

Because the world is a lot more complicated than we care to consider, refugees are not a burden to be borne. They are people who have lost everything. In the words of Jesus: "I was a stranger and you took me in" (Matt 25:35). We must exercise compassion.

"I could return, but . . ." Sometimes people can return, but is it fair or wise to expect them to? In some western European countries, immigration services seem to be using a policy of "wait them out." Refugees wait for interviews about their immigration status. Immigration services let them wait sometimes six months or more without any word on their status.[228] These people may or may not be held in detention centers. They are in "camps," but the camps are often places like empty factories that have been turned into rough accommodations. In one facility I knew of, an empty office building was turned into a "camp." In each room there were two camp-type beds (metal frame with springs and a thin mattress). Each of the two inhabitants of the room had a metal locker big enough to hold a couple of shirts and trousers on hangers. They were given meals, but there was nothing to do. A yoga instructor offered to give free classes in the center. Her offer was refused. The dwellers in the "center" could go to her studio, a forty-five-minute trip by public transport, but she was not allowed to give lessons in the center.

After waiting several months like this, one man we knew simply gave up and returned home. He had hoped to bring his family, but he could not bear the separation and the uncertainty. We have to ask ourselves whether this is fair treatment. What has he returned to?

"I'm returning." *What does it mean?* In the case of the man I just mentioned, what does returning to his homeland mean? He never formally declared himself a Christian (as far as I know), but he attended a Bible study which my wife and I led. One of his countrymen, who is now a citizen in the country I live in, said that 90 percent of the people claimed to be Muslim in that country due to the Islamic regime in power. However, again according to my informant, most of those I met in the center were

not religious Muslims or even Muslim "believers." They said what they had to say, that they were Muslims, to stay alive and survive. Only those who came from ethnically Christian minorities dared to be openly Christian in that country. Any converts from Islam to Christianity risked a death sentence (whether carried out by the state or family). Christians in such countries have some freedom, but also have particular restrictions applied only to Christians and pay heavy special taxes (*jizya* is a term taken from the Quran for this sort of tax) which "Muslims" do not pay.

I met one young man from this country in the Near East at a church service. He was, at that time, an inhabitant of a detention center in Greece. I asked him whether he was a Christian. He said that he had believed in Christ about six months before leaving his country to come to Greece, where he was detained awaiting his request for asylum. He had been waiting fourteen months in the detention center. I asked him about his process. He said that he was being deported in two days back to his homeland. When I mentioned this to a church worker at that church, he acknowledged that being sent back might well be a death sentence.

This reminds me of the days of communism in eastern Europe—and even further, back to the Turkish domination of the Balkans. During the days of Communist Yugoslavia, people became members of the Communist Party and received Party membership cards simply in order to get into the university and to get better jobs. In the mid 1990s, many people publicly burned their party cards and were baptized into the Serbian Orthodox Church or Croatian Roman Catholic Church to show that they had always believed in God and to identify themselves as "Christians"; well, at least as members of the Serbian Orthodox or Roman Catholic church.

Those of us who have never lived under such religious or political oppression may not be sensitive to the pressures it puts on life and would-be immigrants. However, if we would explore our own family history, we might find our ancestors had just such reasons to immigrate.

I'll tell a story. Once there was a small group of Christians who were being persecuted by the main religious body in their country. They were fined, taxed, jailed. Some were even killed. They fled their homeland, crossing a body of water to another country, to find freedom of religion and worship. However, they stayed only a decade in that country. They were not persecuted there, but they felt that their children were assimilating and that their new country was becoming liberal. They returned briefly to their country of origin and then again crossed another body of water to find a new home. Nearly half died in transit and almost half again died due to the harsh winter in their new land in the first year.

Have you guessed who I am talking about? The Pilgrims, or "Pilgrim Fathers." In their day, some of them were even executed for "sedition." They fled to Leiden, the Netherlands, where I now live, in or around 1607, and then to the region which would become New England in America, in 1620. What if, instead of welcoming them to the Netherlands, the Dutch had said, "Too bad! Go back! We don't need problems with England!"

Most of us who are North Americans don't have to go too far back to find that our forefathers fled poverty, war, or religious persecution. The US has been built by immigration. Some people might label that a "liberal" assertion. However, no one can argue that it is a well-documented historical fact.

Freedom of religion and worship, as well as freedom of speech, is a cherished part of our American tradition. How many of our forefathers came to the US for freedom??

I read a biography of William Penn not long ago.[229] Being from Pennsylvania, I was interested to read about him. When you come from "Penn's Woods," naturally you are interested in Penn. The biography showed the ethnic diversity of Pennsylvania even in its early days.

Penn, of course, was a Quaker, and Quakers were heavily persecuted in England. Penn fought for freedom for Quakers, and due to his family background (his father had been an admiral in the Royal Navy), he was not heavily fined or jailed (at least, for very long).

Penn initially invited Quakers to come to Pennsylvania, and many came. But Penn also invited other religious minorities. He allowed, for instance, Mennonites and Amish to come to Pennsylvania from Germany and Switzerland. Central Pennsylvania is well known for the Amish. Moravians as well came to Pennsylvania very early on.

My point here is that the early colonies were welcoming of religious and ethnic minorities. Rhode Island was a haven for Baptists. Maryland was a colony of Roman Catholics. John and Samuel Wesley evangelized throughout Georgia and other American states.

It is interesting but sad to me that many Americans today are only willing to extend freedom of religion to Christians and Jews, or at least that's how it would appear.

However, due to the wars in northern Africa (Libya) and the Middle East (Syria and Iraq), suddenly America is no longer a safe haven for religious minorities. Frankly, many of us Americans are simply ignorant, or we have been hoodwinked into believing that all Muslims are the same. Any Muslim is seen as a potential or "closet" terrorist. All Muslims are believed to want to take over our countries and institute Sharia law. Conspiracy theories abound and our laziness lets us form opinions about things we have not even examined.

When I started to study at the Catholic University (KULeuven) of Leuven, Belgium, I thought I understood what a Roman Catholic was. I had been trained in Lutheran Church Catechism while in high school. I knew the difference between transubstantiation (the Roman Catholic doctrine of communion) and consubstantiation (the Lutheran doctrine of communion). I had read large portions of the Vatican II documents and had come, I thought, to understand what it meant that the Virgin Mary was the Co-Redemptrix.

However, in Leuven I saw a side of Catholicism I had never expected. The Belgian Roman Catholics often seemed very "secular" to me. They attended church (Mass) but only rarely. There were many things I found difficult to understand. I was surprised to find that some Belgian Catholics, for instance, wanted an end to the papacy. They considered it heavy-handed and patriarchal. Some were in favor of women priests. Others argued for married priests. Some openly argued for gay marriage. There was a Centre for Liberation Theologies (devoted to a Latin American radical view) and a Centre for the Study of Augustine, Augustinianism, and Jansenism.[230] This Centre is dedicated to the teachings of St. Augustine, Luther (whose works had been banned and who had been excommunicated by the church), and Jansenius (originally named Cornelius Jansen, the founder of a Catholic Augustinian movement called Jansenism, also called the Port Royal Movement. The famous French mathematician and philosopher Blaise Pascal was a part of it. It was a kind of Catholic "Calvinism").

I discovered that what I thought was Catholicism was more represented by "traditional" Roman Catholics from Africa and Asia. I found that I actually had more in common as a traditional Protestant Evangelical Christian with these friends from Africa and Asia than I did with most western European Roman Catholics.

While at KULeuven, I studied philosophy at the Institute of Philosophy, which had been started by Cardinal Désiré Mercier, a Belgian, as a training school for missionaries to the Americas. I, however, spent a lot of time reading postmodern atheists. I never could understand how Heidegger could be an atheist and also a Roman Catholic—he was even buried a Roman Catholic![231]

My point is that if I can have mistaken assumptions about Roman Catholics, who are also Christians, it is much easier for us to misunderstand another faith. Not all Muslims are the same. The main division is between Sunni and Shi'ia Muslims. Sunni Muslims, such as those in Egypt, for example, rely on traditions which have been passed down from

Muhammad as well as the Qur'an. They also have several schools of interpretation of the Qur'an. On the other hand, Shi'ia Muslims, such as those in Iran, follow an ayatollah who is their prime spiritual leader. Sunni and Shi'ia nations are sometimes, often, at war.

In addition to Sunni and Shi'ia, there are other sorts of Muslims. There are, for instance, Sufi Muslims, who are more mystical in their approach. Within all three of these groups, there are subgroups.

Sunnis from Egypt may not be much like Sunnis from Kenya. Twelver Shi'ia from Iran may not have a lot in common with Sevener Shi'ia Muslims, or Ismaili Muslims, from Pakistan. Ethnic Muslim divisions between Muslim groups are similar to ethnic divisions between Christian groups.[232]

I was invited to a meeting in the EU Parliament for the founding of an organization emphasizing wisdom in world peace. An EU functionary said to me and my friend, a graduate of our seminary, "You are Evangelical Protestants. However, I doubt that your Muslim friends know the difference between Protestant, Roman Catholic, and Eastern Orthodox, much less between different types of Protestants." This may seem a funny anecdote, but how many North Americans really know the difference between Roman Catholics and Eastern Orthodox Christians or between Reform, Conservative, and Orthodox Jews? We dare not be lazy about understanding the Muslim world, especially now that Muslim countries are so much in the news and more Muslim people may be crossing our paths. The Muslim world is very large and diverse, with many different religious groups and practices. It stretches, as we have said, from Spain and North Africa to Indonesia and Malaysia. It has adherents who are from many different ethnic groups and races. It has adherents in all countries on all continents.

A Serbian friend of mine studied at our seminary, Tyndale Theological Seminary here in the Netherlands, where I now teach, in the late 1990s. The "Bosnian" War in the former Yugoslavia was still going on. Outside of the seminary, when he was in Amsterdam he was often asked where he was from. When he said "Serbia," he told of how people would look worried and would seek an excuse to get away.[233] At the time, in order to drive a military campaign, i.e., get the approval of the populace, the news media in general branded all Serbs as beasts or demons in human form—butchers and brutal mercenaries. To be sure, there *were* some who were butchers and brutal mercenaries, but most Serbian young people I knew wanted nothing to do with the war. Many fled Serbia and went to other nations (the UK, the Netherlands, Germany, Sweden, even Russia) to escape military duty.

We tend to bestialize or demonize those we go to war against. Propaganda doesn't allow for fine distinctions. If we see those who are going to war with us as demons, it's easier to bomb them.

However, I have another friend who is a Serb from Herzegovina and who during the war was a refugee. He often introduces himself as "a ferocious Bosnian Serb," which is funny because he is the most *"simpatičan"* (endearing, likable) fellow you'd ever meet. People immediately burst into laughter, shouting, "No way!" He is a generous, warm man, a husband, and a father. He has a servant heart born out of his refugee experience.

Just as not all Serbs were butchers, not all Muslims are terrorists. I am quite troubled these days with the very poor logic I see circulating on Facebook and even on other more reputable sources. To believe these posts would be to conclude that all Muslims are terrorists. Of course, *some* Muslims are and have been terrorists. Perhaps even some *types* of Islam are terrorist ideologies, say Wahhabism. This is just as some Christians were crusaders in the Middle Ages. They went to war for the "sake of Christ." There are some radical groups of Christians today who profess not only the right to bear arms and carry weapons, but also reject government control of weapons, such as the Militia of Montana, and, earlier, the Montana Freemen.²³⁴

I have been teaching a course these past several years called Introduction to Islamic Philosophy. I am not an expert on Muslim philosophy, but I understand the history of philosophy and philosophical conceptions, so I set out on a journey of discovery. I knew that there were "classical Arab" philosophers in Spain during the eleventh and twelfth centuries. I had studied enough "Western" philosophy to know of Avicenna ("Ibn Sina") and Averroes ("Ibn Rushd"), who influenced Thomas Aquinas, the Roman Catholic scholar, and Maimonides, the well-known medieval Jewish scholar, for instance. However, during my study for the course, I have been very surprised to learn of the sheer vastness and variety of Islamic philosophy. If Islamic philosophy is so diverse, how would it be possible that Islam could be so monolithic as some suppose?

Islam faces many of the same problems Christianity (or any religion) does. For instance: What sort of dress is acceptable? Should we watch TV or movies? How does my revelation, my holy book, relate to reason and science? How can my religion handle questions like "Is Intra-Cytoplasmic Sperm Injection acceptable?"²³⁵

As I continue to read Islamic philosophy, I am finding it fascinating to see how different Islamic philosophers attempt to solve some of philosophy's typical, knotty problems. They are thoughtful and reasonable. In the face of this, I can't believe for a second that terrorists such as Osama bin Laden or anyone of his ilk represent the majority of Muslims.

It is true that some moderate Muslims become "radicalized" in Western countries, but I find it quite improbable that a Western Muslim's experience of being radicalized is stereotypical of what all Islam wants and attempts. One such radicalized person has claimed that a verse of the Qur'an which says Islam must conquer all other faiths is *the* key verse in the Qur'an.[236] Muslims, however, do not agree about what the key verse of the Qur'an is. How, then, can he know which verse is the key verse or that his interpretation is correct? He may believe that only the extremist imam that taught him is correct in this assessment of which verse is the key verse in the Qur'an. Or, he may think that one can use historical criticism of the Qur'an and say that Muhammad gave this *ayah* (verse) late in his career and so it represents *the* Islamic view. However, even this second possibility is illogical since extremist Islam doesn't allow for historical criticism of the Qur'an. Rather, conservative Muslims of all sorts believe that the Qur'an was given by God directly to Muhammad. There is, on the ordinary view of the Qur'an, then, no deciding which verses are earlier or later. In fact, a pair of German scholars were put under a *fatwa* (a death sentence) by one extremist Islamic group for engaging in historical criticism of the Qur'an.[237] So, if Muslims even cannot agree on how to interpret the Qur'an and disagree about other things, how can we as non-Muslims claim that all Muslims are terrorists and that this is "the" only correct view? The views of radicalized Muslims are not characteristic of other Muslims.

Another example which contradicts this idea that all Muslims are or want to be terrorists is my own personal experience of Muslims in the Netherlands. This is personal, subjective, and anecdotal evidence, but I can't omit mentioning it because I've experienced it. I have many Muslim neighbors in Leiden. They are Turks, Moroccans, and others: Indonesians, for example.

In our neighborhood, we live together in peace. We visit the same stores. A female young Muslim cashier might wear a hijab, a traditional Muslim head covering. The boys stocking the shelves may be Turkish. The manager is a Moroccan. We have other smaller shops, which are owned by Muslims: a kebab shop, an Islamic butcher, a Muslim baker. I have never been discriminated against or threatened. On the contrary, our neighbors are kind and considerate people. Once, when I needed to get past a Turkish man who had stopped in front of a shelf, although we had no common language he bowed and stepped aside and waved me past with a gracious smile.

There has never been a problem in our neighborhood. There are two mosques near us: a larger one (Moroccan) on our side of the main street and a smaller Turkish one across our main street. Yet, we have had no problems which were caused by religious tension.

Just as we do, these neighbors seek freedom of religion. They want a good life for their children: education, jobs, nice homes, cars, etc. Aside from obvious differences in skin color or hair color, most Americans would not be able to distinguish many of them from Spaniards or Italians.

In the mid 1980s, my wife went to a small seminary, Trinity School for Ministry, which had bought a couple buildings in a dying steel town, Ambridge, Pennsylvania, along the Ohio River north of Pittsburgh. Property was cheap! When the mill had been working there were some ten thousand steel workers in the town.[238] Many of these steel workers had come from many nations, mostly parts of Europe. There were churches of all descriptions still in that tiny town in the mid 1980s, years after the mill closed. There was a Ukrainian Orthodox church, a Greek Orthodox church, an Antiochian Orthodox church, and a Russian Orthodox church. There was a Ukrainian Catholic (not Roman Catholic) church, an Italian-speaking Roman Catholic church, a Polish-speaking Roman Catholic church, a Hungarian-speaking Roman Catholic church and a Croatian-speaking Roman Catholic church. There was a Jewish center and a former Presbyterian church. These communities celebrated (and still celebrate) their diverse religious traditions and cultures. Just as Pittsburgh has long had an annual "Nationality Days" festival, Ambridge has its own "Nationality Days" celebrating this diversity.[239]

At its best, Pittsburgh, as a city originally made up of immigrant steel workers, has long had many interesting things to experience: Italian sausages, German *wursts*, coleslaws and potato salad, Ukrainian *pirogi*, Polish dill pickles and cabbage rolls. However, war propaganda during World War II turned neighbors on each other and fostered paranoia about domestic spies.

My father was beaten up as a child in the elementary school yard in Pittsburgh during World War II. He was a "Kraut," a German. It didn't matter that his father had volunteered as a "Seabee" ("CB," a "Civilian Builder," one of a group of non-military civilians who volunteered to do building projects for the Navy). My grandfather had volunteered as a Seabee since he was too old to volunteer for the Armed Forces, being over forty years old at the time.[240] While my grandfather was in Pearl Harbor fitting pipes on ships to rebuild the US Pacific Fleet, my father was being beaten up for being a German.

Perhaps you might reply, "All of your anecdotes are interesting, but they don't prove much. I still think all Muslims are terrorists." My point is that we ought to and must make distinctions between people who call themselves Muslims. It is true, some Muslims have been radicalized; there is no doubting that. However, assuming that "all Muslims are the same" is, as one of my professors used to say, "just plain wrong." Interestingly, that professor himself could have been an example of this. His surname was Jewish, he was a Jew ethnically. However, his family had been Christian for at least two generations. Assumptions are dangerous. The Nazis wouldn't have cared about his grandfather's professed Christian faith. After all, it didn't help Edmund

Husserl, the well-known father of phenomenology (a sort of philosophy) who had to flee Germany, despite the fact that he was baptized as a Christian as an adult and had had his children baptized.[241] It also didn't help the Jewish philosopher Edith Stein, a disciple of Husserl's, even though she converted to Roman Catholicism and became a nun. She was sent to Auschwitz by the Nazis. Later she was beatified by Pope John Paul II.[242]

Further reading

Bauman, Stephan, et al. *Seeking Refuge: On the Shores of the Global Refugee Crisis* Chicago: Moody, 2016.

Bourke, Dale Hanson. *Immigration: Tough Questions, Direct Answers*. The Skeptic's Guide. Carol Stream, IL: InterVarsity, 2014.

Part III: **Personal Encounters**

Chapter 8: **Personal Encounters**
—My Yugoslavia

"Alas, Sovereign LORD," I said, "I do not know how to speak; I am too young." But the LORD said to me, "Do not say, 'I am too young.' You must go to everyone I send you to and say whatever I command you. Do not be afraid of them, for I am with you and will rescue you," declares the LORD.

—Jeremiah 1:4–8, NIV

I WANT TO SHARE my own experiences of the years that may have been most defining for me and my concern for refugees and people who are displaced by war and suffering—my time in Serbia. I have been told that I should share my own experiences so that readers can experience what I tell as I felt it.

My wife, my two young children, and I went to Yugoslavia and settled in the capital, Belgrade, to learn the Serbo-Croatian language in August 1986. We lived there for three years before the "Bosnian" War, two years teaching at a school for Serbo-Croatian speakers in Vienna, Austria, and two years in the northern Serbian city Novi Sad, returning to Yugoslavia during the war. We hadn't expected our new homeland to implode into civil war as a result of age-old national hostilities. However, we were "safe." We had "blue" passports, US passports. We could leave at any time that we felt in danger. We had a car and a Western income in German marks. The hyperinflation, which ran at 600 percent, did not affect our buying power. We didn't owe on large loans, which nationals had taken in Western currencies. We didn't have to depend on trading local currency, that was hourly devaluating, for "hard currency" (US dollars or Germans marks) that would keep its value from one day to the next. We didn't stay through the seventy-eight days of the NATO bombing of Novi Sad in 1999, where we had lived from 1992–94. We left when we felt called to leave.

We had worked hard to learn the language well and felt enormous love for many people and the nation. Still, we chose to leave.

I'm not sure if I can explain our feelings about leaving, but I'll try. When we first arrived in Belgrade in 1986 we were told by local Christians and non-Christians: "You won't stay!" It seemed to us at times that this was a self-fulfilling prophecy. Almost no Westerner managed to stay beyond ten years. Local Christians were often wary of foreign missionaries.

Still, it surprised us that certain people displayed bitterness about who we were and what we were doing. Once I was in a village at a church youth gathering. I asked a young man to pose for a picture with me. He acidly asked me: "You're going to raise money with my picture, aren't you?" I asked in reply, "You're not paying my salary. How else do you think I can manage to be here?!" Shame and blame is the name of the game in the Balkans. When friends who haven't seen each other for a long time meet, they say, "Why didn't you call? Have you forgotten me?" I think that people brought up in that kind of culture can cope with it. Maybe they don't take it seriously.

We moved to Novi Sad, Serbia, in August of 1992 from Vienna, Austria, when the Bible Institute we taught at closed. We remained in Novi Sad for two years during the "Bosnian" War. We left in May of 1994 and didn't return to Serbia, even for a visit, until June of 2005. I have a list of good reasons for why we did not return. But we did not live there through the bombing of 1999 when Novi Sad was bombed for seventy-eight days. We didn't suffer like locals and refugees (IDPs). Nevertheless, we had gone to live in Yugoslavia, twice: originally, when it was communist (1986–89) and again when it was in a state of war (1992–94). I think that shows we cared. We cared enough to spend nearly ten years of our lives trying to make a difference in Yugoslavia.

I have struggled to figure out what my part was but also what it wasn't. We can't do everything and we aren't gifted to do everything. However, we should do what we can do and what God tells us to do. So, I will tell a few of my stories from our time "on the Red Planet," as my wife and I nick-named Yugoslavia in playful homage to both communism and Mars, the god of war. However, I want to emphasize that the heroes of my story are not my wife and I, or my family, or even my missionary friends (though I admire them all). The heroes of this book are those who stayed—those national Christians who worked and sweated and slaved to provide for the homeless and even stateless people, the Yugoslav and other brothers and sisters who were there through the whole war and the bombing and some of whom continue to work to provide for the elderly and the broken—they are the true heroes.

One more thing: when the "Bosnian" War was blazing, many books were written. I resisted writing a book then about our experiences in

Yugoslavia. Though I speak Serbian fluently, and had been working in the region for almost ten years, I felt that my anecdotes were no more influential than anyone else's. Perhaps I fell to the Yugoslav tendency to despise news reporters who spent a few weeks "embedded" with a Serbian militia and then felt they had enough experience to write the "definitive" book. However, I will now write of our experiences in Yugoslavia, because it and the war there are the motive spring for this book, for why I care about refugees and immigrants at all.

I also write about our experiences in Yugoslavia in the eighties and nineties to help you to see how you might be involved refugees and immigrants now. Perhaps through our experiences you will begin to understand what it means to see the country you love descend into violence and war, and ties of friendship, marriage, and citizenship dissolve with broken lives all around. Many, most of the immigrants and refugees who are coming to our countries have experienced this and much worse. I hope that you will sympathize and care—not about us, but about them.

First trip to "the Red Planet"

My wife, Linda, and I left the US, accompanied by our two children, Elisabeth, then two years old, and Stephen, our three-month-old son, to live in Belgrade, Serbia, Yugoslavia, in August of 1986. We went there as first term missionaries to study the Serbo-Croatian language in order, after learning the language, to teach in a Bible institute for Yugoslav students, the Eastern European Bible Institute in Vienna, Austria.[243] I had studied the Russian language at college and it was judged that I could learn Serbian quickly and well, which proved true. Some imagined us to be walking into real danger, a communist country. Yugoslavia was a union of federated socialist republics. But if anything, Yugoslavia was the mildest of all the "communist" states.

Yugoslavia was prosperous and peaceful. Sarajevo had not long before hosted the Winter Olympics in 1984. The Adriatic coast was a playground of the rich, where people like Sophia Loren and Sylvester Stallone vacationed. Stores were full of goods, both domestic and foreign. Yugoslav passports allowed nationals to travel in many lands. Freedom to work abroad allowed thousands of Yugoslavs to work in places like Austria and Germany, among others.

We had the usual problems which all first term missionaries have. We had to learn not only language, but also the culture of Serbia. In our first three years in Serbia we studied the Serbo-Croatian language (as it was then called). We had babysitters to watch our children and help with cleaning and cooking. We had language helpers to help us learn the language. We were warmly welcomed by Christians in the First Baptist Church where we worshiped.

Eventually I also studied the Macedonian language and preached in Skopje, Macedonia (now North Macedonia). We learned about communication between people, expectations, and something that is always difficult for me: unwritten rules. We loved many things about Yugoslavs—they were warm, hospitable, and jovial. We made many friends, especially as we learned the language. But, as I related above, there were also some dysfunctional things about their culture. (Of course, every culture, even our home cultures, has good and bad things about it.) There was sometimes an attitude among local people that foreigners didn't really care about them and thus wouldn't really commit to staying long-term.

Our goal was to learn the language well and then move to Vienna to be a part of the Eastern European Bible Institute, the aforementioned Bible institute for Yugoslav students. We expected to be in Serbia for four years before moving to teach in the school in Vienna for the rest of our missionary career, which we thought would be about forty years long. We were twenty-five years old when we arrived in Belgrade.

Being in Belgrade, the capital city of Yugoslavia, could be uncomfortable because of political pressures. I am not a political person and have, throughout my career, tried to steer clear of politics and tried not to speak about political matters. We were forbidden by our agency from engaging in discussion of the politics of Yugoslavia and the former republics. We were there to teach and disciple, not instigate. One professor at Trinity Evangelical Divinity School, Dr. J. Herbert Kane, who had been a missionary in China before and after the communists, used to say, "You can keep your mouth shut and do what good you can or you can open your mouth and be forced out. The national Christians will be left behind to deal with the fallout."[244] So we tried to be apolitical. However, we didn't realize that political and nationalistic tensions were rising.

One afternoon we were invited to our landlord's son's birthday party. There were friends and relatives present. We talked in Serbian about why we had come to study the language in Belgrade. I explained that I was a Slavicist; I had studied Russian and wanted to expand my range of Slavic languages. Somewhere in the conversation, we talked about a Serbian church we had seen in Illinois. In the courtyard of the church, which was also a monastery, there was a bust on a pedestal of a fellow we didn't recognize.[245] I ran upstairs to our apartment and came back with some pictures. I showed them to the guests. One man who worked at the phone company, and in fact was a communist and the head of his communist union there, roared at me. "Don't you know who this is? This is Draža Mihailović! He was a Serbian royalist general![246] He was a traitor! What are you, a spy, a provocateur?" I was dumbfounded. I didn't remember reading about him. I had no idea who he was. Our landlord burst into laughter. "You can see that he has no idea who Draža Mihailović was! Ha, ha, ha!" So, I wasn't lynched that day or arrested!

Later, though, I heard from the assistant pastor at the First Baptist Church that he had had a visit from the Internal Police. They had asked him who I was. He told them that I was a missionary. This may not sound like much of a problem, but I was not supposed to be a "missionary" as far as the state was concerned. I held a visa as a foreign student studying Serbo-Croatian. I had been warned by the director of our Bible Institute in Vienna not to say that I was a missionary. In fact, I was so effective in avoiding saying that I was a missionary, that when I finally admitted that I was a missionary to one elder in the Baptist Church in Belgrade, he asked me why I lied to him earlier. I had told him that I had studied Russian and was a Slavicist. What I had told him was true. However, like many people in the Balkans I didn't tell the whole truth, only what was safe and convenient. In retrospect, I had felt forced to lie, and then felt condemned by the elder for doing so. It was a no-win situation, and deeply uncomfortable, which was typical of life under communism in eastern Europe.

I loved Yugoslavia but was always uneasy being there. It seemed that the government always had to have something on me, some reason to throw me out when they decided to. They didn't mind me being a missionary really. They were more worried that I might in fact be a spy. Our Bible Institute director used to say, "It's better if they think you're a missionary than that you're a spy."

This idea about lying, even if for a good cause, was, I found, deeply embedded in the culture. Eventually, to keep a visa, I signed up as a freshman at the University of Belgrade (despite already having a BA and a master's of divinity). I signed up for the Slavic language program in the south Slavic languages. During that time, I was assigned a paper to write on any topic in Serbian folk literature that I chose. I asked a friend, who had been a journalist, what to write on. He suggested that I write on Marko Kraljević, a heroic Serbian figure who had been ruler of Macedonia under the Turkish rule of the Sultans, after the Battle of Kosovo in 1389 when the Turks had captured Serbia.

While writing this paper, I learned that Marko Kraljević had lied to his Turkish overlords and to the Turks in general. Though Marko Kraljević is a hero of folklore, and some of his exploits are mythical rather than historical, the stories about his wiliness encapsulate Serbian attitudes to this day. Lying to one's enemies is called outwitting them.

For example, in one story Marko was languishing in prison in "Arabia."[247] The king's daughter fell in love with him. She promised that she would let him out of prison if he would take her with him. Marko promptly took off his cap, got down on one knee and said, "O my faith! To thee I will be true!" So, the king's daughter let him out of prison. They made their escape on Marko's magical steed, Sharats, the talking horse. Along the way, the story says that Marko looked at the girl's raven black hair, and her long nose, then he took out his knife and . . . slit her throat.

I was, to say the least, confused about the story! I asked my journalist friend about it. He said, "No, you don't understand. He outwitted her. When he swore to be true to his 'faith,' he meant his Serbian Orthodox faith! She was a Muslim. He tricked her!"[248] That he tricked her was seen, of course, as positive. Dissembling is a part of the culture that is deeply ingrained.

Years later, when Slobodan Milošević signed the Dayton Accords knowing that he would break them, I recalled Marko lying to the Sultan's daughter.[249] Lying to an enemy was an acceptable way for a Serb to treat an enemy according to his culture. Such a tactic was considered to be outwitting an enemy. If your enemy believes your lie, too bad for him.

After three years, we took a home assignment back to our home town, Pittsburgh, Pennsylvania, from July 1989 to August 1990. During that year my wife, inspired by Serbia and its church history, finished her master's of arts in religion at Trinity School for Ministry in Ambridge, Pennsylvania, where she wrote her master's thesis on the founding of the autocephalous Serbian Orthodox Church under St. Sava Nemanjić. She did this because we expected to return to Serbia and to minister there.

We returned to Belgrade in August 1990. The world had been turned upside down during our time in the US. The "Communist Wall" had fallen. Missionaries were rushing into places like Romania, Bulgaria, Ukraine, and Russia. I felt torn. My original missionary calling had been to Russia, but we had never been able to go there. But we had just begun our ministry in Serbian and had learned the language.

So, we returned to Belgrade. Because we hadn't been sure when we could return, we had told our previous landlord to rent the apartment he was holding for us. When we arrived, we could only find a small two-room apartment for the four of us. We had no furniture and threw mattresses on the floor to sleep. We also rented the basement apartment from our first landlord. I used the basement apartment as my office. All of our things were also stored there until we could get a bigger apartment. It was a difficult time. The political climate was getting more tense. Rapid inflation began; to economize we ate as cheaply as we could. In Vienna, our team at the Eastern European Bible Institute, where we would teach eventually, was also going through a difficult time. The founding director had left, and the teaching staff was short-handed. I was asked to come to teach at the residence school in Vienna. I left my family on their own in Belgrade, where they were safe and felt fine, since my wife spoke fluent Serbian and we had many friends.

The walls were thin between our apartment and our landlord's. He was a Montenegrin—a tall, handsome man, very big and powerful. His diminutive wife had been a model. They had one son, a toddler. One evening we heard a scream, then an argument. He said, "What?! Why are you screaming? I haven't even hit you yet!" "You're a beast," she said. "I want everyone to know what a beast you are!" We knew that if we called the police, we would be in trouble. The police would ask why we were meddling in the couple's affairs. Wife beating was common in Serbia and throughout the Balkans. More cultural differences that were hard for us to understand.

Later, at the Bible Institute in Vienna, I once saw a young Serbian male student washing dishes. It was a part of chores which he did in partial repayment for room and board. He was wearing a frilly apron. I couldn't help teasing him. "That'll be good practice for you for when you get married," I joked. He replied, "If my wife gives me any lip, I'll give her a slap!" I was rather taken aback, since he was a senior student about to graduate. I asked him if he had taken the marriage and family class! (He had!) But violence has been a way of life in the Balkans as far back as recorded history. The Serbs define themselves as a Christian warrior nation, which sacrificed itself to save the West from the Turkish Muslim onslaught in the Middle Ages and which still stands between the Muslim East and the "Christian" West.

After bouncing back and forth between Belgrade and Vienna for a few months, the leadership of the Bible Institute asked us to move to Vienna. I was relieved to do so, because the atmosphere in Belgrade seemed toxic to me. Slobodan Milošević had let the genie of Serbian nationalism out of its bottle. His hope was to take over all of Yugoslavia, to be the new Tito, the former leader of Yugoslavia.

We had to make adjustments to live in Vienna. Our Bible school operated in Serbo-Croatian, but of course the language of Austria is German. We attended the Yugoslav Baptist Church while there. In many ways we identified more with Yugoslav immigrants: Serbs, Croats, Slovaks, Gypsies/Roma—than with Austrians, even though our last name, Gottschalk, was not uncommon in Vienna. Our personal world was like little Yugoslavia. But the situation was actually more complicated even than that. Our family language, of course, was English. As one of our colleagues used to quip: "I wake up in America. I walk through Austria. And I work in Yugoslavia."

I knew some German, so my life wasn't as hard as it could have been, but learning Austrian culture was not always easy. In general, we existed in the bubble of the Bible Institute. Our students were a mix of nationalities and ethnicities. We had one Serb, one Croat, one Albanian (later "Kosovar"), a handful of Yugoslav Slovaks from Vojvodina, the northern part of Serbia, and a few Bulgarians. While the students generally got along with each other, there were some cultural clashes and some nationalism. Slovaks were used to being a subjugated people, but they were the majority in the Bible Institute, which could make life a bit hard for a Serb. While there was no real antagonism between Serbs and Croats in the school or church, of course one's ties to one's homeland were strong. To some degree we experienced this even as a staff. Some of the teachers had studied in Zagreb, the capital of Croatia, and had learned Croatian. Others of us had studied in Belgrade, Serbia, and learned Serbian. The language Serbo-Croatian was really a combination of different dialects, and war-time stress and propaganda was separating it into two languages. Yugoslavia, the country we had loved, was dying.

I will tell a story to give an example of how the language of Yugoslavia was really several dialects or even different languages. As I learned Serbian I had repeated arguments with one colleague about how to pronounce words. He is a good friend. However, he had studied Croatian in Zagreb. He didn't know some of the differences between Serbian and Croatian. He was a devoted "birder," birdwatcher. Once I remarked that we had a bird's nest nearby. "Bird's nest" in Serbian is pronounced "*gnezdo.*" He corrected my language saying it was "*gnijezdo.*" I had to resort to pulling out my dictionary to show him that I was speaking correct Serbian.

Serbs speak the Ekavski dialect of Serbo-Croatian. The Croats speak the Ijekavski dialect of Serbo-Croatian. In effect Croats elongate some syllables. The Bosnians also speak a different dialect, the Jekavski dialect of Serbo-Croatian. Now all three claim to be separate languages.

The upshot of these linguistic differences is that a "Yugoslav" can tell exactly what nationality you are as soon as you open your mouth. In effect Croats "drawl" and Bosnians have a softer "drawl," that is, they elongate certain syllables. This explanation may seem pointless or even boring. However, during war such distinctions meant life and death.

These sorts of little tensions built up. Tempers were sometimes short. Students were tense.

In general, I didn't suffer any problems from speaking Serbian. However, once in Zagreb I was in the store that sold bread and milk. I asked for "*hleb*" (bread). The sales person looked at me with disgust and said,

"*KRUH!*" To Serbs, "*kruh*" is dry crust. Croats use the word *kruh* for bread. Simply saying "bread" got me in trouble.

While we lived in Belgrade, one colleague had given me a little yellow Langenscheidt dictionary of Serbo-Croatian, or more correctly Croato-Serbian (*Hrvatsko-srpski*). I looked up the word for glue and walked into an office supply store and asked for "*lijepak.*" The clerk there in Belgrade asked me to pronounce it a few times. Then he glared at me and said, "*lepak.*" That is, he corrected my elongated syllable so that I spoke Serbian and not Croatian.

These little differences didn't seem so big when we were first in Belgrade, just an irritation. However, later they became matters of life and death, or at least major discomfort.

You may have read the story in Judges 12 about how the Gileadites fought against the Ephraimites. When the Ephraimites were trying to flee, they would be asked if they were Ephraimites. If they said "No!" then they were asked to say "Shibboleth" (which means flood or stream). Because of the dialect which the Ephraimites spoke they could not say "SH" and said, "Sibboleth." Then they were killed. This minor dialectical difference of speech cost them their lives.

In the Netherlands during World War II the Dutch used a similar linguistic difference to tell German spies from actual Dutch soldiers or Resistance. They would hand a card to a person being questioned and ask him to pronounce the word. They would use a word like "*Schiphol*" ("ship's hold," but now the name of the Amsterdam Airport) or "*Scheveningen,*" which is a port near The Hague. Germans pronounce "sch" as "sh." When the German would say "Shiphol" or "Sheveningen," he would be shot.

My last name Gottschalk is pronounced in German "Got-shalk." However, there are Gottschalks in the Netherlands (some during World War II were Jewish). In Dutch the name is pronounced "KHot-skh-alk." You really have to hear it to appreciate it. You make a sound like you are going to spit from the back of your throat, a hawker, a loogie! Also, the initial G is not pronounced as a G as in German, but as a KH or a ch as in Bach. So, even pronouncing my own name could have been deadly had I been alive then.

The same sort of linguistic features plague former Yugoslavia. In the nineteenth century a Serb linguist, Vuk Karadžić, attempted to unite the South Slavs, the Yugoslavs, by collecting national poetry and songs (like Goethe did in Germany) and by translating the Bible into a dialectic he in fact created. He used Serbian grammar, but used the Bosnian Ijeka-vski for spelling. He attempted to tie Serbs, Bosnians, and Croats together linguistically. Tito did something similar when he had linguists develop the Serbo-Croatian or Croato-Serbian language. However, as soon as Tito died nationalists on all sides began to change the linguistic differences to reassert their individual ethnicities.

These linguistic differences seem small, but they portended greater difficulties. During the "Bosnian" War they separated friends and neighbors, and sometime even families, member from member. One day a student came to me and said, "My uncle has sent his wife home." I was confused. "What do you mean?" "They have been married over thirty years, but he sent her home." "Where did he send her?" I asked. "He is a Croat and she is a Serb," she said, "and he sent her home" to Serbia. It was said that some men even killed their wives.[250] Some killed their children. When the war broke out, it was a civil war. Brother killed brother and friend, friend. So at least he didn't kill her. Whether what this uncle did was kind or not, I can't say really.

We watched the news anxiously. First Slovenia seceded from Yugoslavia, then Croatia. The Yugoslav National Army sent tanks to the Danube River, which was the border of Croatia and Serbia, but they stopped there. However, when Bosnia seceded the real war began. Serbs were enraged and wanted to protect the 30 percent of the population of Bosnia that was Serbian. Croatia was bad enough where many were Serbs: in Lika, along the coast of Croatia and in the mountains in that region, and in Banat along the border with Bosnia. However, Bosnia was worse, having a higher percentage of Serbs.

Sadly, the situation with our team at the school was not sustainable. The last straw was financial. Eventually, after we had been living in Vienna for two years, the team decided to close the Bible Institute due to lack of funds. Some of us elected to return to what was now former Yugoslavia: some to Croatia and some (as we did) to Serbia.

Return to "the Red Planet"

So, we chose to return in the summer of 1992 to Serbia, to "rump" Yugoslavia, what was left of the former UFSRY (Union of Federated Socialist Republics of Yugoslavia). We moved to Novi Sad, a city in northern Serbia. Novi Sad had once been the capital of the autonomous region of Vojvodina within the Republic of Serbia. It was the most Protestant area of Serbia, since many ethnic minorities, like the Slovak Brethren and Lutherans, lived there.

What is it like to live in a country at war? We moved back just after Yugoslavia had been dissolved. Although we were not Serbs, after living in Serbia, speaking Serbian, and working with Serbs since 1986 we felt in many ways like cultural insiders. However, we soon became aware that although friends and neighbors accepted us warmly, politically we were still very much seen as foreigners: nationals of one of the opposing forces. The US and NATO opposed the war being carried out by the Serbs. Daily news on TV and radio spewed anti-American rhetoric, blaming foreign influence for the war. Although our children knew the language, we decided to home-school to keep them out of potentially uncomfortable situations.

We had not returned to Belgrade, but moved to Novi Sad, the capital of Vojvodina, the northern region of Serbia. Vojvodina is the bread basket of Serbia. It is largely a farming area, though there were also an oil refinery and a military and air base nearby Novi Sad.

At one time, Novi Sad had been part of the Austro-Hungarian Empire. The Empress Maria Theresa had driven Czech and Slovak Brethren believers to the edges of that empire as it then existed, which is the region around Novi Sad, called Vojvodina. Slovaks in Vojvodina are Brethren, Baptist, or Lutheran. There are other ethnic groups in Vojvodina also. Tito had been given territory out of Romania, Hungary, Austria, Italy, Bulgaria, and Albania, all of which had been Axis Powers in WWII. As a result, there were Hungarian Reformed Christians and Romanian Protestants, as well, in Vojvodina.

When we lived in Novi Sad we worked mainly with two groups: the Christian Evangelistic Centre in Bački Petrovac and the Christian Fellowship in Novi Sad. We taught classes for young people at the Christian Fellowship: discipleship, apologetics, marriage and family, and other classes. We also offered some remaining students from the closed Vienna school courses they needed to finish their diploma program.

We rented two apartments: the second and third floors of a small building. We used the second-floor apartment as our home and the third floor as our classroom and guest room. There was an internal staircase between the apartments and an external staircase to the ground floor.

As with all new buildings in that area, the stairs were made of marble, since marble was cheaper than wood in Serbia! It is said that the Roman Caesars had chopped down all the trees in earlier centuries. The building was brand new. Our friends said that the owner must be in the mafia, because he couldn't have had this much money otherwise during a wartime economy!

What was life like in "rump" Yugoslavia during the "Bosnian" War? In some ways, easier. I was given a religious worker visa without a problem. On the other hand, day-to-day life was difficult. Yugoslavia was under UN sanctions. No oil could be imported. A black market was going full tilt, but the gas stations were empty. You had to buy gasoline on the roadside in 1.5 liter Coca-Cola bottles, or buy from someone else.

We had an acquaintance, a young Christian in the village. He was an ingenious lad. He put a propane gas burning unit in his car. He would drive across the border to Hungary using his liquid propane. He would fill his gas tank with gasoline and then fill the tank in his trunk with propane gas. He went back and forth leaving the gasoline in drums in his chicken coop. His business flourished until customs agents got tired of the crowded borders and imposed a tax which made his trade unprofitable.

Natural gas for heating was allowed only two hours per day: one hour in the morning and one hour in the afternoon. Each time the main gas valve in the neighborhood was turned off the safety valve in our gas meter dropped. This meant that the next time the gas came on, you had to open the gasket, raise the valve (while the gas hissed out) and then close the nut again. After that you had to jump into the dirt floor of the basement (no stairs) and re-light the furnace. This procedure was repeated twice daily. It kept the house at about 55 degrees F / 13 degrees C. The family huddled in the boys' bedroom during the days for homeschooling during cold weather.

Since natural gas was rationed and fuel oil was scarce, people used electric space heaters. However, the electrical grid wasn't prepared for such demand. Transformers on utility poles regularly blew out, with a lot of "fireworks"!

Normal goods in stores were scarce. The people of Vojvodina had voted against Milošević. As a result, though they were the farmers and brought in the harvest, nothing was given to their stores. Everything was sent south to Belgrade and further south to the rest of Serbia.

This was a disaster for many ordinary, hardworking people. For example, we had a friend who worked in the department store. He was being paid in coupons since they had no cash and banks didn't work. He asked Linda to come and buy her food in the grocery section of the department store where he worked, using his coupons. Then we paid him for the worth of the coupons in German marks, which was the *de facto* currency at that point. Among other things, for instance, we ended up buying lots of margarine, which we put in our freezer, just to find things that we needed from their stock! When the store was depleted, he framed a couple of pictures for us as a small job. We were just trying to give him things to do so that we could share our marks with him.

People, who, like him, had loans for their houses which they had taken in hard currency, like US dollars or German marks, had to repay these loans in the same currency. So, with hyperinflation running wild, the Yugoslav dinar was worthless. For example, a 5,000,000 dinar bill which was issued at 9 AM would be worthless by 12 PM! One day, my wife exchanged several marks for a large number of Yugoslav dinar in the morning in Novi

Sad and then we drove to Belgrade for a team meeting. We went to Mc-Donald's (yes, there were McDonald's in Serbia and they were open during the war) and to her shock the money had devalued so much during the morning that it was almost worthless—certainly not enough to buy lunch! She had an emotional meltdown and felt shattering guilt as she realized that her "carelessness" had wasted money that would potentially have been very important to a national. The McDonald's lunch would already have been a luxury that most nationals would not have been able to enjoy and now even that had been wasted. We had heard on the news that some Serbs were committing suicide because their assets had lost all their value. In that moment, she reflected later, she had "gone native" to such an extent that she was reacting like a national.

Such hardships were only one side of life under sanctions and war. Another aspect is that everyone seemed to be armed. Things like hand grenades and ammunition, were for sale in the open-air market. Serbian Christmas is January 7th, as it is for Russians and other Orthodox Christians. Serbian New Year's Day is January 14th. It is the custom of Serbs to fire weapons into the air when celebrating the New Year, weddings, etc. In 1991, I traveled down from Vienna to Belgrade to teach a modular class. We met in the apartment of a fellow missionary. It happened over Serbian New Year's. I was looking out of the window and watching the fireworks and hearing the gun shots. A Serb friend said, "Get away from the window. You'll get shot!" I thought he was joking. He said, "Have I ever joked with you about such a thing? People get shot every year. You're a foreigner." He had a point. When a Serbian general in Bosnia was asked what he would do if NATO forces bombed, he replied "I would take every NATO blue helmet captive and . . . ." He drew his finger across his throat.

On one Serbian New Year's while we lived in Novi Sad, we were home quietly by ourselves. I heard a machine gun firing somewhere nearby. I turned out the light and lay down on the floor on the mattress we had as a bed. Twice there had been shootings in front of the drugstore in front of the hospital. Some black marketeers brought in drugs which were needed: for instance, insulin. They sold the drugs for hard currency. Twice, black marketeers had been ambushed and killed and their money stolen.

In short, living in Yugoslavia at war was nerve-wracking. There were daily fly-overs by NATO jets doing reconnaissance. Hearing jets scream above your head, even if you're not on the front, is unsettling to say the least. Besides the jets, there were also helicopters of the Yugoslav (Serbian) forces, carrying wounded soldiers from the front, which was about ten kilometers away (seven miles). Helicopters came and went all day from the front to the military hospital in Novi Sad. Even though we were not in the war zone per se, we were always aware of the war.

Because of sanctions against Yugoslavia ("rump" Yugoslavia), there were no international flights into Belgrade. Whenever a person wanted to visit us, or a guest teacher was to come to teach a class in our apartment that was a classroom on the third floor, they had to fly to Budapest, where they took a bus or train, or waited for us to come by car and pick them up.

Once, a guest teacher was coming from Amsterdam. He flew to Budapest. Because there wasn't even normal food in the stores in Novi Sad, I went early to Budapest and did some shopping for staples for my family. I bought milk, orange juice, peanut butter, and other things we needed. When I picked up my friend in Budapest at the airport, I explained that either we could stay overnight at a small hostel in Budapest, which would mean unloading all the groceries out of the car and taking them inside the hostel (otherwise, they'd be stolen) and then repacking the car in the morning, or we could drive that night back to Novi Sad. If we left immediately, we would arrive around 3 AM, but he could sleep till afternoon as our classes would be in the evening. He thought we should just drive back to Novi Sad.

So, we set off. We had to stop at the Yugoslav border of Hungary and Serbia. We had to present our passports. Then I had to produce the letter, which said that I was allowed to import goods duty free despite the sanctions on Yugoslavia, for the customs officer. After that I had to purchase car insurance from a Yugoslav insurer, since, again due to sanctions, my international insurance, which was Austrian, wasn't any good in Serbia (tit for tat). We managed all of this in about an hour, which was a good turnaround.

I had chosen a small road through the countryside to avoid traffic. Also, the smaller border was easier to get through quickly. Because we were on the small road, we had to drive through a village. We reached the village, at about 1 AM. There was a military check point at the main intersection in the town. I hadn't thought about it, but we were about one kilometer, less than a mile, from the front between Serbia and Croatia. The military check point wasn't a surprise and it didn't really bother me, but there was a soldier who seemed to want to extort money out of me. Eventually his commander told him to let me go. After his commander had turned his back, the soldier pointed his rifle, which was hanging on a strap on his shoulder, at my friend and said in Serbian, "He doesn't have his seatbelt on." Again, trying to get some money out of us. My friend asked alarmed, "Why is he pointing his gun at me?" "He says that your seatbelt isn't fastened," I said. "But it is!" he said, as he quickly opened his jacket, which was covering the seatbelt.

I wasn't too bothered by the event. I was used to soldiers and guns. It was more an irritant to me than a threat. I knew the soldier wouldn't shoot us. However, to someone from outside it was frightening.

Even in telling this story, I feel many confused and ambivalent feelings. If I tell how a soldier pointed his rifle at my fellow professor while at a routine military check one kilometer from the front, it sounds dangerous. It wasn't as dangerous as it sounds, actually.

When I drove back into Serbia from Budapest, I often traveled the same road. This road went past a graveyard. I noticed that every time I passed it there were at least a half a dozen new graves. Though the front wasn't in Novi Sad, it was very close by.

There were also many people hiding from the military police, mostly young men who didn't want to serve in the army. Every Yugoslav citizen was required to carry a "booklet," a sort of internal passport that showed whether he had served his military duty or not. If a Yugoslav citizen was found without a "booklet," the assumption was that he had destroyed it to avoid the draft. Such men were sent immediately to the front to fight.

Every evening in Novi Sad there is a custom of taking a walk, called the "korso," around 6 PM on the main walking street of the city. Everyone takes a stroll down the main street and looks in shop windows, sees and is seen. This custom continued through the war. Every so often, every third or fourth day, though not with any pattern, a blue military police van would roar up the street and stop. Blue camouflaged military police would stop every man and ask for his "booklet." Whoever did not have a "booklet" or a "booklet" showing that he had served his military duty on the front was trundled off in the van and sent to the front. While it was disconcerting, it never involved me directly, as I was a foreigner and to them I looked foreign. As a result, they never approached me. Still, this was a constant reminder of being in a country at war. Imagine living every day with the fear of being arrested and sent to the front!

Two requests which were made of us at this time were being asked either to carry someone in our car out of Yugoslavia to avoid the military duty or to house either a draft dodger or a refugee (IDP). As we had a car licensed in Austria and we were Americans, people reasoned that we could carry an extra person in our car and only wave our blue passports at the border, and be able to get someone out without the Passport Officer knowing what we were doing. It may sound like the Underground Railroad, but there was nothing glorious about it. If we had been caught, we would have had a stamp put in our passports that would have prevented us from returning to the country. We would have had in effect our temporary residence visas revoked on the spot. We would not have been able to return, even to get our things out.

The situation with housing either draft dodgers or IDPs was also difficult for us. We had rented two apartments, living in one and using the other for a classroom and guest room for visiting teachers. Sometimes the guest room was free, but we always used the classroom, nearly on a nightly basis. There was no way to accommodate someone staying there on a long-term basis. If we had housed a draft dodger and were discovered, again, we would have had our temporary residence visa revoked. Whatever good we could have done as teachers of Bible and theology would have abruptly ended. Sadly, we felt at the time that we had to say "no" to these requests. Of course, our hearts went out to these internally displaced people/refugees. We wanted to help, but . . . . We did not support the war in any sense; of course, we felt for those who did not want to fight.

My wife, Linda, and I are gifted and experienced teachers. We taught these refugees, these young people what we knew: the Bible, discipleship, apologetics, church history, theology. At times, it seemed like what we did was pointless. People were homeless and starving, unemployed and desperate, but we taught "Bible courses." Other people and other groups brought aid and helped in more practical ways, and we tried to support them in it. But I think this shows a key principle: you and I should do what we can, what we are trained for and gifted to do, and what is at hand to be done. Not everyone is a teacher. Not everyone is a counselor. But anyone can have an impact in a refugee's or immigrant's life by caring, by being there, by doing what can be done.

We left Novi Sad in May of 1994, not because of the war, but because I felt called to pursue more education on a higher level. The students we had wanted to get through the program had finished and it was time for our regular home assignment. After one year in the US, we moved in August of 1995 to Leuven, Belgium, where I studied at the Catholic University in the Institute of Philosophy. I got my MA and eventually in 2004 my PhD. Keeping in mind our intention to return to Serbia, we attempted to return to Novi Sad in 1999. However, the NATO bombing made it unwise for Americans to return at that time and so our mission forbade it.

After much soul-searching, in 2000 we decided to move to the Netherlands. Why the Netherlands? My seminary advisor in the US, Dr. Arthur P. Johnston, had started a seminary near Amsterdam (Tyndale Theological Seminary) and he invited me to join his teaching staff. Also, we made the decision so that our children would have English-language high school and a Dutch-speaking environment (they had learned Flemish/Dutch in our time in Belgium). After our turbulent years in Serbia and Austria, my wife in particular thought that they needed a more peaceful environment.

We thought again about returning in 2006 to Novi Sad to teach at an existing school there. We visited in June 2005 and were warmly welcomed by our former students, both from the Eastern European Bible Institute, which had been in Vienna, Austria, and young refugee people we had taught in Novi Sad, who were now pastors. We were very excited and prepared to return. However, we decided that we could not return for a variety of reasons. Also, we remained in the Netherlands for our younger son to finish high school and eventually college, and for my wife to pursue a PhD at Leiden University.

Actually, we are amazed to note that there were such long-lasting good results from our two years in Novi Sad during the war. In our visit in 2005, we saw that the formerly-young people were, ten years later, pastors and elders in various churches in Vojvodina and other regions. One student had even started a crisis pregnancy center and a pro-life campaign. Their marriages seemed strong. There was much to be thankful for! We weren't there very long, just two academic years, but we did make a difference using the gifts we had, a difference in their lives and their futures.

This, then, was my Yugoslavia. First, it was a union of federal republics of diverse peoples. Then, it descended into war and madness. It became a place of ethnic hatred and wanton destruction. Hopefully by my telling of some of our experiences, you will understand some of the confused and ambivalent feelings we had about cultural differences and trying to fit into a new home. You can see how difficult it is when a country you love, the country which has become home, descends into war. You might be able to imagine through our recollections how confusing and scary it is when violence and financial instability surround you, and then multiply that at least ten-fold to try to envision how refugees from war-torn places feel. I hope that our recollections help you to sympathize with immigrants, refugees, and displaced people in their difficulty.

Further reading

To understand the civil war in the former Yugoslavia, see:

Mojzes, Paul. *The Yugoslavian Inferno: Ethnoreligious Warfare in the Balkans*. New York: Continuum, 1995.

To see how reconciliation might be affected, see:

Volf, Miroslav. *Exclusion and Embrace: A Theological Exploration of Identity, Otherness, and Reconciliation*. Nashville: Abingdon, 1996.

To understand the Serbs' attitude towards Muslims, see:

Andrić, Ivo. *The Bridge on the Drina*. Reprint ed. Chicago: University of Chicago Press, 1977.

Chapter 9: **Personal Encounters with Refugees**

REFUGEES USUALLY ARE PEOPLE who are fleeing war or violence or persecution. They aren't happy to flee. Often, they are driven out of their homes literally in the dead of the night and forced to run. They first flee somewhere away from immediate danger. Usually that place is a temporary safe haven. It might be something as flimsy as a tent set up in a swamp. Such places have hardly any sanitary facilities or even running water, let alone heat.

If they are accepted after being initially processed, they make their way to a temporary asylum center. Depending on various conditions they are interviewed again (and sometimes again and again) by government officials. If they are deemed true refugees, they are allowed to move to another facility (say an abandoned factory) where they will await a more permanent place to live (a small apartment).

Once these refugees become actual immigrants they have a lot of things to learn: the language of their new country, a job skill they can make a living at, customs and laws and regulations, etc. They must accept some things which in their cultures were unthinkable, for example topless beaches in the Netherlands . . . (not in the US, however).

My heart has been broken many times over the decades as I have gone from one desperate situation to another. What I knew vaguely as the son of someone helping a Vietnamese refugee woman, to being a graduate student working with Russian immigrants in Chicago, to watching thousands and thousands of IDPs cross into Serbia from Croatia and Bosnia in cars and on tractors pulling their belongings, has become now too normal.

Here in the Netherlands, where I live now, I meet many immigrants and many refugees. They live nearby. Many of my neighbors are immigrants. As well, some are descendents of refugees who have fled persecution in their homelands, as did Huguenots who came to Leiden when the Roman Catholic Church in France persecuted them.

My concern is that we do not suffer "donor fatigue" before we begin to try to help. With our modern news media, we see situations developing before we know what they mean. For a person like me who has lived in a country at war (Serbia) and worked in a country at war recently (Ukraine), I understand all too well what people have suffered. I understand their unwillingness to open up and say much of anything beyond banalities. They are shy to say where they are from exactly or what their religion really is. I also fear sometimes that people are telling me what "I want to hear," i.e., the "safe" "line." But, I understand why they might be afraid to tell the "truth."

But where does compassion for refugees and internally displaced people come from? Is it something we are born with or just feel intuitively? Can it be learned? My wife and I learned compassion for refugees when our mothers helped refugees.

When we were teenagers our small Lutheran church in Pittsburgh, Pennsylvania, sponsored a Vietnamese family. Actually, it was our "Luther League" (our youth group) which sponsored the family. The husband had been a police chief in Saigon. He and his wife and four children (soon after, five) were able to escape when US armed forces helped "friendlies" to escape. They had to spend a long time waiting in the water until they were evacuated by helicopter. One of their children was born *en route* as they fled and eventually reached the US.

Being a refugee is not only being physically removed from your home. It is entering a new culture. In the case of most refugees there is no time to prepare for emigration or immigration. One is thrust from one's home and inserted in another place. All is new and strange. For example, one day this family came to a worship service in our church to show respect and gratitude for our church helping them though they were a Roman Catholic family. At one point in the service the minister wearing his clerical robes extended his hands forward with his palms up and raised them in a sign for us to rise from our seats. The family was shocked. This was an extremely rude gesture in Vietnam. Why would a "priest" make such a gesture?

The family was exceedingly grateful to the church for their help. The weather in Pennsylvania, however, was hard to get used to. They kept the thermostat in the home the church gave them set very high all winter. We were of German descent and this was considered outrageously spendthrift. "Don't they know how high the heating bill will be?" (People from a tropical area are not used to cold. Just ask my students from Ghana who are studying in the Netherlands!)

The relationship between the family and the church was not always straightforward. The wife became pregnant again. Some parishioners felt four children was plenty. "Why do they need any more children?" they asked. It was also hard for Lutherans to understand them as Catholics just as much as it was hard for Americans to understand a culture in which more children is a blessing.

My mother and my future mother-in-law tried to help this family as much as they could, to befriend them and help with clothing, give them rides to the doctor, and helping in many other ways. They especially spent a lot of time helping the Vietnamese wife learn English, among other things. She learned quickly. Their children excelled in school and eventually, as I recall, all got scholarships to college.

The husband, however, did not fare so well. He had been an important person in Vietnam, a police chief. Now he was no one. He could not speak English. He was embarrassed to try. He spoke French fluently, but no one in our church spoke French. He had no marketable skill. Eventually he left his wife and returned to Vietnam. He couldn't make the change. As with many immigrant marriages, theirs didn't survive.

Our little church tried to do its best. Its best was better than the nothing many churches did. They weren't without judgmental attitudes and their own limited horizons, but they tried to help this immigrant family, and the family was helped to a large degree. Though the family was glad for the church's help, eventually they moved to California to be near some of their relatives, who had also immigrated, and to be in a warmer climate. The children excelled in high school, university, and graduate school. They have found the American dream, but their father returned "home." When we help refugees, we must be prepared for cultural differences and even decisions that we cannot or do not understand.

While our mothers had shown us a model of caring for refugees and immigrants, later in life we also encountered other refugees and immigrants. When I went out to Illinois to go to seminary, I found out about a small ministry to Russian immigrants in Chicago and wanted to work with them as a volunteer. Before I got involved, I didn't realize that these Russian immigrants were Jews, but in the process of working with them I learned a lot about *Yiddishkeit* and Russian Jewry.

Immigration of Soviet Jews began after Senators Edward Koch of New York and Clifford Case of New Jersey drafted legislation "allowing 30,000 special immigrant visas for Soviet Jews."[251] The policy of détente increased the number of Soviet Jews allowed to immigrate into the US. President Jimmy Carter hoped to give Soviet Russia favored nation status, but the Soviet invasion of Afghanistan prevented this. Still, in the 1970s, 64,000 Soviet Jews immigrated to the US. A person who was as little 1/16 Jewish could apply for asylum in the US on the basis of religious persecution, as I recall. This policy was applied into the late 1970s. Fewer Jews immigrated from Russia until another wave of Jewish *Aliyah* from Russia took place in the early 1990s.[252]

I moved to Chicago in August of 1980 and was involved with ministry to these immigrants. It was quite a learning experience. The first thing I learned was that most of these people were not religious refugees. They were "Jewish" somewhere back there, enough to qualify for a visa, but most were not interested in being Orthodox Jews. Though the immigrants were usually sponsored by the Hebrew Immigration and Aid Society (HIAS) in coming to the US, they shed or rejected whatever requirements being Jewish meant.

Usually these people went first to a "transit camp," either in Traiskirchen (south of Vienna, Austria) or in Rome, Italy. They had to be processed thoroughly before they were allowed to enter the US. An organization, like HIAS, had to sponsor them so that they could come to the US. This is a fairly typical pattern governments follow with refugees: immediate camps where first interviews take place, transit camps where more in depth interviews take place, and finally placement.

Most of the Russian Jews I met had come to Chicago to find the "American Dream." They expected the US to have streets paved with gold. Slushy Chicago streets in the dead of winter didn't seem so nice! Apartments that these people could afford on their limited welfare amounts were not of a very high quality.

It's one thing to have exalted ideas about helping others, but when the rubber meets the road sometimes there are challenges. I had studied the Russian language in college. Our director had a master's degree from Harvard and knew Russian also. One day, an elderly woman entered our small center. Sadly, she had been a chemical engineer in Russia, but couldn't get a job in the US in her field. However, now she was looking for an apartment.

She talked a mile a minute in Russian. She kept repeating one word: *tarakany*. Our director couldn't understand that one word. That was the one word I *did* understand: "cockroach"! I had translated parts of a novel where the word was used when I was taking a college class. So, since I understood that one word, he sent me to help this woman look at an apartment and make a list of repairs. It's a funny story, especially since she didn't have to worry about cockroaches, as it turned out. Trying to translate her rapid-fire speech to the superintendent, including her concerns about (as I recall) a broken shower curtain, unsafe electrical outlets, and a refrigerator to be repaired, at one point something seemed to fuse in my brain. She kept badgering me as I tried to explain to the "Super"/concierge what she wanted, reminding me not to forget anything on her list. I got so rattled that I turned around to her and said, "Be quiet!" in English. Then I turned to the building superintendent and repeated her list in Russian! Laughing, he told me it didn't matter, he had understood.

Another young Russian immigrant woman we were helping was upset that her landlord had raised the rent on her apartment. She complained that her welfare payments were not going up! "How could he ask for more? The government wouldn't allow it! They aren't giving me any more money! How can I pay more?" We patiently explained that the landlord was a private citizen and could raise the rent on his property. She refused to agree. She persisted in paying her rent at the old rate. This was in the dead of winter. Her landlord waited till the date in the spring when he was allowed to by law (when "winter" ended) and then put her belongings on the curb (those he hadn't confiscated as payment for the rent she had withheld). She was completely dumbfounded and confused, and suddenly homeless. Being an immigrant often means not understanding what is happening around you or being "discriminated" against. At times the confusions are humorous, but other times they are just sad.

Two Russian men meeting on the street in Chicago would "bear" hug each other and kiss loudly on the lips, and then go arm in arm together down the street. Imagine burly, square-chested, typical Russian men doing this! Such humorous differences are not all so bad.

On the other hand, some situations are sad to the point of despair. Two Russian sisters arrived in Chicago. One had been a doctor and the other an engineer. To become a doctor in the US would have meant for the former doctor in the USSR that she would have had to pass medical board exams again, and this meant at least several years in medical school and going through internship and residency. Who had money for all of that? The doctor eventually took a job as a day care worker. She was happy that she had work and she loved the children. Her sister, the engineer, didn't fare so well. She became seriously depressed.

Another Russian Jewish family came from a very large city in Ukraine. Their son was deaf. They hoped for a better life for him. The husband had been the chief editor of the largest newspaper in his city in Ukraine. But he couldn't speak English. He had to work as a longshoreman loading and unloading trucks. He sat for hours in his darkened room with the curtains drawn and smoked cigarettes. He was frustrated and started to beat his wife. She left him. He had no one and nothing.

Novi Sad, "rump" Yugoslavia

Besides our own experiences with refugees and displaced people in the former Yugoslavia, I want to highlight some of the praiseworthy people who headed up work with them.

Although as I've said, our main job in our time in Yugoslavia/Vienna/Serbia was to teach Bible courses, as a part of the school in Vienna or out of our Novi Sad apartments, some of our friends were working with refugees and internally displaced people who were in need due to the war. When we moved back into Serbia, Serbia was a part of what was called "rump Yugoslavia," i.e., what was left of the old Union of Federated Socialist Republics of Yugoslavia, which was Serbia proper and the Republic of Montenegro. Many people had been displaced due to the civil war and breakup of UFSR Yugoslavia.

My wife and I joke that if you ask someone in the Balkans why something in the last decade or so has happened, they tend to begin with an answer something like, "Well, in the eighth century . . ." or "Well, in 1389 . . .," "In the nineteenth century . . ." or "Before the 'War' [they used to mean WWII] . . . ." Historical perspective is very important to people in the Balkans and seen as essential to explain why anything is the way it is. So, indulge me as I give you a little Yugoslav history here.

Why were there refugees/internally displaced people (IDPs) in Serbia in 1991–2000? Because there was a civil war. Why was there a civil war? When we had earlier lived there in Belgrade, Serbia, from August 1989 through May 1990, Serbia was a republic of Yugoslavia. The UFSRY (Union of Federated Socialist Republics of Yugoslavia) was a post–World War II state, which was established after the Allied Powers awarded General Josip Broz Tito, leader of the Communist Partisan fighters, with the whole territory of the South Slavs for his success in fighting the Nazis during World War II.

Unfortunately, the country of Yugoslavia had a short history. Earlier Serbia had been five hundred years under the domination of the Turks from its defeat at the Battle of Kosovo in 1389 until the end of the nineteenth century. Serbia had been a vassal state of the Sultan. Twice they rebelled against the Sultan and finally achieved a state, when after World War I in 1918 the Allied Powers awarded the Serbian leader, in this case the King Peter I (Karađorđević), a kingdom: to be precise the so-called "Kingdom of the Serbs, Croats, and Slovenes." The Allied Powers also awarded the Serbian king with territories taken from conquered Axis countries: Italy, Austria, Hungary, Romania, Bulgaria, and Albania.

Though some had had a dream of a pan-Yugoslav or pan–South Slavic state, the various ethnic nationalities making up first the Kingdom of the Serbs, Croats, and Slovenes and later the Union of Federated Socialist Republics of Yugoslavia (UFSRY) were not happy to dwell together. After WWII Marshall Tito managed to create a ponderous system of government which allowed for a set of checks and balances to curb the power of the Serbs and allow smaller groups to have a say in the governing of their country. The republics would take turns holding the premiership of the Presidium and thus each have a voice. Tito also divided Serbia into three parts. He made Vojvodina, the northern part of Serbia, which is largely composed of many ethnic minorities—Slovaks, Czechs, Vlachs, Romanians, Hungarians, and others—into an autonomous region within Serbia with a vote of its own in the Presidium, the supreme governing body of the Union of Federated Socialist Republics of Yugoslavia. He also made Kosovo, which had been the birthplace of the Serbian nation and scene of the famous Battle of Kosovo, a separate autonomous region within Serbia. He also allowed Albanians to immigrate into Kosovo from Albania, though it was never an officially recognized policy. Tito's goal was to weaken the Serbs' strength. The Serbs were about 36 percent of the populace in the former Yugoslavia.[253]

The result of Tito's experiment was an unstable peace which lasted beyond his death until the late 1980s, when Slobodan Milošević arose to power in Serbia proper. (This was happening just as we arrived in Belgrade in 1986.) A Serbian nationalist, Milošević wished to take over the whole of Yugoslavia. He tapped into Serbian nationalism, which had been repressed during the time of Tito (witness the story I told in the last chapter about the taboo topic of Serbian royalist Draža Mihailović). He held enormous open-air rallies, swaying the populace with his nationalisitic speeches. He also engineered a change in the constitution of Serbian Republic of the UFSRY, taking the autonomy of Vojvodina and Kosovo away from them. This simple move guaranteed Milošević control over all of Yugoslavia. Serbia, as a result of this change of constitution, gained three votes in the Presidium. Serbia could also always count on the army, which had a vote, and Montenegro. Montenegro is a mountainous region, which is home to a small segment of ethnic Serbs. There were six republics in post–World War II Yugoslavia: Slovenia, Croatia, Serbia, Bosnia and Herzegovina, Macedonia, and Montenegro. Then there were the two autonomous regions: Vojvodina and Kosovo, plus the army. There were thus nine votes in all in the Presidium. If Serbia had three votes and could count on the army and Montenegro to agree with them, Serbia could control all issues that would come to the Presidium. In other words, Serbia could rule unchallenged.

When Milošević's intentions became clear, in early 1991 Slovenia and Croatia seceded from the UFSRY. (This was when we were living in Vienna and teaching at the Bible Institute there.) Shortly thereafter Bosnia and Herzegovina and Macedonia seceded from the UFSRY. The so-called "Bosnian" War began not long after that. The result of the civil war in Yugoslavia was floods of refugees across the Balkan Peninsula. Croats fled Bosnia into Croatia. Serbs fled Croatia, Bosnia, and Kosovo into Serbia. It was a horrible humanitarian crisis.

When we returned to Serbia in August of 1992, we met and worked with many refugees . . . well, they thought that they were refugees, but their status was actually more blurred. They were ethnic Serbs who had lived in other parts of former Yugoslavia and now fled. They were not safe in their home republics. (Those former Yugoslav republics are countries now: Croatia and Bosnia and Herzegovina or in the case of Kosovo, a UN Protectorate.) They fled into Serbia sometimes carrying only what they could put into one bag. Some told stories of having to leave with only a few hours' notice. Imagine, if the US were to have another civil war, that someone whose grandparents had been born in Pennsylvania, but who himself had been born in New York state, had to flee south, without their possessions, never to return to New York.

There were, probably, about seven hundred thousand refugees who poured into Serbia over a two- or three-year period.[254] This created a big problem for the regime of "rump" Yugoslavia.

In actual terms, these people should be called "internally displaced persons," not refugees, since they didn't (technically) leave their homeland. The UNHCR makes a distinction between "internally displaced persons" (IDPs) and "refugees." IDPs are people who have had to flee their homes and/or regions due to war, but remain inside the boundaries of their home country. A more recent example is the Ukrainians from Donetsk fleeing to Zaporozhye. The Internal Displacement Monitoring Centre figures there are still seven hundred thirty thousand internally displaced persons in Ukraine as of the 31st of December 2019.[255] They also figure that there are at least two million more Ukrainian refugees who have fled to Russia, Poland, Belarus, Moldova, and other countries.[256] In any case, whatever these Serbs who fled into Serbia in 1991–99 were called, they were homeless and poorly cared for.

In former Yugoslavia, some Christian agencies worked hard on behalf of displaced people in need. While in the former Yugoslavia/Serbia in 1992–94 we worked alongside two agencies: the Christian Evangelistic Centre in Bački Petrovac, led by Ondrej Franka and Vladimir Majersky, and the Christian Fellowship church in Novi Sad, pastored by Vera and Daniel Kuranji of CAMA Ministries.

Rev. Ondrej Franka was co-director of the Christian Evangelistic Centre in Bački Petrovac, a Slovak village in the north of Vojvodina, Serbia, former Yugoslavia. Ondrej and his coworkers were very involved in evangelizing IDPs in Vojvodina and in caring for them physically through extending aid and in caring for them spiritually.

Ondrej notes in an article he wrote: "As Slovaks in Serbia, we can say without bias that the genocide was rampant on all sides."[257] The Slovak population has been in Vojvodina since the seventeenth century when Slovak Protestants were driven out of the Austro-Hungarian Empire by Empress Maria Theresa.[258] The Slovak Protestants were the majority and were dedicated, in the main, to the teachings of Martin Luther.

Ondrej, who had extended us an invitation which officially allowed us a visa to work in Yugoslavia from 1992–94, points out in his article:

> This civil war produced several million displaced people and hundreds of thousands of refugees who poured over the borders on all sides of the conflict area. Taking their meager possessions or nothing at all, they entered neighboring countries with the hope of finding peace from oppression and suffering. Now the question was, who will take care of these refugees?[259]

Along with other evangelical churches, the Baptist churches and Brethren assemblies among the Slovaks reached out to these refugees with both physical and spiritual aid. It was a very difficult time for everyone, with black outs and brown outs of electricity, restrictions on natural gas, and sanctions that meant no available gasoline at service stations. The greatest hardship was an action taken by Milošević's government to punish Vojvodina for its voting against him in elections. Though Vojvodina is probably the richest and most productive farmland in Serbia, the stores were empty of basic goods, which were produced in Vojvodina: bread, milk, eggs, oil, etc. Ondrej and his coworkers were involved in a program called "Tell and Feed" where they extended food and other physical necessities and spiritual aid.[260]

Circumstances were very grim for many people. In Bački Petrovac, near the Christian Evangelistic Centre, there was an abandoned brick factory. It was turned into a makeshift refugee center. Wires were strung across the huge expanse of the space making six "rooms" in which six families lived, almost all of which had three generations living in a small space, perhaps three m. by four m. (9 ft. x 12 ft.). There was no central heating. There were no sanitary facilities, except an outhouse. It was a mean existence. I held a Bible study for these people for a while. They were simple people from villages in Bosnia. Some were illiterate (among the elderly). Some were young teenagers who had no future.

Aside from IDPs, Serbia itself became a very poor place. As Ondrej chronicles:

The imposed international embargo, sanctions and economic collapse of Serbia brought many down to the level of poverty. People in the cities were suffering the most, because of the scarcity of food. Here again the evangelicals responded by setting up "soup kitchens" where free meals were served anytime to anyone who was in need.[261]

During this time, another member of Ondrej's church took me around to preach in village churches where there might be only a few believers. Once I asked a fellow who organized the aid from the church in one small village, "How many people come just for the food?" He said, "A third. A third come only for food. A third come both for food and worship. A third would come even if there was no food." This might seem heartless to some, to "force" people to listen to a sermon to receive physical aid. However, these believers knew that physical help can only go so far. There are hidden needs as well as the need for food.

Some criticized evangelical churches for forcing people to convert to Protestantism in order to survive. Ondrej responded pointedly to this comment:

> Slovak evangelical Christians, being a minority themselves in Serbia, have strived to present God who in Jesus Christ embraces all people alike. Even though they have to pay a price for this, they uncompromisingly continue. In the process, a lot of threats and other kinds of violence are experienced by the local body of believers.[262]

I remember about this time that Rev. Dr. Aleksandr Birviš, longtime pastor of the "First" Baptist Church in Belgrade, responded to criticism from the Serbian Orthodox Church, which alleged similar charges that Protestants were buying converts. Birviš, though himself a Baptist, had studied at the Serbian Orthodox Theological Faculty in Belgrade during the Communist Era. He replied: "We have done nothing wrong. We help the poor and needy. This is what Christ requires of His people. Let the Orthodox Church join us in well-doing."[263]

Vera and Daniel Kuranji of the Christian Fellowship were also tireless workers, both in working to meet the physical needs of the refugees and in sharing with them the gospel of Christ.[264] We worked closely with them and their church. Most of the people we worked with were young people, whom we trained, as we mentioned, teaching them the Bible and Christian doctrine. The stories they tell of these young people, and the stories of others will illustrate what happens when you are a refugee.[265]

Serbs fleeing bombing and attacks on their homes in Croatia or Bosnia fled into Serbia. Those who arrived at the border of Serbia by train were met by armed troops or military police. In one case a woman and her daughter were separated from her mother and other daughter. The mother and one daughter were sent north into Vojvodina (northern Serbia) and the grandmother and the other daughter were sent south into Šumadija (southern Serbia). Her husband was taken away immediately at the border and sent back to fight on the front. He could call on the phone once every two weeks or so, and speak with her briefly. It took the mother two years with the help of the Red Cross to find her mother and other daughter and be reunited with them. There were no mobile or cell phones then. Phone lines were often cut, as well. Computers were uncommon then too.

We also worked with two brothers, whom we taught, who were from Sarajevo. Their mother was a Serb, but their father was a Bosnian. To keep the boys safe and to flee Sarajevo, which was under siege, the mother brought the two boys to Vojvodina to stay with relatives and to go to high school in Novi Sad. They could only get letters to their father by sending them through a UN "Blue Helmet" Peacekeeper, who was a Norwegian soldier. As I recall, this was about once every other month.[266]

One of our graduates from the school in Vienna was from Novi Sad, so we saw a lot of her after we moved to Novi Sad. The church that we were involved in, the Christian Fellowship, was doing refugee work delivering food and goods to refugees, who had no aid from anyone else, since some western agencies would not help Serbia. The church had help from a UK charity, which brought down two trailer trucks full of discarded or outmoded clothing to be distributed among refugees. The church's yard was set up as a bazar, with a checker at the gate. The pastor explained that some people, who weren't refugees, would come and take things and then resell them at the open-air market. Therefore, all refugees who were to get clothing, etc. had to present a ticket which the pastor had given them. As I was there in the church yard, our former student approached me. She introduced me to her uncle, who had been born in what is now Croatia. His family had lived in the Lika area, he said, for five hundred years. But he wasn't familiar with Vojvodina, the region he was now in. She said, "You know Vojvodina better than he does." She said that she had urged him to take two white shirts. He had taken only one. He proudly said, "I have two shirts. I can wear one and wash the other." He had lost everything: his home, his livestock, his lifestyle, his land . . . but one shirt was enough.[267]

Working among and with refugees was a strange and wonderful experience. Sometimes people, who have literally nothing, are more thankful and generous than people who have a lot. One couple had arrived from

Bosnia. He had been an engineer there. His wife worked in the forestry service. One night they were warned to flee their home in Bosnia with what they could carry as a bombing campaign was going to start. They fled in their car and watched their new home go up in flames.

They made their way to Novi Sad. They had nothing, except their car and what they carried. His wife found work in the forestry service in Fruška Gora, near Novi Sad. The husband found a job in a plant, making bombs. They had nowhere to live. One Croatian man in Novi Sad met them and said, "I have a mud wall house in a nearby village. It was my mother's house. It has no central heating, no electricity, no running water in the house and only an outhouse, but you're welcome to have it rent free."

By comparison, we lived in a new building, which had probably been built with war profits. Next to us was a small house. It was a home to squatters. A Serb family had arrived from Bosnia. The woman was a middle-aged mother. Her husband had started to drink and run around with other women. He couldn't face being no one and nobody.

I could go on with many other stories, but the point of what I want to say is that no one wants to be a refugee. One day suddenly you are driven from your home, which is probably destroyed, and you end up somewhere rootless. You flee because you must: to save your life and/or to save the lives of your children. War is a disease that kills countries and lives. It doesn't discriminate between "good" and "bad." It maims, destroys, and cripples. The crippling isn't just physical. It's often much deeper and much harder to deal with.

Bosnian Serbs who fled to Serbia were despised. They speak a different dialect than Serbs in Serbia proper do. If you think of how southerners in the US "drawl," the idea is similar. As soon as you open your mouth, you are a boob from the hills, a hillbilly. In the twisted viewpoints of war, the victims became the cause. A friend who fled from Sarajevo to Belgrade said that when he opened his mouth people turned away or abused him. "Why have you come here? Weren't there enough mouths to feed? Why aren't you on the front?"

This same scenario is going on right now in Ukraine. Those who have fled the area where rebels and Ukrainian forces continue to fight, despite a ceasefire, are considered a problem and a burden. There is "donor fatigue" in Ukraine among Christians who feel that they have given all they have, and there's little left. There is not enough aid for all the "internally displaced people."

Various aid agencies were trying to address this situation. Westerners like Dr. William Steele and his wife, Debbie, of the International Mission Board of the Southern Baptist Church, USA, agreed with the UNHCR in Belgrade to distribute aid to 125,00 Serbian refugee children in Serbia proper. They provided school supplies worth $850,000 which were distributed through evangelical churches.[268] Most of the items were purchased in Russia and Bulgaria with a total of eighteen forty-foot containers of supplies delivered—one million pencils! Steele partnered with evangelical churches to distribute items normal for school (backpacks, notepads, paper, pencils, protractors, etc.). Local churches received no funds except to cover their costs. The students who received the supplies were not required to attend any services or be church members. Steele's example is one of a person from a smaller agency (IMB SBC) helping a larger agency (UNHCR) to do its job well.[269] He and his wife blessed many children during this terrible time of war and deprivation. They served during a harrowing time at great personal cost.

Other missionaries under the International Mission Board of the Southern Baptist Convention at that time were Randy and Joan Bell. Working along with Bill and Debbie Steele, Randy's focus became bringing aid to refugees in the Republika Srpska, the Serb enclave in Bosnia. Since Bosnian Serbs were seen as the enemy, no agencies seemed disposed to help Serbian displaced people driven out of Bosnia into the Republika Srpska. Randy, however, answered the call and earned the nick name "Bosna Ekspres," the "Bosnian Express," for carrying aid to Republika Srpska. I retell their story because it shows just how grave the situation of many IDPs, "refugees," is and how praiseworthy people like the Bells are for their service in this situation.

Randy and Joan arrived in Belgrade in October 1994. They were originally to have worked as church developers and helped with discipleship in the Baptist Church. One of their daughters was born there in Belgrade. Along with Bill and Debbie Steele, the Bells found themselves thrust into refugee work. No matter what you had come to do, with the floods of refugees everyone was asked to take on new responsibilities to help people in dire need.

Randy and Joan were asked to work on the Serbian side of Bosnia and Herzegovina. They worked in Republika Srpska. Their coworker Bill Steele was responsible for Bosnia and Herzegovina and Croatia. They took Bibles and money for food to the Serbian refugees in Republika Srpska. They also took money to give people to buy small livestock: goats, pigs, and sheep. These Serbian refugees had been pushed out of Croatia. The infrastructure in Bosnia and Herzegovina was very poor: bad roads, no water, no electricity, no heating, etc. Many refugees were squatters in abandoned and in some cases bombed out houses. The IMB built a school for children.

Randy found no problems in working with the government of Republika Srpska. The IMB had the goal of helping all refugees anywhere in the former YU. Dragan Simov, a native of Belgrade and later our student at Tyndale Theological Seminary in the Netherlands, helped Randy in this work.

There was a period of difficulty when politicians Biljana Plavšić and Radovan Karadžić were contending for power over Republika Srpska. Plavšić was favored by Western powers. Karadžić was favored by Slobodan Milošević. There were sometimes friction and contention between their supporters. [270] This impacted ministry also. On one occasion Randy and his companion waited all night at the border at the city of Banja Luka. They were stuck at UN check points. UK forces had deployed large contingents, including tanks. The contending forces for Plavšić and Karadžić were armed. Some had Kalashnikovs. Many trucks (lorries) were lined up waiting to cross the borders, but they were not allowed to enter. As well many people had been bussed in, probably by Milošević from Belgrade, to demonstrate in his favor. Many of these people were refugees. They were probably paid for their participation.

Randy had no way to call his wife that night that he and Dragan sat at the border between Serbia and Bosnia. There were no cell or mobile phones then. She did not know where he was or how he was. It was harrowing for her not to know what was happening and he could not tell her. At some point the UN forces allowed the people to loot the trucks, which were lined up, including Randy's truck and its supplies. This was done by UK and Dutch NATO forces, and perhaps others, to relieve the tension of the crowd. The NATO forces, thus, used Randy's aid to solve their own immediate problem. Helping refugees is sometimes very dangerous. Many times, it is also quite frustrating and difficult.

Getting to Republika Srpska of itself was hard. The roads were bad and the conditions very difficult. There were many border crossings and problems with finding fuel.

Bread of Life, a relief agency in Belgrade, gave Randy a visa to work in Republika Srpska. However, the lack of infrastructure caused political instability. Many agencies feared being involved there.

Very few people in the West understood the situation. They could not understand how there could be Serbian refugees from Croatia and Bosnia in Serbia, let alone in Republika Srpska. As a result of the demonization of the Serbs by western media, it was hard to convince people of the need. Randy and Joan were among the few Westerners who understood the situation.

Joan had dubbed Randy the "Bosnian Express." Twice a month Randy drove from Belgrade to Banja Luka and Prijedor, carrying packages and money.

They recall that you don't realize at the time how much stress you are under. You do what has to be done. It was also difficult to help when everyone wanted you to help them. You couldn't help everyone. You didn't have enough resources or time or strength.

Though they were never attacked or robbed, they did not feel very safe. The neighborhood that they lived in, Bežanijska Kosa, was a sort of upscale neighborhood on the outskirts of Belgrade. It was home to "mafia" (drug and gun runners), and singers and entertainers with money. In a country at war where lawlessness rules, such folks flourish.

Another family they knew represents the fate of many refugee marriages. The father stayed in Sarajevo to try to protect his property from squatters or damage. The wife and children moved to Belgrade. She was a language teacher in Belgrade. Eventually their marriage fell apart and they were divorced.

Randy Bell's keenest memory about refugees was a time just after their own youngest daughter was born in Belgrade. They knew a family of refugees from Knin, a large city in the Lika region of Croatia. The father had been taken by paramilitary forces and forced to fight for a half a year.

When Randy and Joan had a meal with this family, the mother was struggling to cope with two daughters and no husband, since her husband was fighting on the front. This mother rarely heard from her husband. Randy and Joan had hired one of the daughters to baby sit their three daughters. Earlier in the year the two daughters and the mother had become Christians through the *Hram Sveta Troica* (The Temple of the Holy Spirit), which was a large Pentecostal church in Belgrade.

The mother and two daughters lived somewhere out in the outlying suburbs of Belgrade, in an unfinished basement, since they had little money. However, they invited Randy and Joan to lunch.

The mother prepared food mainly from things that she could find in the fields around their house. They had snail soup. They had salad made from greens found in the field. They had a sort of berry bread made with flour from aid agency Bread of Life and berries found in the field. They sat at a table in the yard to eat.

What struck Randy most was that despite the hardship of their lives, this family exerted itself to give traditional Yugoslav hospitality to their friends, though they had nothing much to give. The mother used her ingenuity—finding food in the fields—and what little she was given—flour—to make a meal for their guests.

The situation of this family was in many ways typical. The husband was separated from his family and forced to fight. Fortunately, he was older and was only forced to serve in the army for about six months and then released.

Also, they had difficulty finding housing. There just was not enough housing for refugees. This family was forced to live in an unfinished basement. Still, they were so grateful to Randy and Joan that they gave the best of what they had.

Randy and Joan were evacuated twice: once in October of 1998 and finally again in March of 1999 just before the NATO forces bombed Belgrade. They have served in Slovenia since their evacuation from Serbia.

Many of the young people we worked with in Novi Sad eventually managed to make lives for themselves in Serbia. Some, though, left Serbia. Many people left Serbia and the other former Yugoslav states. Even before the war, when we lived in Belgrade from August 1986 to May 1989, people joked about the "lottery." The US and other countries have a visa lottery system for choosing people to whom to give immigration visas. I recall that it was something like 1900 people a year.[271] Our friends used to say that people would give anything they had to get out of Yugoslavia.

There are all sorts of refugees and immigrants. Some refugees are religious refugees, fleeing for freedom to practice their religion or fleeing outright persecution. Some refugees are refugees fleeing war. Their homes and towns have been destroyed. Sometimes the lines between those fleeing war and those who are persecuted for their religion or ethnicity aren't clear, as in the case of religious minorities like the Yazidis in Syria, who have long been persecuted and were driven to a hill top to die.[272] In the end no one wants to be a refugee.

Chapter 10: **Personal Encounters**
—"Letters from camp"—Moria

Letters written from Lesvos, Greece, about my time working
in the Moria Migrant Reception and Identification Centre

IN ORDER TO UNDERSTAND what migrants/immigrants/refugees really
go through I thought it would be good to go and serve as a volunteer in
a migrant detention center. A friend of mine from seminary coordinated
short-term teams who go to the island of Lesvos, Greece, to help with the
migrants in the Moria Migrant Reception and Identification Centre. Moria
was a minimum-security prison. It is mainly dirt and concrete along with
miles of hurricane fence topped with razor wire.[273] Volunteers had various
jobs which they could do. I will detail some below.

Moria and other detention centers or refugee camps in Greece were set
up to deal with the wave of migrants who arrived at the height of this migration in 2015.[274] In 2015, 850,000 migrants arrived on Greek shores. To stop
the trafficking of migrants, Moria and other detention centers were set up
to register and house migrants until they could be processed or until other
places could be found for them. A deal was struck between Turkey and the
EU in 2016 by which Turkey would build two refugee camps on their border
with Syria.[275] Turkey also agreed to repatriate anyone who was rejected by
Greece.[276] The deal never worked. After an attempted coup of Recep Erdogan, the Turkish premier, which many in the EU supported, Erdogan ef-
fectively reneged on the deal. In 2016 there were fewer migrants arriving in
Greece 170,000.[277] However, that number was far beyond the capacity of the
detention centers.[278] As of May 2018 there were more than 7,300 detainees
in Moria which should have had no more than 3,000.[279] In October 2018 the
New York Times reported that there were 9,000 held in Moria.

On August 11, 2019,

Alternate Minister for Citizens' Protection Giorgos Koumoutsakos, who is responsible for Greece's migration policy, [said] in
an interview with Kathimerini [that] more than 20,000 people
are currently stranded on the Greek islands of Lesvos, Samos,
Chios, Kos and Leros.

He also said that

just during the period covering the first half of this year [2019],
there have been 30,500 new applications [for immigration vi-
sas]. During 2018, more applications were submitted on Lesvos
and Samos than in Austria and Finland respectively. As a result,
those that enter the country [Greece] today will have their first
programmed interview in roughly two years.[280]

Earlier rules said that detainees could only be held for six months,
but no more than eighteen months, the reality was that it could take up
to at least a year or longer to be processed.[281] Migrants thought that they
could go immediately from Greece to Germany or another European
country. However, by the time I was there in 2017 they could only hope to
receive the right to settle in Greece. This caused a lot of aggravation among
the migrants.

Probably the most eye-opening part of working in Moria was the despair.[282] People arrived on the island of Lesvos having paddled a rubber boat
across a small part of the Aegean Sea from Turkey expecting to enter the
promised land. They discovered that they were escorted into a prison. They
are allowed to go outside of the center, for instance, to go into town, once
they are processed, but they have to stay in the center until they are either
moved to the mainland of Greece or sent back to Turkey. The length of time
for processing is at least three months to a year or more. Single men wait the
longest. Families from war torn countries have the shortest wait.

The frustration level was palpable. EuroRelief, the organization I went
with, tried to help the center staff by giving out meals, by fixing plumbing,
and other manual tasks. To some degree volunteers were seen as a sort of
unofficial police since some roles, like checking papers at the gates to the
housing areas, is a sort of policing.[283]

Whatever I thought I would find, I found something I never expected.
Some migrants become so frustrated they voluntarily returned to Turkey.
Some caused riots.[284] All found ways to survive: to beat the heat, to find a
space for themselves, and if possible to speed up the process.

I worked in the Moria Reception and Identification Centre for two
weeks. I was a part of a group organized by Greater Europe Mission. GEM
was the organization that my wife and I joined in 1984 and served with for

thirty years. We know the couples who work with GEM there well. Our friend, Kim, had found his life's calling there in Moria. He was convinced that God put him right there for that time. They were working alongside a Greek evangelical mission, EuroRelief. A couple former students of ours from Tyndale Theological Seminary in the Netherlands, a pair of Greek brothers, pastor's sons, were also involved with EuroRelief. GEM was recruiting and sending teams to Moria, all year round up until the destruction of the camp in September 2020.[285] The refugees keep coming. Though the Centre was burned down, there are still about 13,000 Persons of Concern on Lesvos waiting to be housed or moved.[286] It remains an explosive situation. The boats keep crossing the small channel from Turkey to Greece. There is no end in sight!

A Volunteer's Diary

July 11, 2017

Dear praying friends,

It's been a strange day. We set off to the refugee camp to do our shift 4 PM–12 AM, but there were police cars roaring in, and refugees and relief workers along the road. Some had been evacuated. There was a dark billowing cloud of smoke rising above the camp. Fire vehicles came along.

We were told to wait in our vehicles and then told to return home and be on call. Later we, men, were asked to return. There had been a riot, perhaps not as serious as it sounds, but there were Molotov cocktails thrown into the offices of the UNHCR and the EuroRelief headquarters.[287] Relief workers were evacuated. Some lost backpacks with passports, wallets, and cameras. The EuroRelief office was completely destroyed.

Some particularly Africans/Congolese/French-speaking Africans felt that they were being shortchanged somehow by EuroRelief, and felt that EuroRelief was eyes and ears for the police . . . They were threatening to attack the EuroRelief offices.

EuroRelief lost its computers and records, besides the individual things [personal items] lost. EuroRelief has teams from YWAM (Youth With A Mission), GEM, I58 (Is 58 Mennonites) and other groups. There are some Dutch folks here among them.

I don't believe 1/3rd of the camp was destroyed [as reported by some], at least not sleeping quarters or housing areas. A big structure, which was a shade structure, was burnt up and other smaller offices. I don't think any housing was lost.

Groups are more or less housed together: families, single women and/ or women with children and no husband, unattended minors, African men, Asian men, and Arabic speaking men. There is another hillside / an olive grove with tents and a shade structure. There is a completely separate camp in another location for families who have been processed.

I was on "Kitchen" in the Arabic-speaking single men's area last night. I think my job was mainly to prevent theft of hotplates there. I then went to New Arrivals, where people just off the boats come.

The families in New Arrivals were moved today to other quarters to allow new arrivals, who came last night, about seventy-five. Smugglers in motorboats bring people within swimming distance of the north shore of the island and then throw a child into the water to get people to jump out and save it. Then the smugglers leave and may or may not throw the refugees' belongings in or just steal them. Others give thirty-five or so refugees a rubber raft and say, "Row to that set of lights." Refugees are in Turkey, which we can see from Lesvos. They have to cross about five km or less to reach Lesvos, Greece. They are then picked up and brought to the camp.

There seem to be easily discernible three sort[s] of refugees: those who are fleeing war, usually with their families, some have injuries or obvious handicaps due to war damage; the second are those seeking economic improvement; and thirdly dangerous characters who have been soldiers elsewhere or just hooligans, some may be criminals.

As of March 2017, they cannot hope to leave Greece. One third to two thirds will be deported back to Turkey. Those who are safe and processed will be allowed to move to Athens and eventually become Greek citizens. No one moves on to Germany or other countries [as in the past].

Though the EU gave Turkey about four million Euro to house and keep refugees and send them back to Syria or wherever [they have not]. [It was actually three billion Euros.[288]] The Turkish government is not happy now with the EU and the US, who have complained about the coup which took place there.[289]

When we, men relief workers, got into the camp there was a strong police presence, and all EuroRelief folks seemed to be there. There were a couple fist fights among some single men refugees and shouting matches, but no serious incidents.

My shift with the family section was mostly calm and involved playing, horsing around with bored little kids. It became a game to "escape," get through the bolted gate and then make us chase them. I was ok with it until it turned into one kid throwing stones at other older kids. One kid collared me from behind and hurt my neck. I angrily told him, "NO!" I finally grabbed the little instigator and carried him inside the family area and made him stay. At that point I asked to be relieved. [We were not to touch or be angry with the POCs (People Of Concern) in the center.]

I then moved up to the area where the fire had taken place and saw the damage to the EuoRelief office, as well as the other burned ISOBOXES. [An ISOBOX is a shipping container fitted to be an office or a dwelling.] There were a lot of crowds of angry, mostly young men shouting. There wasn't any more violence.

Some relief workers went off with a leader to take some clothes and things out of a container to safe keeping. I went back to the family area again.

Pray for Jeremy, Missy, and Megan. They are in charge of EuoRelief's efforts. The firing of their container/office has hit them hard. Those of us serving there are affected, but not a lot.

The whole business was started by the stewing of some young men from Africa. There is some tension between the [some other] nationalities and French-speaking Africans who feel short changed in distribution of goods and feel their cases are not dealt with in a reasonable time and way.

My main impression of the situation is that families are moved on more quickly, but that vetting is very thorough. No one moves through without adequate vetting.

Second is that single young men get through even [more] slowly. It's not uncommon for a young man to wait up to fourteen months to be denied, much less accepted.

Anyone suspected of criminal background or just being an economic immigrant will be refused.

The remaining image of the day is the razor wire at the top of all fences and facilities. The sound of the day is the noise a metal bolt for a gate sounds like when it is slammed shut.

I let people in and out of one section, but at night I can go home or at least back to my room, free.

Thanks for your prayers!

Warmly in Christ,

Phil

July 12, 2017

Dear all,

To correct some impressions. First, not all African[s] were involved in the riot. Some refused to take part even when threatened. Some from other nations were also involved. Some were arrested. There is a more serious place of incarceration within the camp.

Second, I have learned that this was the fourth time there was rioting (really on a small scale) and a fire. News media has exaggerated the numbers. There were several hundred evacuated and some weren't evacuated at all and there was no problem. [No one was injured.]

The impressions from the day before yesterday was heat and dust. The camp is all concrete and stones. There are a few trees. There were many shade structures with air conditioning. One was ruined. This is July in Greece with blistering sun and temperatures in the upper 20s [Centigrade] (low 90s [Fahrenheit]).

There was a drama unfolding yesterday that struck me. The people from New Arrivals, who arrived Sunday night, had to be moved to more permanent housing, but there is significant overcrowding now. There are few unaccompanied minors now. So, some families and women with children live in that area.

A couple waited some hours while a negotiation went on to find space for this couple. Those in the room said there was no space. Eventually they were convinced to allow the new couple to move in. The couple took one look at the space and said it was too small, about one mattress size in a room. They refused the room and complained. The drama continued until eventually a few others from their nationality convinced them it was only temporary. So, they moved in.

When quarters are close, tempers flare. There were a few "dust ups" [fist fights], which the police stopped quickly. The police seem to have a sense for allowing people space, without letting things get out of control. Sometimes refugees think they are entering a Western country only to learn they are being put in what is really a prison. They have entered Greece illegally and are interned first and processed, before those who have been approved may leave. Many are deported.

Today started with delivering lunch in the Olive Grove, where there are mainly Africans, French speakers largely, it seems. They are in tents which hold about ten, and a large main tent, which is usually air conditioned with a hundred and fifty inside. They make separators with their blankets and so have sort of cells. Some are neat. Some are a wreck. The area outside is covered with trash. There is resentment at waiting and no desire to clean. On the other hand, we had help from one young man named Boris (pronounced in a French way [Bah-reese with the accent on the second syllable]) in delivering the lunch. It was chicken and everyone liked it and took seconds. Meals have been usually more or less starch, chick peas, or rice with some flavor (grape leaves) with feta cheese and

Greek bread. It is ok when it's the more starchy sort, but usually most folks don't like the starchy sort of meal. They don't seem to like Greek bread, which is like a flour tortilla, or the feta cheese, which is often served. They like yellow cheese, they said.

The main complaint was no electricity. However, someone in the main camp had "hot-wired" the generator to run day and night. It runs on fuel oil and should only run 6–12PM. So, all the allotment for the fuel oil has been used already for the whole month. The military supplies the fuel oil. They aren't contracted to give more. So, no air conditioning.

One job I had was shoveling up fist sized rocks. There had been a re-taining device for a hill side near the bleachers, which was wire with rocks inside. The rioters broke the wire and threw the rocks. When throwing rocks began and the fire was started, the police used tear gas to disperse the crowd and contain the situation. So, we were given the task of shoveling up all the rocks and dumping the over a hill side away from the bleachers.

I helped a bit with another part of the clean-up efforts, emptying out the old ISOBOX of the EuroRelief office. I showed my skills with a hack saw! ;-)

Later there was a problem with a toilet in the New Arrivals area. I went to help. The toilet plunger issue was easy. The real problem was that the waste water drain from the sinks had come off the wall and parts were lost. The result was pipes for the drain were on the floor and when the toilets were flushed, the pipes on the floor ran raw sewage onto the floor.

I surveyed the situation and ascertained what plastic pipe was need and hangers (and bricks). I could not finish the job, because it was too late to go to the hardware to buy parts. I will finish tomorrow, at least a make shift repair as there is no time to dry stuff out and correctly glue it in place.

The problem is the result of the wall being fiberboard. The water on the hangers caused them to fall out, which resulted in the pipe dropping and the fixtures falling apart. (Hence the bricks.)

People are washing their clothes in the sinks and splashing the walls.

Image: the New Arrivals structure . . . It's again a steel structure with tent-like walls with one hundred bunk beds. There were seventy-five new ar-rivals on Tuesday and over a hundred Wednesday. The weather is good. So, more come. New Arrivals has this large structure for sleeping and showers and these three toilets . . . The facility wasn't intended for the volume.

It's a constant cycle of one group handing out clothes, blankets, and ba-sics. Then the refugees are processed with health checks, initial interviews, issuing of badges, bracelets, and eventually documents. Then they move these folks out to other areas. I'm not sure how many leave each day, but the wait is usually about twelve to fourteen months minimum.

I went back to the Olive Grove again at dinner time to distribute dinner with a fellow from Philadelphia, Pennsylvania, and the daughter of my seminary friend, who is also here. Boris was out. He was "praying," I was told. I and the fellow distributed food to the tents and then put a meal on each bed in the rooms. There were two hundred meals delivered, but about thirty to forty were left.

So, it was a long day full of odd jobs. I had been told not to expect two days to be the same.

Thanks for your prayers and encouragement.

Warmly in Christ,

Phil

July 13, 2017

Dear praying friends,

Remember when you went to camp as a kid for a couple weeks in the summer? You slept in a tent with a bunch of other kids of your same sex and a camp counselor.

Now imagine that the temperature is 95F and the sun unrelenting. The tents hold ten when small and one hundred to two hundred when large, and the "campers" stay as long as eleven to eighteen months. In the winter it's cold and snows, but you're still in the tent. There are porta potties at best and camp type showers.

Remember how you hated camp food? Now make it twice as bad, mostly rice, chick peas, beans . . . Once in a while you get a chicken leg with a thigh. Imagine being forced to drink butter tea with cardamom for every meal and instead of the bread you like, you are given a flat unleavened frisbee disk. The food never improves. The fruit you are given is past due. The only vegetables you see are carrots in the chick pea and carrot stew.

Power comes and goes. It is rationed for 12 PM to 6 PM to run air conditioning, but either the wires aren't right or there's no power.

It's near 100F in our "shade structure" with no air conditioning. People constantly ask, "Tell you supervisor—no power!" "I'm nobody," I told them.

The image for the day—feces floating on the floor of the bathroom I'm working in. The smell—actually the stinking, large containers full of garbage.

Mark, a teammate, and I bought parts and tools and fixed two sinks (S joints, flexi tube) and seated a faucet. We discovered a toilet wasn't seated. So, another trip to the hardware (but Greek spinach pie for lunch!). Took the toilet out. Wrestled out the screws. Drilled tap holes. Reseated the toilet. Flushes fine now. No more muck on the floor.

We were working in the toilets in the New Arrivals, a holding pen, where people, who have arrived on land in the night or morning, are brought to be processed. There are four toilets for 150 people. They wash their clothes in the sink and plug up the drain. Then the water starts to back up and run out ... Water seeks the lowest level. One hundred new arrivals came last night and another fifty this morning. An endless cycle ...

It must be a real shock to find yourself, not in the paradise you expected, but locked in a bull pen with razor wire and chain link fence. For a bed you get a bunk bed in a room full of one hundred or more other new arrivals.

Now, I'm the toilet man, having fixed the New Arrivals toilets! Mark and I walked up to level two to fix the toilet in room nine, but found that my friend, Kim (m), had already fixed it. Walked down the long, hot hill. The whole camp is on a 45-degree angle from the bottom to the top. There are six levels. The doctor is on the fifth. (Logic?) The last housing is at the top at sixth. Some sleep in old Quonset huts.

We went back down to the temporary Info center. EuroRelief has been given a temporary spot, which is a police office. They have to leave asap. Many EuroRelief temporary workers are cleaning the burned mess out of the old container. Eventually tonight or tomorrow or mañana a new ISOBOX will come to be the new Info center. Info is where shifts start and end. You sign in and out. I pretty much decided I was detailing myself today.

When someone said there was a shower which wasn't giving any water, up the hill ... I didn't volunteer. There is a cistern/well at the camp. There is a main line from the city, but this part of Greece needs to develop the water mains ... However, there's an economic crisis in Greece. So, no new water mains.

If they run the pump from the well all day, the well runs dry. Then there is no water. If they run it all day when there is no water in the well, the pump burns out.

I actually find the repairing stuff fun. It's much harder to communicate with people. Hand and foot and a bit of English, German, or Russian ... Someone thought I was Air Force, because of my chino pants, white shirt, black shoes, and floppy sun hat. I just burst into laughter. Right, me!?!

I realized how easy it would be to become callous to the refugees. Some don't look so poor. Others are angry and abusive, when they can be. It's discouraging, but we came to serve.

It made me think of a prayer I pray from time to time from the Book of Common Prayer, Prayer 37 "For Prisons and Correctional Institutions."

It struck that it would be easy to become jaundiced and to trust no one. It would be easy to see them all as shiftless or sneaks. But this isn't true and even if it were that's not how I should relate to them. They may be sneaks, some of them. They may be frauds, some of them.

37. For Prisons and Correctional Institutions

Lord Jesus, for our sake you were condemned as a criminal: Visit our jails and prisons with your pity and judgment. Remember all prisoners, and bring the guilty to repentance and amendment of life according to your will, and give them hope for their future. When any are held unjustly, bring them release; forgive us, and teach us to improve our justice. Remember those who work in these institutions; keep them humane and compassionate; and save them from becoming brutal or callous. And since what we do for those in prison, O Lord, we do for you, constrain us to improve their lot. All this we ask for your mercy's sake. *Amen.*[290]

But many of the new arrivals are people fleeing war and destruction. Some show it with depression, others anger, and some with even joy. Some are happy to be away from places of war. They aren't happy to be in "prison": the chain link fence, razor wire, and clanging bolt shot to lock the doors behind them. Many hate having to show an ID all the time. But most realize that this is a temporary stop.

Due to it being no one's home, no one cares for it. So, we volunteers try. For a week or two we stop a leaking toilet. Two weeks from now someone else will do it.

There are a lot of us running around doing various jobs. The hardest is finding places for new arrivals to move from New Arrivals to temporary housing, so that new arrivals can enter the New Arrivals area.

There is an army of other workers and service people who arrive each morning or evening. Police change shifts. After the riot and with so many new arrivals, there are more police. There is a detail of riot police visible every day.

There are also nine-to-five workers [in the camp]: UNHCR processors, Red Cross and other doctors, who do physical examinations, various interpreters and legal people, a variety of police helping from various countries, including one Dutch prisoner transfer truck. There must be a hundred cars on the road in front of the camp. People who are well dressed and with fancy hand bags come and go. Perhaps psychiatrists or EU officials. It's a veritable army of people to manage and process.

The EuroRelief people are like worker bees or worker ants. They come to Info for their shifts: 8 AM–5 PM, 12 PM–9 PM, 4 PM–12 AM, 12

AM–8 AM. Only the police are around during the night. People volunteer for shifts watching a gate (checking IDs and opening and closing the bolt on the gate, and opening the chain link fence door; CLANG). It's a prison. It grates. Tempers flare. "No ID! You police!!" There is time in some places to play with children.

I actually had a long talk with a translator from Afghanistan. He speaks Farsi, Dari, and Urdu. We had a long philosophical and theological conversation. He said that he was an atheist. But we talked about Omar Kayyam (whom he maintains is an atheist). I gave him Pascal's Wager in the end . . . What an unexpected conversation!

A new batch of EuroRelief volunteers are here today. Newbies! After four days I am an old hand . . .

There seems actually to be an army of Mennonite sisters who run this place! I(s)58 and others. Also there are Dutch women YWAMers among the leaders.

Please pray that in the midst of all of this, as the days drift by, and I can't remember what day it is due to starting on Sunday and swing shifts that I remember the goal is not just to stop a leaking sink or toilet, but to engage with people.

Warmly in Christ,

Phil

July 14, 2017

Dear praying friends,

Today's reflection . . . More toilets, well one more again. Somehow after I anchored one, the other came loose. The result of the toilet rocking was the same. I tried to anchor it without putting new pilot holes in . . . It isn't seated solidly . . . Duh. The sinks and drains seem fine.

Someone broke the door handle/lock mechanism on one stall. Whoever it was stole the face place . . . So, it can't be repaired without being replaced. We went to the hardware store in town to try to find one . . . Umm, too expensive and having to cut new channels in the metal door . . . I don't think so. We went for a simple bolt lock . . . Too small, we went back to the hardware. We got a larger simple bolt type lock . . . I needed a shim (furring strip) . . . There were no shims at camp. I wandered around looking for a piece of wood and a drill (tools migrate, as the office migrated, from temporary shelter below to up to above the bleachers) . . . By the time I found the drill and a piece of wood, it was too late to start the task. I still needed a drill bit, but it wasn't in the set . . .

The real news of the day was a visit by the American ambassador to Greece. I guess that's why two Greek ladies came to hose down the bathrooms in New Arrivals.

I don't know if the group of fifty Africans, who came to the main gate to the police and UN offices to complain of no electricity for days thought that they would see the ambassador, but they didn't. Someone did address them and they dispersed peacefully.

The Greek cleaning ladies said they do the New Arrivals toilets all the time. I haven't seen them yet. Girls from College Church in Wheaton were laboring with poor supplies. Someone told me that there had been a garbage men and cleaners union strike which just ended.

A hundred more people arrived in the night. It's been clear as a bell with a near full moon. Nice time for a row in your boat.

Due to the sudden influx of refugees the old shade structure has been turned into a tarp-covered frame with individual tents. There are six or eight tents, which hold about ten to twelve.

Some families have been taken to the other sister camp nearby, due to the overcrowding.

It's both discouraging and sort of par for the course. It's like almost all mission work I have done. You are expected to make due with what you have, even if it's particle board that's going to fall apart. You do a rough and ready job and get 'er done! However, you know that by next week or even tomorrow, something will be broken or vandalized.

As I look over the two bathrooms I see all sorts of signs of ill-use or abuse. I can tell that once upon a time there were two utility sinks there for washing. The holes in the wall tell the story of the wastewater pipes connecting to the drain. The wastewater pipe has been capped. There are no more utility sinks. So, the refugees wash their clothes in the hand sinks and clog the drains, and splash water onto the wall and ruin the hangers . . .

I honestly believe many of the refugees do not understand how a flush toilet works. They don't seem to understand how to push the button, though at least one person seems to enjoy breaking things.

Some of the new arrivals are so kind. They carry in bottles of water to flush the toilet. [Actually they used the water in the bottles to wash with. There was no toilet paper. They left the bottles all over the floor.] Others do it wherever they want.

Sorry to be so focused on the bathroom in New Arrivals. The four stalls get very heavy use with more than a hundred using them. There are also separate showers.

Sometimes there are real emergencies. One young woman in the New Arrivals was pregnant. She was in great pain. Eventually she was taken to the hospital.

Sometimes the emergencies are not so real. One woman called for a doctor to see her sick daughter. Rather than have them carry the little girl up the long hill, he walked all the way down the hill to see her daughter. He asked the mother to describe the symptoms. Then he patiently explained that the condition wasn't urgent, but chronic, and they would see the girl during doctor's office hours. New Arrivals is on the lowest level near the UN and other offices. The doctor's office is on level five allll the waayyy uppp the hillllll Uff!

In my Yankee way I want to jerry rig things and get it done. However, the problem is both unsolvable and systemic. The New Arrivals toilets [ISOBOX] wasn't designed for so many people and not for people who can't understand a button to push to release the water from the tank. I can't fix that. I can put a Band-Aid (plaster) on a cancer, but I can't solve the problem.

The whole refugee situation is like this. Wars create millions of refugees and many more millions of Internally Displaced Persons (IDPs). The camp is a small place, but has a large volume to deal with. It is a couple hours of rowing in a dinghy from Turkey. It's a favorite route, though the refugees don't always know what is happening. They don't seem to know they can only hope to become Greek citizens, at least those who arrived after March 2017.

I cannot solve the problem, but maybe for two weeks the bathrooms will work . . .

Tomorrow we get some plywood to put behind the sinks so that we can anchor the pipes!

One other good thing is having Greek spinach pie or pita for lunch! Since we (Mark and I) keep running back and forth into town, we can get lunch there! Yum! 8-)

Thanks for your prayers and encouragement.

Warmly in Christ,

Phil

July 15, 2017

Dear praying friends,

The word for the day is tired. Seven days straight of work is too much, even if you don't have night shifts. I've tried to keep sleeping regular from at least

0000 to 0600. We've had swing shifts from 0800–1600, 0900–1700, 1600–0000. Thankfully they absolve the seniors [like me] from the 0000–0800 shift.

The feeling for the day was deflated, but then a rebound of sorts. Here I thought I was the important plumber, but the real plumber was ahead of me by a day. He was installing new tanks above the toilets. I don't know why he didn't seat the toilets that were rocking and leaking, but . . . well, it stinks.

Anyway, even though he and I hadn't even met, somehow the Lord coordinated our different efforts. He's done some contracting. So, he's way ahead of me on knowledge and ability. Anyway, I did what I could.

My compatriot, Mark, who is quiet, kind and silent most of the time, is a pretty much exact opposite to me, well at least the quiet and silent. Today we finished a project to install a sliding bolt lock on the bathroom door in New Arrivals. There didn't seem to be many people there. With the cleaning of the shade structure framework after the fire and putting tarps over it, they put up a dozen tents under it which took pressure off the New Arrivals housing.

A neat thing happened when we got to the toilets at New Arrivals with this fellow Aaron, the real plumber. As the young ladies and a guy (one young lady was from 158 the Mennonite group) were cleaning, one of the refugee ladies started to help and told them she would be glad to help any time they needed her. Also, a young man offered to help and did. It was nice to see people be willing to help.

It's rather amazing, but the new "Info," the office of EuroRelief, is now right up where the riot and fire occurred. It seems bizarre to me that the powers that be would put Euro-Relief closer to those who targeted them, than they were before. The Lord knows.

From what I see of EuroRelief, the head is a fellow named Jeremy. He is a quiet southerner born in Biloxi, Mississippi. He floats around and oversees. He also does large ordering and overall organization. He is also between EuroRelief and other organizations. There are a number of young women, a few Mennonite (obvious by their long dresses and lace head coverings) and a few typical (loud, self-assured, dynamic) Dutch young ladies (don't get me wrong I think they're great). They run the place. There are today hordes of volunteers. So many today that one shift was sent home.

Saturday was quiet and the main gate was open. People strolled in and out. It was like a day off for everyone. No one was processed. No hordes of UN and other staff running around. Just Saturday in Greece.

Before I went up to the camp I had to buy some drill bits and then go to the carpenter nearby the hardware store to get a furring strip. He waved me to his son who speaks English. The son said, "Have a look, if you find what you need take it." I found what I needed and he gave it to me for free with a smile and a hand shake. Everyone is related here in the village. The women in the hardware are related. Papa sits quietly in the store. Father and mother and sister are working. His son and daughter also work there.

More and more I feel I don't have any clue what is going on here. I'm too far down the pecking chain to understand anything. I don't need to. Today I fix a sliding bolt lock and do a variety of other small tasks.

The Women's Section has been very difficult. There's a lot of posturing, shouting, and weight thrown around, but not by all. We were asked to look at the plumbing in a couple rooms. It was pretty easy. Ordinary type European shower head and hoses, which need to be replaced. A sink drain which needs to be swapped out. There was one issue I couldn't think how to solve: a pipe from the toilet tank above down into a Turkish-type toilet. The place where they joined was leaking badly, clean water, but . . .

We set off with old parts in hand to the hardware to discover that it was closed. Stores were open from 0700–1400. Oops I forgot. We had to return and apologize to the women in section C, and put back the old stuff. We'll have to go Monday to get parts and return.

Actually, I thought the women would be mad, but I think the fact that we were there and showed that we were trying to help made a good impact. The people in the camp feel hopeless and abandoned. So, for some it's an excuse to show you who's boss! "I won't show my ID card!" For others it's a time to wait. Some seem better able to wait.

Water was turned off most of the day after we got there, probably from 1200–1700. It was due again to the well and the water level. If the water level is too low it will ruin the pump to run it. It's hard to tell what's leaking if you can't see a leak. But some things needing repair were obvious like a shower hose where the plastic inner hose is exposed.

People often stop me at random and tell me, "Chief, we have no water! Water, we need water! (Or electricity)." I guess because I am older I must be important. Or they confuse me for Jeremy. I have replied, "Me! No, I'm no chief! I'm a peon! I'm a worker bee down on the bottom!" It helps to defuse their anger with laughter.

Tomorrow we get to go to a church, which was started by longer-term folks here. It is frequented by Africans and some others. It's great to see people who are believers, including refugees.

Weary! A good Saturday night to rest and Sunday to be recreated! Good Sabbath to you all!

Warmly in Christ,

Phil

July 16, 2017

[N]'s (a teammate's) update

Hello everyone,

Thank you for all your prayers! The team is doing well and we've officially made it half way through our time serving at camp. Now that I have a better picture of the overall landscape I will do my best to give you a reasonable summary of our environment, our situation, our role in all of it, and how to pray for us over the remaining week.

OUR ENVIRONMENT

When a migrant or refugee (important to note the difference) enters the camp it is because they have entered the country illegally (by boat) and therefore must go to this camp to be detained until processed by the Greek/ EU authorities[, UNHCR, International Organization for Migration (IOM) and Red Cross/Red Crescent]. The camp is a federal prison. It isn't "like a prison," it's a prison: a large complex of reinforced concrete and double-lined fencing with razor wire at the top. Not exactly "the promised land." The complex is subdivided into separate compounds:

New Arrivals—everyone goes through to be documented by the police then handed off to us to be given food, their first set of sleeping bag(s), blanket(s), toiletries, etc., and a place to stay inside one large tent for the first few nights until they can be relocated to the Lower Level or Levels 1–4 for the remainder of their stay.

Lower Level—for families, parentless children [unaccompanied minors], and single women.

Levels 1–4—for single men divided by common languages and non-warring factions as best as possible, but not always realistic.

When we arrived a week ago there was an estimated 2,600 occupants representing over forty nationalities and dozens of languages. The general "vibe" of the camp is a mix of fear, uncertainty, and anger (thus the riot after we arrived). It's also very hot and there's a limited amount of water we can issue to refugees per day. [We gave out bottled water ½ liter—twice a day to POCs.]

OUR SITUATION

Since we arrived last Saturday, there's been about seventy-five to one hundred new arrivals per day (more than usual). Finding the appropriate space has been a growing problem, exacerbated by the fact that the riot burned down a residential tent that already displaced dozens of people. So, there's a growing tension of managing the current population while finding room for the incoming crowd.

OUR ROLE

We have many jobs to perform each day. They include guarding the entry gates for each of the compounds; distributing food, clothing, anything we can; side projects like clearing recently burnt structures and building new (temporary) tents in their place; managing the New Arrivals compound by making sure people get what they need as best we are able to; and doing what we can to maintain a secure environment.

HOW TO PRAY FOR US

1. Peace—Everyday some kind of fight breaks out somewhere in camp. Usually it's an argument that just escalates into a brawl between two parties that ends before police arrive. Pretty benign but frustrating to experience.

2. Compassion—It's easy to serve those who are grateful. Many have expressed gratitude but more don't and some constantly complain. The team has been very good about loving in spite of this, so this request may be more for me. (While guarding in the Lower Level compound the other day I [N] was playing with about eight super hyper boys. One bit me pretty hard and I saw red. I'll leave it at that.) [I wasn't bitten, but I gave up watching the kids when one jumped on my back from behind and hurt my neck. Phil]

3. Thankful—God has provided safety in a hostile environment. We have many friends inside the camp, most of which are refugees that watch over us as much as we them.

4. Renewal—Each day the team feels tired but satisfied and ready for tomorrow. There has never been a clearer example of needing/receiving our daily bread both physically and spiritually.

Again, the team is doing well.

Written by [N], a teammate.

July 16, 2017

Dear praying friends,

I already sent a summary letter by a teammate today, but I want to add a few thoughts about church on Lesvos.

There is a church called Oasis. It's run by I58, which is more or less a Mennonite group. See their Facebook page (I58).

The church service was singing mainly in English with some in French and Farsi (Iranian). The pianist was a French-speaking African, who also served as the translator. There were a lot of songs to start and it was incredible worship.

The congregation was one-third Farsi speakers, one-third French speakers (Africans), and one-third other (I58 workers and others).

The sermon was in English with translation into Farsi and French. There were interactive parts where members of the congregation answered questions like: "Why would anyone follow Jesus? Why would you follow Jesus?"

I asked the fellow beside me what his status was. He said that he was being deported back to his home country in two days. He has been a believer for about six months before coming to Greece and another year and a half while in Greece. His return to his homeland could mean death.

Another young man gave his testimony and was to be baptized that afternoon. He was baptized by a worker from his nationality and the American administrator.

I had lunch with some of the I58 folks learning more about them. Later we went to their center where they had ice cream and then a devotional and prayer. Some of them had to go off to a 1600–0000 shift.

After that I left to go back to my room to rest and think and connect with Linda [via e-mail].

Tonight, I go in search of octopus to eat at a restaurant.

I'm not sure what tomorrow holds. My roommate heard that some Africans were planning and promising a repeat of last Monday's riot and fire . . .

I appreciate your prayers!

Warmly in Christ,

Phil

July 17, 2017

Dear praying friends,

Today was an interesting day. Thanks for your prayers. We were on "Standby" for an hour awaiting to be evacuated.

I was frustrated to sit while we were on "Standby." We were on the lower level where the Family Section, unaccompanied minors, and Women are. This section is always locked down in emergency to protect them. The sections are carefully monitored to keep out people who might hurt or abuse them. The police station is right there too.

On the same level are the sections for the UNHCR, IOM [International Organization for Migration], Red Cross/Crescent, etc. The police would not allow any riot to reach that level, as we evidenced even last week when there was the fire.

Then the boss, Jeremy, said it was safe on the lower levels, where I was, to go ahead with work. So, I went back to plumbing.

Apparently, the Standby was caused by a threat of a riot by some African young men. Later they asked for a negotiation, and someone spoke with them. Then they asked to stage a peaceful sit-in. They did. Then the heat got too much and they took over the only shade structure left and wrote Congo RDC Unite Amour Paix [Unity, Love, Peace]. I think they need to learn what the last two words mean!

I spent the morning replacing shower hoses and shower heads. I still couldn't fix all of the problems in the Women's Section. Jeremy, the boss, came down and gave it a look. He said that the one problem involved heating an old lead pipe and shoving the new plastic pipe into it to make the seal. That was beyond me. I looked at another leak, but it would require finding the main water shutoff for the Women's Section. Jeremy said that he'd never seen one.

I think this effort to try to do something small but kind is helping to defuse some of the pedantic behavior of some of the women. In general, they seem to be pretty docile, and even kind. Most of the women in that section are African. Some are pregnant and some have babies.

We gained another "plumber" today, a Swiss German engineering student named Daniel. He got his first ride to the hardware store. Now he knows how to find it.

It's hard to justify the time and expense of repairing things that will [be broken] again [deliberately]. But, if it lessens tension and helps people see that we aren't just guards at the gates, perhaps that will help overall.

On another front, my roommate, Z, left at 0500. I had to get up at 0600, and only barely made it out of bed by 0700. However, now I have my own room! :-)

Tonight, we will meet together as a group for dinner at 2000 which is normal meal time in Greece. Last night I got my octopus in red wine with a side of French-fried zucchini and nice soft bread.

In terms of practical life, I was washing clothes out in the sink. I wanted to wash both pairs of trousers I was working in, but then I realized that I washed the same pair twice! It's not so much the work, but the heat. Working with plumbing is actually cooler, because I am inside and it's wet! ;-)

Earlier in the day one of my work shoes decided to quit. The sole was flapping off the front. So, I put duct tape around it. One of the POC (Persons of Concern—they are not refugees yet) thought it was bizarre to see me taping my shoe, but there was no other solution. 8-)

Thanks for your prayers!

Warmly in Christ,

Phil

July 18, 2017

Dear all,

We were evacuated today at @1200. There was a riot because some Africans are unhappy. They have been ramping it up. Military riot police went in and the fire fighters.[291] We may go back later.

Thanks for your prayers,

Phil

July 18, 2017

Teammate's report

Subject: Lesvos Team Update/Prayer Request

Hey Everyone,

Just wanted to report that the team is still doing very well. I do, however, want to make an urgent prayer request for an overwhelming peace to fall upon this refugee camp. The last two days have had organized and peaceful protests in front of the Greek Immigration office in the middle the camp.

Today, however, what started as a peaceful protest turned into a march through camp that escalated into a destructive riot that led to the evacuation of the Family compound of the camp. As of this writing, Greek riot police were still in the process of suppressing the rioters so fire crews can go in and address burning structures. No volunteers from any agencies were injured and to the best of our knowledge there are no reported injuries among any refugees. One pretty touching moment was that several African refugees formed a human wall in front of the main gate where Greek police were guarding the Family compound (which is full of mostly Arab families) while the remaining volunteers evacuated.

So, at this time I would ask prayer for the following:

1. Peace in the hearts of all refugees.

2. Forgiveness in the hearts of those who may have lost their homes or belongings during the riot.

3. Wisdom in the hearts and minds of Greek authorities (police and military) to respond timely and appropriately as tension builds in or to prevent more loss.

4. Justice for the instigators of these violent riots

As a side note, take caution to what is presented in the media as reliability is questionable. Thank you for your prayers. Blessings!

[N]

July 19, 2017

Dear praying friends,

The sound of the day was children laughing. The feeling of the day was relief.

Yesterday's riot ended with police intervention. Somewhere between thirty and forty were arrested.

Fortunately, the newly arrived/newly housed refugees who were/are in tents under the old shade structure were safe, and weren't vandalized or the tents destroyed or torched. It must have been a harrowing experience for those already traumatized by war. Some families were evacuated and then returned.

Oddly enough my backpack and tools [which had disappeared from the EuroRelief ISOBOX] reappeared. I don't know who thought to rescue them, but they reappeared this morning, and I needed them. [I had left them in a shed near the bleachers where EuroRelief workers locked up things for the night. Everything had been looted.]

I started out the day guarding the gate to the unaccompanied minors area. It was very early and most of the boys were asleep. So, things were peaceful.

Little children played in the area in front of the Family area in front of the gates laughing and running. Just near them one man, who must have feared to return to the single men's section, was sleeping on the gravel by our gate. It might be that he was a new arrival without any place to go, since there was no one to meet him and get him to New Arrivals. I honestly thought he was dead as he didn't move when his phone rang at least two dozen times. A section head checked his pulse and watch him breathing. "He's alive," he said.

Many officials from many agencies are here now making sure people are being treated fairly. Yesterday when we tried to keep some French-speaking African women in at the time of the riot, they threw stones (gravel) at us. We let them go. Then we were evacuated.

Later today I was asked to do plumbing again. We had to go to the hardware store. My friend also needed two extension cords and multi-strips. We had to buy wire, multi-strips, and plugs. I wired them up. Then I went back to plumbing.

I was working in the Family section. I had to shut off the main water to the room. That involved digging in the gravel about a foot and a half, and finding the cover over the main valve. Strangely, there seemed to be waste water in that hole and maggots. The valve was under water about seven inches. Thankfully, I had my extra strong rubber gloves. I turned off the water.

We replaced the faucet unit with the shower valve. I turned it on and they said it was ok, but leaking a bit. I thought it was just tightening the nut, and so I closed the hole and replaced the gravel.

However, we had somehow left out a washer. Then I had to uncover the hole again. I get performance anxiety. A man was watching the whole time. I kept fumbling around and forgot the washer. Anyway, we got it fixed and went to the next room. I was able to replace a shower head and a hose, but other problems were beyond my ability.

In the middle of the first job we were asked by some Spanish aid work-er whether we could come to Section C Women to look at room four. These were the women who had thrown gravel at us.

I had exchanged the hose to their shower earlier in the week, but somehow the shower head was cracked. I had a used one which worked fine. When they saw it, they complained, because it was old. They wanted a new one.

Also, they had clogged the sink with cooking grease, fat, and guck. I emptied the flexi-pipe and told the man that they had put cooking stuff in the drain and showed him. Why didn't they put it in the toilet (Turkish)?

They also had broken the valve you lift up to get shower to work. They had done such a good job that it would not let any water through. I explained that I had just fixed such a faucet, but I didn't/don't know where the shut off valve is, and can't replace the faucet unit if I can't shut off the water. Also, I mentioned that our boss, Jeremy, had said that he had no idea where the shut offs were. I told the man I had done all I could.

I suspect it was all a game to humiliate me and my friend, who helps me with plumbing. They wanted us to do the repairs again and knew they could force us by having the Spanish aid worker step in. He was understanding.

I explained that the people in room four weren't happy with the used old shower head, but it worked. He said, "Is it operational?" I told him it was. We didn't have any other supplies. Evacuating twice has depleted our supplies and each repair means a trip to the store.

As we were trying to leave a very nice young lady from Utah, who is a volunteer like us, who speaks French well, came out of room four with the shower head I had just installed. "They say that it doesn't work," she said. I showed her how to work the on off button on the handle. I'm sure they lost the washer when they took it off. So, it will leak.

We are off tomorrow. So, I don't have to worry about it. It's all a silly game.

They won't eat the food served, which I admit is monotonous: beans and rice, feta cheese, Greek bread, and peaches (they must be in season). They use the money they are given to buy food and prepare their own food. Lots of prepared meals are thrown out every day.

My sanctification was challenged with these women. They are imperious and ridiculous. They want asylum and want to immigrate, but they act entitled.

At the same time, I am glad that others in the camp work alongside us. Many of the Persons of Concern (or POCs since they are not yet or may never be refugees) volunteer to help when there is a project. Other people are clearly refugees from war zones. I know the look.

Thanks for your prayers. A day off tomorrow and then one more work day, and home.

Warmly in Christ,

Phil

July 20, 2017

Dear praying friends,

Today was my rest day. I got up a bit later 0800.

I had breakfast and then went out for coffee: a double Greek coffee. Then I went to the hardware store to buy some parts, etc., but especially duct tape to fix my shoe one last time.

I bumped into Anna and Hanna, who run the EuroRelief shifts. They are both Dutch.

After that I ran into a few guys who are from another team or solo with EuroRelief. We had a wonderful lunch of grilled fish.

Then I went to the store to buy laundry detergent. After that I washed my clothes. I will give some away when I leave. There is a ministry called the Warehouse, which gives clothing to POCs (People of Concern).

I had dinner by myself earlier than normal at 1930. Then I met my friend Ivan, who is the team leader. We've been friends since seminary from 1982. We went to Serbia together in 1986.

The big news of the day is that the ring leaders of Tuesday's riot, about thirty, were tried and convicted. They will be deported back to Turkey soon. Those convicted were from Senegal, Guinea Bissau, Nigeria, and other countries. Apparently, no Congolese were involved or arrested.

There are lots of media reports of police brutality. Articles may have mostly true facts, but spin them. The pictures accompanying the articles are often from several years ago or not even of the camp or event.

There were some unpleasant encounters on Wednesday. Please pray that I can end this time well. Pray especially as I try to give some witness to the French-speaking women.

Thanks for your prayers and support.

Warmly in Christ,

Phil

July 24, 2017

Take-Away from Camp

What I learned this week is that I am not at all selfless and am very proud and used to deferential treatment.

People were praising me for fixing toilets and specifically for fixing plumbing for African French-speaking women who had thrown gravel at me the day before. I replied that I was motivated by spite. I wouldn't let them believe that they had gotten to me, and I would heap burning coals on their heads.

I realized this week that I am accustomed to being important or someone important. I am a missionary, an ordained pastor, a professor, a PhD. When you are at the camp, you are nobody. You are another EuroRelief orange vest. UNHCR people, IOM people, and others look past you, as if you weren't there. I guess I looked awful with stains on my clothes of obvious origin and I may have smelled. No one of them looking at me would've thought I had a PhD. Why would a PhD do such a thing as seating toilets in a foul environment?

And I couldn't explain. I wasn't allowed to "witness" in the camp. I could not say, "Jesus' love compels me." Only my behavior said anything: when I was angry at a kid throwing rocks or angry at the teens who knew I could not push back, or angry at the idiotic, imperious behavior of African French-speaking women who wanted to make the stupid American fix the same thing for the third time.

I didn't mind doing the stinky jobs. When I was done with a job, something worked. When I seated the toilets and fixed the exhaust plumbing below the sinks, at least for a while the refugees in New Arrivals had toilets and sinks that worked.

The image for the day is the New Arrivals in their cage: hurricane fence and barbed wire with little kids playing nearby. They did their laundry to wash the sea water out of their clothes in the hand sinks in the bathroom. They hung their clothes on any available place, even on the barbed wire.

What I didn't do was smile as I worked. I never do. I didn't take time to chat, if I could. I never do.

Many times, there was no common language. I surprised one African young man by knowing Russian. He knew a bit. I don't speak French and he didn't speak English.

There were times that people said "thank you." There were many times when they did not or some even cursed me in Arabic (the teenage boys).

I wanted to explain things, who I was, why I was there, but I couldn't or wasn't allowed. My actions had to speak louder than my words. Sometimes they did to my detriment.

They told us that we had to get it through our heads that we were not there to be liked. Guarding gates and demanding ID cards doesn't win friends.

At other times people helped us, but misunderstood. The section head for the single women's housing went out of his way to learn the information I needed (where the main shut off valve for the water was) and bought the part (spigot/shower unit). I asked for a young lady to accompany us into the room. He thought I was afraid of the African French-speaking women, because they had thrown gravel at us the day before. I wasn't afraid of them physically at all. I was afraid of a false sexual harassment charge! He was left thinking I was afraid of them and called me "brave." He completely misunderstood and I couldn't say anything.

I like to talk. ;-) I talk a lot. I like to talk about me.

In camp I couldn't talk about me. "I have a PhD! I am a professor!" Even when I could explain, it didn't matter. No one cared. The African French-speaking women just wanted to humiliate the Americans. Actually, it's impossible to humiliate someone who doesn't care. I didn't care about their stupid, childish games, like staying in the shower running the water for a half an hour when I wanted to get in and fix something. At least it was air conditioned in the room!

I found that neither of my master's degrees nor my PhD prepared me for the jobs I did. My time spent with my father doing home repairs and my Boy Scout training were more important.

I am a servant, God's servant. Many days I am not such a good servant. I have my agenda and my goals. I learned at camp that I need to listen to him more and shut my trap. (Good luck, right?! ;-))

I need to do what he assigns each day. My pride doesn't matter, but he does and those he died for do. I must find my joy in serving him and them, even if they humiliate and demean me. He loved us when were still unlovely.

We had a team dinner last night to debrief. I found it painful. Everyone was sharing about playing with kids or connecting to people. All I could think about was pain and misunderstanding, not just my pain, but the pain of all the POCs (Persons of Concern; no one is a refugee until their case is finished). So many broken lives, so many stories.

One Syrian teen is bald and has lost one eyebrow. He lost his entire family in the war. They were killed before his eyes. Where does help and hope come from?

The New Arrivals and those transferred to more long-term housing were often shocked to be either locked up in the "cage" (the fenced-in detention holding area) or to be forced to take a small and inadequate space. However, they had to adjust. Thankfully, people don't stay in New Arrivals more than a day.

The good weather means that many boat loads of people have come in the last two weeks, but the last two weeks have been hard for everyone. The first riot resulted in the EuroRelief ISOBOX/office being torched and almost all lost. Also, it terrorized already frightened people fleeing war. There is no love lost between factions: Arab speakers, Farsi speakers, and

Africans. The rioters were mainly Africans: Senegalese, Bissau-Guinean, Nigerian, and others.

The second "peaceful" demonstration on Monday, and then the riot again this past Tuesday was terrifying to New Arrivals. There were about one hundred angry African young men shouting, chanting, putting gravel in bottles, and then banging them on the ground. They demonstrated, a sit-in in front of the processing area, all the while holding up the process of registration. Then Tuesday the riot police from Athens stopped the second attempt of these instigators at a riot. There was a much lesser degree of destruction as a result of the riot. Thirty to forty of the rioters were arrested, quickly convicted, and deported.

However, it was still terrifying to the newly settled people in the new section of tents under the old shade structure. We feared that they would be forced out and their tents torched, but they weren't, thankfully.

More tents go up on any space flat enough and big enough. New tents went up in the Olive Grove. New tents are in the Family section. It's bizarre, but there's no more space.

I don't have any great answers. I wanted to know, if I could know, how the UNHCR determines the truth of a refugee's statements. I don't know precisely, but they can check stories. If there are relatives already there, they can verify. In this computer age, databases are huge and search engines strong. Usually there are interpreters in the camp who are from the countries affected. What I know is that no one is approved who has not be thoroughly screened. Just after one arrives in the camp one is screened and given an initial approval letter for remaining in the camp until one's case ends. Then then next work day one is checked for health by the doctor. (I think they are Red Cross.) One is interviewed more thoroughly. Then you wait between four and eighteen months. Families seem to be processed more quickly, but they often are just moved to a less rigorous camp only for families. Young men wait and wait and wait.

On a grander scale, Greece must deal with the camps and refugees. Other EU countries don't want any more refugees. Anyone arriving on the island now can only hope to get asylum in Greece, not citizenship. That is another longer process. Those from before March [2017] can hope to go to another EU country. The EU has paid almost $350,000,000 to Turkey [actually 3 billion Euro] to settle refugees on the Syrian border and try to repatriate the refugees to Syria. They have received the money, then had a coup. The result is [that the traffickers,] those who help refugees and others cross the 5 km to the island here, are not stopped.

I think it would be best for people to come to help at the camp who know Arabic, French, or Farsi. At the same time, I was amazed at my older teammates. They were respected for their age. People were open to them, and they were kind and encouraging to people. They also jumped right in. They even helped to put up tents and clean bathrooms. They added an element of stability to the EuroRelief teams there. There were probably six to eight teams these two weeks with up to a hundred volunteers.

The difficulty now is that many NGOs have left the camp, since the flow of refugees has slowed. The other NGOs carried some of the tasks (housing refugees more permanently, i.e., negotiating to get new people into overcrowded spaces), paying for some things (items given to New Arrivals: a set of clothes, blankets, backpacks) and manning the gates in front of the sections.

I think the people most grateful [for our help] were the Greek police. They know that those who were manning the gates are seen as "police." All orange vests (EuroRelief) are seen as "police." In a way we are. We do man the gates and control people going in and out. We deflect some of the animosity from the police. They know it and seem grateful. They also kept us safe, forcing us to evacuate when trouble came.

At the same time, some of the POCs were often grateful for our help with plumbing or whatever, e.g., putting the volley ball nets up, putting up tents, or delivering the food. Most were grateful. Only some angry young men and some African French-speaking women, it seems, were unhappy.

Despite what videos on YouTube say there is no soporific drug in the food. [I ate it too. I would know.] Also, by comparison the food was nourishing, if not always exciting. Also, POCs are not abused. The police only used violence when things really got out of control, i.e., after a riot, a fire, and another riot. I think they are remarkably forbearing.

Some agencies for refugee rights immediately descended the day after the riot to be sure conditions were ok. They wanted to see whether the complaints of the demonstrators were true. I have to say that many POCs say what they know will get sympathy: "I was abused by my husband and fled," or "I was a Christian (or gay) and had to flee." Maybe I am older, sadder, and wiser, but I think we must not accept or publish POCs' comments without verification. I read some news articles, which were irresponsible. These authors cited POCs' stories as if they were gospel truth with no balance or verification. They even used old pictures, some from two years ago. News reporters aren't allowed in the camp. It is a prison or at least a detention center. These reporters were looking for a story and sensationalizing. The truth is stark enough. The UNHCR and others, e.g., Save the Children, have access and tell a different story.

I want to repeat my admiration for our boss, Jeremy, and his shift leaders: Missy, Megan, Anna, and Hanna. We "peons" don't understand why we are called upon to do what we do. However, we obeyed their orders. Those of us only here for a week or two can't hope to grasp the situation. We must follow the rules and instructions we are given.

One POC was wearing a ball cap that said in large white letters, "OBEY." I doubt he has any idea what obedience means. Some POCs showed an attitude of entitlement. Others, however, were grateful, like the Syrian female new arrival who jumped in and helped clean the bathroom in the New Arrivals cage.

I have great admiration for the Mennonite folks from I58. The young ladies wore long skirts or dresses (all on the same pattern) and white doilies for a head covering and running shoes. It was sort of like a nun's habit. The POCs in the main respect them. Their presence was like an immediate calming element.

EuroRelief is composed of Greater Europe Mission, YWAM (Youth With a Mission), and I58 (Mennonites) teams. The core are the longer-term GEMers (our friend Kim [m]), the I58 folks, and the YWAMers (the Dutch young ladies). Those here longer-term have picked up a lot of burdens from the abandoning NGOs and done a great job.

I was just a small cog in a bigger machine. I used what skills I had, rough and ready though they were, to help calm the waters a bit.

For a final thought . . . I was in the hardware store in the village where we stayed, Panagiouda, many times in the last two weeks, asking for help to get the right parts, returning sometimes three times a day. The hardware is a family business. Grandfather, who has had a stroke, sits in a chair to one side. Father, mother, and the father's sister work there, along with the two sons, who are learning the business in the summer. We had some talks as the weeks went by.

"Why do they hate us?" asked the mother. I don't think the POCs hate the Greeks, but they hate being locked up. The POCs have to learn that they have entered the country illegally and so have to go through a long process of verifying their stories. Eventually, they can hope to get refugee status and be allowed to move to Athens to settle.

The village [Panagiouda] is a lovely quiet place by the sea. It's unsettling to move from the camp to the village each day. The camp is hurricane fence and razor wire. The village is little boats and kind, "salt of the earth" kind of folks. It's disorienting.

The Greek economy is in shambles and the EU is using restructuring of loans as a means of forcing Greece to deal with the constant flood of POCs, even if the flow is less than before: now a hundred or so a day, before thousands a day. The route to Italy for POCs has taken over a lot of the flood of POCs.

As you pray for the POCs, pray also for the Greek people of Lesvos, who are bearing the brunt of the flood of refugees. Their normal tourism is way down.

Pray also for the Greek Orthodox Church. When [four] Nigerians showed up to a service here, they were told to go away. They moved [on] to the Roman Catholic church.

Pray for the salvation of the Greek people here in this village and other places where the EuroRelief and other agencies are working.

Finally, pray for those of us, who have been there and will never be quite the same.

Warmly in Christ,

Phil

July 26, 2017

Dear praying friends,

I appreciate the various and numerous responses to my missives from the camp. I am grateful for your prayers during that time and your encouragement since.

I left the impression that I feel bad about myself. I did and do in the sense feel bad about myself in that I was unable to communicate God's love through my actions, at least at times.

I discovered that most of my training and giftedness had not prepared me for many of the tasks I was asked to do. I did, though, find that I had some skills I could use to help people there in the camp.

I was able to use my rough and ready plumbing skills to help people, particularly the new arrivals and some French-speaking African women. At least for a while the new arrivals won't be greeted by a disgusting bathroom, even if they don't understand how the plumbing all works.

The French-speaking African women were in the main imperious and ungrateful, but hopefully they sensed something different in Mark and me as we helped them. We tried as best we could to love the unlovely in a practical way.

I know that all of our repairs will be undone in a matter of weeks. That is the nature of the place. People come and go. The situation is always more or less a crisis. Disappointment is palpable. However, at least for some, for a while those we helped will have more humane conditions.

So, I don't feel "bad" about myself, so much as sobered. I was and am inadequate to the circumstances there at the camp, but we all were, more or less. The tide of would-be refugees is less, but it continues. Those in Greece struggle to care for the constant flood of people.

I am grateful to God for the training I have and the ministry I have at Tyndale and at Zaporozhye Bible College and Seminary. I have prepared and worked towards the sort of ministry I have in both places for more than forty years. I feel as though I have finally reached the culmination of my calling.

One of our good friends of many decades, Kim, who works for EuroRelief, said he felt the same way about the camp and his ministry there. He is a great team leader, having spent decades leading GEM EuroTeam short-term teams. He is an encourager. He also has great building skills. I'm glad for people like him who have found their niche at the camp. I'm also glad that I have found mine too.

Hopefully our actions in the camp did speak louder than our words and that there were more positive actions than negative ones. Thanks again for your prayers and kind encouragement.

Warmly in Christ,

Phil

A sad epilogue to the Letters from camp

On September 9th, 2020 the Moria Migrant Detention Centre on the Greek island of Lesvos was burned to the ground. 13,000 POCs are without housing. Though Moria is gone and people cannot go there to serve, there are hundreds of such refugee and migrant detention centers worldwide, where POCs endure similar things.

Conclusion: **Walk a Mile in My Shoes**

Do not judge lest ye be judged . . .

—Matthew 7:1

WE OFTEN CONSIDER PEOPLE who are different from us to be dangerous. People who look different, perhaps with darker skin or different features, may seem like a threat. People who speak another language may unnerve us, since we cannot understand what they say. Perhaps we think the religious creed of a particular group makes them our mortal enemies.

Dutch people love different cultures, and enjoy things they consider to be *multi-culti* (multicultural). However, one young Dutch "new Netherlander" (*nieuwe Nederlander*, a designation for those who have recently immigrated or who are children of immigrants) said rather bitterly, "The Netherlands is multi-culinary, not multi-cultural. They don't want our religion or languages. They just want our food."

The government of the Netherlands wants immigration. It also encourages multiculturalism. However, some Dutch people fear the loss of "Dutch" culture. They are afraid that immigrants are changing Dutch culture and their country. The point of the "new Netherlander's" comment is that such people don't mind small changes, like the introduction of new foods or music, but they are afraid of changes having to do with more fundamental issues, like religion or social order.

The history of the United States is also one of immigration. Yet, each wave of immigrants met opposition and sometimes open hostility because people were afraid that these new arrivals would change their culture and country. Differences of race, religion, and culture fed fears of those who did not want change.

Often we make judgments based on fear or misinformation or ignorance and then start campaigns to enthrone our misapprehensions. We need to rethink what we are doing and ask why we think these things. We need to inform ourselves, not merely find propaganda which supports our uninformed opinions.

We have a right to form opinions about others and must do so. Sometimes, people mistakenly think Christianity teaches that judging others is wrong. In fact, Jesus does allow for making distinctions. He says, however, that when we judge we must remember that whatever measure we use to judge with is the measure that will be used when we are judged. Often, we tend to think that judging others is wrong. However, Jesus is not saying we should never judge whether someone's ideas are wrong or their behavior is wrong. Rather, in this context, he is saying that we cannot be like the Pharisees, Sadducees, and other religious people of his day who judged others with harsher standards than they judged themselves.

> Do not judge, or you too will be judged. For in the same way you judge others, you will be judged, and with the measure you use, it will be measured to you. (Matt 7:1–2)

Just a bit further on in the text Jesus says:

> So, whatever you wish that others would do to you, do also to them, for this is the Law and the Prophets. (Matt 7:12)

This "Golden Rule" is probably the most well-known statement Jesus made. Whatever anyone thinks of Jesus, whether he is Savior or simply some good teacher, almost everyone sees this command as a universally good thing.

If we take either Jesus' explicitly Christian view, or a Jewish, Old Testament view, or even Kant's secular, rational view,[292] the implication for our treatment of refugees and immigrants must be the same: treat them as you would like to be treated if you were in their place.

How would you feel if *you* were driven from your home? Your home was bombed and there was nothing to return to. Your town (put its name in *here* in your mind) was destroyed by bombing. The economy in your country was shattered and destroyed by war. Schools were destroyed or shut down. Your children had no future in their homeland. Your church was bombed and you were discriminated against or even persecuted for your faith.

Perhaps, at its most fundamental, we are afraid. We read and hear things on the news which horrify us, and so some right-wing groups try to magnify this fear, until we freeze in fearful paralysis. It's quite common for us to throw up our hands and simply avoid the issue or try to preserve our own way of life by ignoring those who are refugees.

It is normal to feel fear of the unknown. I include here a long reflection by an American friend of ours, a middle-aged woman married to an EU citizen here in the Netherlands. There was a refugee "camp" nearby her home, which was an amusement park with cabins which the state had temporarily rented for the purpose. I'm including her thoughts because she speaks eloquently of all of the emotions she experienced when she met refugees. Here she writes of her fears about how Muslim male refugees would relate to an American woman and then of her relief from fear.

I have had a lot of fears, both rational and irrational with regards to the young bearded men roaming the streets of our village. What were they saying? What were they thinking? What had they experienced? What did they want out of their new lives, what did they hope for? Did they hate Americans? British? My head was filled with pieces of random and possibly dubious information such as, "Women in the Middle East don't look a man in the eye." So, I practiced averting my eyes and tried to give a welcoming smile at the same time.

I was more than curious as I had read many articles about the situation with the refugees, some more scholarly and informed, like *The Economist* [a British magazine like the *Wall Street Journal*], and some not, like the *Daily Mail* [a British tabloid newspaper on the level of the *National Enquirer*].

A church in our village, the N. Church, had advertised a drop in center for the local refugees twice a week. After attending a concert at the N. Church, I realized how close to my home it was. As I prayed about going to the drop-in center, I felt that God was saying, "Go, do not be afraid."

Now I will write down some of the things that I have observed and learned for others who might be struggling with fear as I have been.

1. It's wonderful to see the Dutch Christians in action at N. Church. N. Church is within walking distance, though a good long walk, from the camping center, where approximately 750 refugees are housed. The church has created a peaceful haven for the refugees. Quite a few church members are in attendance and things run smoothly. When you enter the church, you are greeted and given a name tag. The church people have a little chat with each new person and [get to] "know" who is there, both refugees and visitors like me. They also create an atmosphere of freedom to move about, talk to people, bring food, play with the children and so on. A man, one of the refugees, sits at the piano and plays chord progressions with a Middle Eastern flavor, while another man strums along on the guitar.

In one room several computers are set up, as well as a "haircut" chair, an ordinary wooden chair that you would see in a classroom. A man comes in regularly and cuts the hair of the refugees for free. The men look nice, beards trimmed and clean cut.

The other day, the N. Church arranged for a saxophone quartet to play for the refugees and visitors. It was a beautiful concert and the large number of refugees, as well as the other visitors were mesmerized as they listened to the classical music by Grieg and others. The pastor knew just which one of the refugees was a saxophone player and arranged for him to meet the musicians afterwards. Someone also managed to find a saxophone for the man, who is quite a good musician. He played to his heart's content during the following drop-in session.

In the kitchen you will find ladies mostly from the British School on Tuesdays and the American School on Thursdays, who lay out the food that people donate, and serve coffee and tea as well.

One of the ladies, a grade school teacher, spoke about how her class baked muffins twice a week for the refugees, and followed a Syrian recipe. One of the children, when asked, "What is a refugee?" said, "A referee for the football team."

2. I am impressed by the manners and friendliness of the refugees. When I ask what food the government supplies, the refugees have been very careful not to complain and to emphasize how nice the Netherlands is. This was a relief to me because at the hairdressers I had heard people talking about how the refugees had been complaining about the food and ". . . if they didn't like it they should go back to where they came from." I had overheard this conversation before ever going to the drop-in center and had felt incensed at such complaints. I must report, however, that I have spoken to many refugees about food, because it is a relatively safe topic. I have come to believe that the refugees are truly grateful for what they receive and if not, have the good manners not to say so.

Speaking still of manners, I have also observed that the refugees are trying to adopt Dutch ways. In each conversation, each person extended a hand and looked me in the eye, whether male or female. This is what I have found with almost any Dutch person that I have met.

Before going to the drop-in center, I had worried that being a woman I would feel awkward in a room filled with male refugees. I found, to my surprise, that there was no awkwardness in women speaking to men. I concluded that as a woman of my age [40s], I am like a mother figure to many of the men, who are in their 20s. I therefore also concluded that young women should stay away from the drop-in center. However, a young attractive married woman has been coming to the center recently and I have noticed no difference in the way she is treated.

A little more on the topic of women in general . . . Up until recently there were only men at the camping center. Now there are five families from Syria, Eritrea, and central Asia. The women are with very small children (mostly toddlers) and cannot come to the drop-in center regularly for lack of car seats, a situation which my friend B is working on. Some of the women go without head covering and the others wear different types of covering. The Syrian women spoke of the horror and total destruction of Syria and that it would take many years before it was functioning again. One very young woman with a baby spoke, with tears, of being separated from her husband and the fact that she didn't know what country he ended up in, but that she hoped that one day they would be reunited.

It is also true that a portion of the men do not seem to be interested in speaking to the Westerners, but eat, play games and behave in a very civilized manner. Why wouldn't they? Some of these people speak neither English nor Dutch and others are possibly devout Muslims, who will not speak to a woman.

The police dropped in to the center one session. The village police station is just 1.5 blocks from the N. Church. The police officers, one man, one woman, got a cup of tea and walked around and chatted to the church people and to some of the refugees. It happened to be a day when the center was full to the brim with people . . . a good weather day when more people were willing to walk the ten or so blocks to the church. People seemed pretty comfortable with the police in attendance, even though the officers by no means blended in with their fluorescent green striped jackets.

3. The refugees at the drop-in center are from many different people groups: Iranian Kurds, Iraqi Kurds, Iraqi Arabs, Iranian Christians, Eritrean, Afghani, Syrian, and more. For those that imagine an Arabic Muslim group of men, just on the verge of uniting and organizing against the infidels of the West, think again. I have learned that the refugees speak a number of different languages and often find it hard to communicate with one another. Nevertheless, I have not been aware of any tensions between the groups at the center in my six visits.

Also, there are various religious groups represented. The Kurds have been among the friendliest of the people at the center and to my surprise, some of them are quite anti-Islam. When I am told these things, the men look at my face for a response. My answer is, "I know nothing about Islam" (as I think it would be counterproductive and possibly dangerous to be misinterpreted or misquoted on that topic). The Afghani man says, "ISIS bad, very, very bad, everyone" (then he draws his finger across his neck), "EVERYONE!" Then he shakes his head, gets up and walks away. A Kurdish man then tells how he wants democracy by putting the sentence into his handheld device and having it translated. After I read his screen and shake my head "Yes," I write into his translator, "I want freedom and safety."

From an Iranian Christian man I have learned that he estimates that there are around 50 Christians among the 750 refugees. He has told me of the persecution in Iran and his fear of being killed if he were to stay there. He draws his finger across his neck as he speaks. I asked him if he felt afraid at the camping center or if there were people hurting the Christians there and he said, "No." He stays in a bungalow with his brother. He tells me that he attends a Christian church closer to the camping center.

I was quite worried about revealing that I was an American. At first my plan was to let the men believe that I was Dutch. In conversation, someone revealed that I was an American. "Please don't tell anyone." I said to the Iraqi man that I was speaking to. "I know that Americans are not very popular." He looked at me and said, very emphatically, "I would DIE for the Marines at the base near my village. I would DIE. You don't have to worry. Don't worry." I had a hard time getting his words out of my head. He obviously felt very loyal towards the American military. The next session he brought an Iraqi man up to me and said, "This man likes Americans too." Over time I became more comfortable and though I don't broadcast it, I don't feel afraid if someone asks me where I'm from. Probably some are not pro-American in a group that size, but there is a far distance between not liking someone and wanting to do them harm. I get the feeling from the refugees that they are here to escape hell on earth. Most of them seem to think that death was certain if they stayed.

In Closing

I don't comment here on the decisions that politicians have made or will make. What is best for society on a large scale is a different topic and one that I don't feel qualified to write about. I simply have no choice but to react to the events in my own village, however. No reaction is still a reaction.

Before attending the drop-in center, I would see groups of male refugees walking down the street of our village and my imagination would sometimes get the better of me. Now when I see the men walking around, I look at their faces and sometimes recognize them. There is a smile and a hello and a mutual recognition, "Hey, I know you!." My fear levels have dropped considerably. I hope that theirs have too.[293]

Often, we are afraid. But, what are we afraid of? A stereotype propagated by news media to sensationalize the situation? Among the people whom we least need to fear are the refugees, who, as is obvious here, don't like ISIS and other terrorists. They have suffered at their hands.

Former immigrants helping current immigrants

It's probably not surprising that Mennonite churches are often quick to respond to the needs of refugees and immigrants. Even though most Mennonites immigrated to the US very early, some before the American Revolutionary War, they recall what it was like to be a community persecuted for their faith. They remember their history of being driven from their land and homes. Thankfully, they are not alone in their reaching out to immigrants.

Apart from our heritage and length of time in our homelands, we who are Christians sometimes seem to forget that we are temporary dwellers, aliens, and strangers on the earth. We become far too comfortable with our earthly status. We should question where our wealth is: is it in heaven or is it in an earthly bank? God promises to bless those who share: "Give and it shall be given back to you—pressed down and shaken together" (Luke 6:38).

We also seem to forget that all that we have is a stewardship, not an ownership. "What you have is not your own" (1 Cor 6:19).

God entrusts us with wealth, with health, with homes, with cars, with many blessings, so that we can be a blessing to others. He gives sun, rain, seasons, etc. to everyone, regardless of their relationship to him. He is benevolent and perfect, and calls us to be benevolent and perfect as he is perfect (Matt 5:48).

What I am asking for is a heart of compassion. I am asking for you to share and care. I believe that this is what Jesus asks of us.

I have a student at the seminary I teach at in Ukraine who is from Crimea. Since Russia has annexed Crimea, he cannot return home. He would have to give up his Ukrainian passport and change his citizenship, taking a Russian passport. So, he remains in Ukraine helping refugees (well, actually, according to strictly technical terms, we have described these "refugees" earlier in this book as internally displaced people or IDPs).

When he sits and listens to these refugees share their pain and loss, it is not just words. He can envision the streets and the houses. He knows the villages and the towns. When someone comes from a neighboring city that is still under siege and uninhabitable, he can name the streets and neighborhoods, because he's been there.

Though he lives now in a two-room apartment with his family of four, he is generous seeking help for others. He is a kind, gentle soul. He drives himself and his team of helpers mercilessly, not because he's making money or because someone is watching, but because he knows the pain and loss each person he meets is facing.

His country, Ukraine, was torn in two. Part of his country, Crimea, was seized or seceded (depending on whose version), but it doesn't matter. What matters are those who hurt, who have lost all, who are damaged, internally destroyed, cast away, considered useless or unimportant.

When we've been there and we can see the people in their villages and towns . . . when we can name the streets (at least before they change the names once again) . . . when we can envision the situation, the homeless, the aged left destitute, the handicapped, the maimed . . . it changes our entire view of the situation. It's not just names and figures. It's not just pictures on the nightly news. It's people like you and me. People who bleed and suffer.

I will end with another reflection from our time in Yugoslavia. As a young couple with a two-year-old and a three-month-old, we went to Yugoslavia, the nicest, most developed country in eastern Europe. But beneath the lovely coast and the ski slopes, even despite the Olympics, which had just taken place in Sarajevo, Yugoslavia was a powder keg.

Tito had capped the keg successfully throughout his reign and for a decade afterwards, but the powder was dry and ready for igniting. Nationalism raised its ugly head. People who were intermarried with other ethnic groups faced off. It was horrid.

Neighbors turned on neighbors. One young lady, an internally displaced person in Novi Sad, said that one night in her village in Bosnia, she was wakened by "friendly" forces, who told her and other ethnic Serbs to flee because the village was going to be attacked. She and her sister fled. They would eventually finish high school in Novi Sad and then move to Belgrade later. They could not go home again to Bosnia.

In 1992, I talked once to some Serbs who were internally displaced from Croatia into Vojvodina, the north of Serbia. They spoke of their long

CONCLUSION: WALK A MILE IN MY SHOES 197

march across Croatia from near the Croatian coast in the Lika region, across the plains bordering Croatia and Bosnia to Serbia, a trip of at least 465 km or 290 miles. They had been warned by "friendly" forces (mercenaries who were Serbs, but had fought earlier in Angola, among other places) that they should flee into the hills. These displaced people were farmers, simple folks. They took what they could and fled. The second day they were told, "Go further into the hills, the fighting's getting closer!" So, they went further up. On the third day they were given the same orders. They eventually realized that this was not a temporary retreat, but a forced march out of Croatia. They were robbed of anything of value by "friendly" forces. They said that jets flew over them while they were crossing Croatia, flying so low that they could read the fuselage. They were marched with no provisions or water or cover for weather. When they reached Serbia, they were driven north and south and not allowed to enter Belgrade, lest there be a riot.[294]

Imagine these people. Simple people. Farmers, farmers' wives, children, left homeless, left without livestock, left without hope. The refugees, who are coming to the US, the UK, the Netherlands, Belgium, Germany, Italy, Greece, and Spain now, those who flee war, are similar people. Many are simple people, ordinary people, people who in some cases have also been robbed of all they have and owned.

We can praise God that we have not suffered any of these things. We can show our gratitude by helping others who have.

There was a Japanese diplomat, Chiune Sugihara, working in Lithuania at the time of the Second World War. He was faced with thousands of Jews who wanted to flee the Nazis and extermination. He issued travel visas to several thousand Jews. In the end he saved six thousand Jews. He was not a Christian. When he was asked what his motivation was to risk his life, the life of his family, and his career (which he lost later after the war as a consequence), he replied:

> You want to know about my motivation, don't you? Well. It is the kind of sentiments anyone would have when he actually sees refugees face to face, begging with tears in their eyes. He just cannot help but sympathize with them.[295]

We, as individuals, cannot do everything. However, we can make a difference in one person's life or in one family situation. Even if we contribute a little to a charity of our choice which works with refugees, that is a start. Give up one meal eaten out in a restaurant and give that $50 to a group of your choice that helps refugees.

We can be involved on a personal level, helping individuals. Those near a refugee center can get involved in visiting refugees who for all intents and purposes are incarcerated, i.e., they cannot leave until their cases are decided. They have a lot of time on their hands. They need language helpers to learn the language of their potential new home countries. I have seen Muslim refugees with flashcards of Dutch vocabulary words pasted on their lockers in their tiny rooms in an old office building turned refugee center/camp. Most of the refugees want to integrate. They want to fit in, though many also want to keep their own religious beliefs and practices. Just as my friend visited the drop-in center near her home, so you could take an afternoon and go to chat with your new neighbors and drink tea. The news media shows us either raving fanatics or immediately distressed, grieving people, but it doesn't show us the "limbo" most refugees inhabit between fleeing for their lives and finally receiving an immigration visa. It appears that at least two to five years pass in the process of investigation before a potential immigrant can leave the detention center and find a place to live and start a new life. There are so many ways to help, even small ones. Perhaps you have an old instrument you don't play. Maybe you could donate it to the refugee center or to some refugee you know.

Perhaps, like Pastor Jon Carlson and Forest Hills Mennonite Church, your church or community organization could sponsor a refugee family, providing them with a place to stay, with help finding furniture, with helping to get children in school, etc. Remember my story about the Vietnamese family our little Lutheran church sponsored when I was a teen. It doesn't take a large or a wealthy group. It takes a group with open arms and open hearts. The final results of such kindness far outweigh the costs involved. The children of that Vietnamese family are now high-powered, high-earning professionals. They are all that America wants in immigrants: educated, determined, talented, polite, kind.

"Ah, come on! You're just laying it on too thick! That's not realistic. They aren't so grateful." Am I? The children of this Vietnamese family I mentioned called and have written to my mother-in-law regularly to talk with her, an important person who helped them in their early days in America, remembering her birthday, remembering her kindness. They definitely are grateful for the help they received.

Maybe you could go to help refugees in a war zone. This may sound crazy, but simple people of faith can make a huge difference when they are simply available. Maybe you could go for a week or two, in teams like the one I went with go to places such as Lesvos, or for a couple of years to help some national relief organization in their efforts, moving boxes of aid, arranging it for distribution, processing requests, keeping the books . . . . This is what Alice and Mark Jantzen did when they came to Belgrade, Serbia, to help Bread of Life when Bread of Life needed them most. Quiet, unassuming people, willing to lend a hand wherever and whenever asked, are always welcome.

I'm not asking you to bankrupt yourself, giving away everything you have. Only one person could do that, God, Jesus himself. And yet, there have been those who have done exactly that. C. T. Studd was a very well-to-do gentleman in England in the late nineteenth century. He was a champion cricketer with a distinct possibility of a professional sports career.[296] But he gave away his inheritance, about $500,000 in today's currency, to follow God's call to reach those who were beyond the reach of the gospel. He and six other Cambridge students became known as the "Haystack Seven," since they met at a haystack to pray. They literally went out to the four corners of the earth to help those in need. Now, ironically, the four corners of the earth are coming to us in northern Europe, the UK, the US, and Canada. Studd and others went to far lands to serve—are we willing to go next door to meet and help those brought by terrible circumstances to our nations?

There wasn't any distinction made in the time of the work of Studd and his fellow students between "relief" efforts and "missions" efforts. All who engaged in such mission helped in all ways: material, spiritual, and educational.

You may not be called to do as C. T. Studd did, to give away your inheritance, but you can give liberally from what God has given you. You can also obey the Great Commission by reaching out in love and service to those who are now at our doors. As you weigh the message of this book, and its call to reach out to refugees, migrants, displaced people, and others in need, remember Jesus' words:

> For I was hungry and you gave me food, I was thirsty and you gave me drink, I was a stranger and you welcomed me, I was naked and you clothed me, I was sick and you visited me, I was in prison and you came to me . . . . Truly, I say to you, as you did it to one of the least of these my brothers, you did it to me. (Matt 25:35, 36, 40)

Further reading

On what it's like to be a refugee:

Eakin, Hugh, et al. *Flight from Syria: Refugee Stories*. Pulitzer Center, 2014.

Endnotes

1. "Terrorism," https://www.lexico.com/definition/terrorism.

2. Westcott, "American Muslim Organizations Condemn Shooting."

3. Nowrasteh, "Terrorism and Immigration," 2.

4. Abutaleb, "Rampage Betrayed Islam."

5. "Ahmadiyya Muslim Community," updated October 10, 2018, http://www.ahmadiyya.us/about-ahmadiyya-muslim-community.

6. Given the arsenal they amassed, one wonders about why "gun control" would be such a bad idea.

   "Burguan said the couple had two assault-style rifles, two semi-automatic handguns and 1,600 rounds of ammunition in their rented sport utility vehicle, when they were killed. At the townhouse, police found another 4,500 rounds, 12 pipe bombs and bomb-making equipment. One bomb was rigged to a remote-control device. The guns were legally purchased in the United States, said Meredith Davis, a spokeswoman for the Bureau of Alcohol, Tobacco, Firearms and Explosives" (Abutaleb and Baertlein, "Militant Links to Shooters").

7. Takei, "They Interned My Family."

8. "Somali Armed Group Al-Shabab Should Not Carry Out Amputations," https://www.amnesty.org/en/latest/news/2009/06/somali-armed-group-al-shabab-should-not-carry-out-amputations-20090622.

9. Mujahid, "Islam's Manifesto of Universal Brotherhood."

10. Huda, "World's Muslim Population".

11. Heller, "Rightsizing the Transnational Jihadist Threat"; see also Jones et al., "Evolution of the Salafi-Jihadist Threat."

12. Trump, "Executive Order Protecting the Nation from Foreign Terrorist Entry into the United States," order 13769.

13. See the previously cited CATO Institute report, Nowrasteh, "Terrorism and Immigration," 2.

14. United States Court of Appeals for the Ninth Circuit No. 17-35105, D.C. No. 2:17-cv-00141, http://cdn.ca9.uscourts.gov/datastore/opinions/2017/02/09/17-35105.pdf.

15. United States Court of Appeals for the Ninth Circuit No. 17-35105, D.C. No. 2:17-cv-00141, http://cdn.ca9.uscourts.gov/datastore/opinions/2017/02/09/17-35105.pdf.

16. Trump, "Executive Order Protecting the Nation from Foreign Terrorist Entry into the United States," order 13769, sec. 7 (a).

17. Trump, "Executive Order Protecting the Nation from Foreign Terrorist Entry into the United States," order 13780.

18. Trump, "Executive Order Protecting the Nation from Foreign Terrorist Entry into the United States," order 13780. "In 2016, the Secretary of Homeland Security designated Libya, Somalia, and Yemen as additional countries of concern for travel purposes," sec. 1 (b)(i).

19. Trump, "Executive Order Protecting the Nation from Foreign Terrorist Entry into the United States," order 13780. "'(III) whether the country or area is a safe haven for terrorists.' 8 U.S.C. 1187(a)," sec. 1 (b)(i).

20. Meek et al., "US May Have Let 'Dozens' of Terrorists into Country."

21. Brown, "Bungled Background Checks."

22. "'The assistance of the refugee community was crucial to this investigation,' Dwight Holton, who prosecuted Mohamud, told Portland Patch. He also argued that the failed terrorist's status as a refugee was in no way connected to the carnage he concocted. 'His radicalization had precisely nothing to do with his refugee status,' Holton said. 'He didn't radicalize until much later. His interest in terrorism had absolutely nothing to do with his refugee status. He was radicalized long after he became a United States citizen'" (Silverstein, "Trump's New Travel Ban").

23. Nowrasteh, "Terrorism and Immigration," 1.

24. Nowrasteh, "Terrorism and Immigration," 8.

25. Nowrasteh, "Terrorism and Immigration," 6.

26. "8 USC 1157: Annual admission of refugees and admission of emergency situation refugees; Title 8-ALIENS AND NATIONAL-ITY CHAPTER 12-IMMIGRATION AND NATIONALITY SUB-CHAPTER II-IMMIGRATION Part I-Selection System," https://uscode. house.gov/view.xhtml?req=granuleid%3AUSC-prelim-title8-section 1157&num=0&edition=prelim#0-0-0-190.

    The point is still the same: the president has the right to set the limits of immigration.

27. Connor and Krogstad, "Resettling 110,000 Refugees This Year."

28. Rush, "'Private' Refugee Resettlement Agencies." NB: This is a site biased towards low immigration. Rush notes that most funding for refugees comes from the government no matter who does the settling. She says that these agencies are pushing for higher immigration. She notes that if there is lower immigration these agencies will receive less funding. The implication is that their concern for allowing more refugees is due to their desire for more funding or to limit loss of funding. Frankly this seems extremely cynical to me.

29. Stella, "Church Welcomes Syrian Refugee Family."

30. Grier, "Supreme Court on Trump's Travel Ban."

31. Trump, "Presidential Proclamation Enhancing Vetting Capabilities," proclamation 9645.

32. "First Amendment—U.S. Constitution," https://constitution.findlaw.com/ amendment1.html.

33. "Facts and Case Summary—Korematsu v. U.S.," https://www.uscourts. gov/educational-resources/educational-activities/facts-and-case -summary-korematsu-v-us.

34. "Evacuees had only a few days to get their affairs in order before they had to report to the Portland Assembly Center that was part of the internment process. Homes, businesses, and farms had to be disposed of on extremely short notice. Bargain hunters, fully aware of the situation, stood ready to purchase the property and belongings at a fraction of their true value" ("Oregon's Japanese Americans Learn Their Fate," https://sos.oregon.gov/ archives/exhibits/ww2/Pages/threats-fate.aspx).

35. "Facts and Case Summary—Korematsu v. U.S.," https://www.uscourts. gov/educational-resources/educational-activities/facts-and-case -summary-korematsu-v-us.

36. Hurd and Schwartz, "Supreme Court Travel Ban Ruling."

37. "Trump v. Hawaii, No. 17–965," argued April 25, 2018; decided June 26, 2018, 38, https://www.supremecourt.gov/opinions/17pdf/17-965_h315.pdf.

38. Paul and Selk, "Supreme Court Struck Down a WWII-Era Travesty."

39. "Refugees were not very successful at killing people in terrorist attacks on U.S. soil. Of the 25, only 3 were successful in their attacks, killing a total of 3 people and imposing a total human cost of $45 million, or $13.27 per refugee visa issued. Two of the three refugee terrorists were Cubans who committed attacks in the 1970s; the other was Croatian. All three were admitted before the Refugee Act of 1980 created the current rigorous refugee-screening procedures" (Nowrasteh, "Terrorists by Immigration Status and Nationality," 23).

40. "Asylum seekers usually arrive with a different visa with the intent of applying for asylum once they arrive, so they are counted under the asylum category. For instance, the Tsarnaev brothers, who carried out the Boston Marathon bombing on April 15, 2013, traveled here with a tourist visa but their family immediately applied for asylum, so they are included in that category" (Nowrasteh, "Terrorism and Immigration," 3).

41. "Boston Marathon Terror Attack Fast Facts," *CNN*, updated 1118 GMT (1918 HKT) April 10, 2016, http://edition.cnn.com/2013/06/03/us/boston-marathon-terror-attack-fast-facts.

42. Bergo, "Emmanuel Levinas."

43. See for a lovely introduction, see Davis, *Levinas: An Introduction*.

44. Sartre, *Being and Nothingness*, "Bad Faith," 47–70, "The Look," 252–302, esp. on shame 259–66.

45. Lacan, *Fundamental Concepts of Psychoanalysis*.

46. Deut 6:5; Lev 19:18.

47. Daum and Rudavsky, *Hiding and Seeking*.

48. Daum and Rudavsky, *Hiding and Seeking*.

49. There are now 79.5 million displaced people in the world. UNHCR Figures at a Glance https://www.unhcr.org/figures-at-a-glance.html.

50. Desmond, *Being and the Between*, 194–200.

51. See Merleau-Ponty, *The Primacy of Perception*, "Eye and Mind," 159–69.

52. Nowrasteh, "Terrorists by Immigration Status and Nationality," 1.

53. The BBC says that the odds worldwide are 300,000 to 1. "Small Data: What Are the Chances of Being Hit by Lightning?" *BBC News*, March 17, 2014, http://www.bbc.com/news/blogs-magazine-monitor-26583325.

54. "The Jews regarded the Samaritans as ethnically impure and repudiated them, and in the time of Ezra and Nehemiah marriages that had been contracted between Jews and Samaritans were broken up." Kruse, *John*, John 4:9.

55. Marc Chagall, *White Crucifixion*, 1938, Art Institute of Chicago, http://www.artic.edu/aic/collections/artwork/59426.

56. Wassily Kandinsky, *Cannons*, 1913, http://www.wassily-kandinsky.org/Cannons.jsp#prettyPhoto.

57. Aquinas, *Summa Theologiae*, I, Q.44.

58. Spencer, *The Principles of Ethics*.

59. Sartre, *Being and Nothingness*, "Bad Faith," 47–70, "The Look," 252–302, esp. on shame 259–66.

60. Heller, "Rightsizing the Transnational Jihadist Threat." See also Jones et al., "Evolution of the Salafi-Jihadist Threat."

61. North Way Christian Community, "Part 2 - Obadiah - Pastor Scott Stevens."

62. "What is it to be drawn by delight? Delight yourself in the Lord, and He shall give you the desires of your heart. There is a pleasure of the heart to which that bread of heaven is sweet. Moreover, if it was right in the poet to say, Every man is drawn by his own pleasure,—not necessity, but pleasure; not obligation, but delight—how much more boldly ought we to say that a man is drawn to Christ when he delights in the truth, when he delights in blessedness, delights in righteousness, delights in everlasting life, all which Christ is?" (Augustine, *Tractates*, "Tractate 26 (John 6:41–59)," para. 4).

63. Stott, *Christian Mission in the Modern World*.

64. https://www.samaritanspurse.org.

65. Feinberg and Feinberg, *Ethics for a Brave New World*.

66. Volf, *Exclusion and Embrace*.

67. "Zwei Täter wegen Sexualdelikten zu Bewährungsstrafen verurteilt," *Spiegel*, July 7, 2016, http://www.spiegel.de/panorama/justiz/koelner-silvester-nacht-erste-schuldsprueche-wegen-sexualdelikten-a-1101870.html.

68. **Euronews [Interviewer]:** *So you don't think anything needs to be done against those who protest, who burn refugee shelters? The xenophobia is giving a terrible image of Germany to the rest of the world . . .*
     Thomas de Maizière: Oh yes indeed, there is much to be done. We're seeing a significant increase of politically motivated crimes coming from the right wing: insults, hatred, violence against asylum seekers and the institutions that help them. (Ripper, "Germany Wants Camps to Sort Through Migrants.")

69. Mayntz und Quadbeck, "Erst 30.000 Flüchtlinge haben einen Job," an interview with the head of the German Federal Office for Migration and Refugees.

70. I cannot find an article which attests to the use of this phrase per se, as 1986 was before archived newspaper articles online, but the article below attests to the sort of antiforeigner attitude of Jörg Haider and his Freedom Party Austria (FPÖ). Cohen, "Rightist Is Firing Up Vienna's Election with Slurs." See also Höbelt, *Defiant Populist*.

71. Farley, "9/11 Hijackers and Student Visas."

72. "Theo van Gogh (film director)," https://en.wikipedia.org/wiki/Theo_van _Gogh_(film_director).

73. For further information see "Summary Report: The State of Education 2016–2017," Utrecht, 2018, https://www.google.com/url?sa=t&rct =j&q=&esrc=s&source=web&cd=11&cad=rja&uact=8&ved=2ahUKE wjqtpm29_DjAhVCL1AKHSpaAdAQFjAKegQIBhAC&url=https%3A %2F%2Fenglish.onderwijsinspectie.nl%2Fbinaries%2Fonderwijsinspect ie_eng%2Fdocuments%2Fannual-reports%2F2018%2F11%2F14%2Fthe- state-of-education-in-the-netherlands-2016-2017%2F116806_IvhO_ The%2BState%2Bof%2BEducation_Hfst1_TG.pdf&usg=AOvVaw32fAejn 4YvgssScSVl9VNO.
     See also Meijer, "Government to Fund New Islamic School"; and "Education Minister Threatens to Remove Funding from Amsterdam Islamic High School, Accused of Terror Links," https://www.dutchnews. nl/news/2019/03/amsterdams-islamic-high-school-leaders-have-links-to- terrorists-security-service.

74. Stella, "Church Welcomes Syrian Refugee Family."

75. Author's italic and bold face.

76. Stella, "Church Welcomes Syrian Refugee Family."

77. Stella, "Church Welcomes Syrian Refugee Family."

78. "Local Partners," http://www.northway.org/Pages/Outreach/lamp.aspx.

79. Misra, "After-School Program for Refugee Children"; and https://www.joinourbridge.org.

80 Misra, "After-School Program for Refugee Children"; and https://www.joinourbridge.org.

81. Stella, "Church Welcomes Syrian Refugee Family."

82. Central Agency for the Reception of Asylum Seekers (Centraal Orgaan opvang asielzoekers), https://www.coa.nl/en.

83. "2002 was a peak year in the central reception of asylum seekers, both in terms of the number of asylum seekers (more than 70,000) and the numbers of staff and the reception locations. These numbers gradually fell during the following years. About 15,600 asylum seekers are now (March 2012) in reception" ("COA History," https://www.coa.nl/en/about-coa/history; valid as of Feb. 2020).

84. "Statistics," http://www.asylumineurope.org/reports/country/netherlands/statistics.

    Vluchtelingenwerk Nederland gives a somewhat different number, a bit lower: "In 2016 vragen 18.171 mensen asiel aan in Nederland. In 2015 zijn dat er 43.093. Het grootste deel daarvan is afkomstig uit Syrië (2.158 personen) en Albanië (1.664)" ("Bescherming in Nederland," https://www.vluchtelingenwerk.nl/feiten-cijfers/cijfers/bescherming-nederland).

85. "Refugees," http://www.unhcr.org/pages/49c3646c125.html.

86. "Figures at a glance," https://www.unhcr.org/figures-at-a-glance.html.

87. Walker, "A World Indifferent to Refugees."

88. "Internally Displaced People," http://www.unhcr.org/pages/49c3646c146.html.

89 "Internally Displaced People," http://www.unhcr.org/pages/49c3646c146.html.

90. Wong, "Sunni Arabs Driving Out Kurds."

91. Su, "Yazidis Languish on Sinjar Mountaintop."

92. MacKinnon, "Burmese Regime Blocked International Aid."

93. MacKinnon, "Burmese Regime Blocked International Aid."

94. "Emergencies," http://www.unhcr.org/pages/503352e46.html.

95. "Mission Statement," https://www.unhcr.org/4565a5742.pdf.

96. "Global Report 2018," 6, https://www.unhcr.org/5d0a1ce47.pdf.

97. "Global Report 2018," 4, https://www.unhcr.org/5d0a1ce47.pdf.

98. While the persecutions were worse in Germany and Switzerland, Menno-
    nites were at first persecuted in the Netherlands. As a result, some fled.
    "Whereas in other parts of Europe they were either completely wiped out
    or after severe persecution reduced to a small percentage of the population,
    in the Netherlands the Anabaptists, after the first half century of persecu-
    tion, were permitted to develop in comparative peace and live in accord
    with their type of faith, their un-dogmatic Christianity, which was true to
    the Gospel but without binding formulations and was especially strong in
    its practical aspects" (Van der Zijpp and Brüsewitz, "Netherlands).

    "In the early-to-mid 16th century, Mennonites began to move from
    the Low Countries (especially Friesland) and Flanders to the Vistula delta
    region, seeking religious freedom and exemption from military service.
    They gradually replaced their Dutch and Frisian languages with the Plaut-
    dietsch dialect spoken in the area, blending into it elements of their native
    tongues. . . . The Mennonites of Dutch origin were joined by Mennonites
    from other parts of Germany including the German speaking parts of what
    is today Switzerland" ("Russian Mennonite," https://en.wikipedia.org/w/
    index.php?title=Russian_Mennonite&oldid=934101789).

    See also Unruh, "Dutch Backgrounds of Mennonite Migration." As
    noted in Penne and Foth, "West Prussia."

99. See Hartzler and Kauffman, *Mennonite Church History*. Krehbiel, *General
    Conference of Mennonites*.

100. Dower, *Ethics of War and Peace*, 3.

101. "About MCC," http://mcc.org/learn/about. Emphasis original.

102. "Vision and Mission," http://mcc.org/learn/about/mission.

103. "Vision and Mission," http://mcc.org/learn/about/mission.

104. Bender and Neufeld, "Mennonite Central Committee (International)."

105. "Where We Work," http://mcc.org/learn/where.

106. "Annual Report 2019 for the MCC in the United States," 5, https://mcc.org/
     sites/mcc.org/files/media/common/images/2019_annual_report_in_eng-
     lish.pdf.

107. Shenk, "Protestants Reclaim Cultural Heritage in Yugoslavia"; Shenk, "Is
     This the End?"

108. Mennonite Central Committee, *Workbook* (1991), 80.

109. Will, "Refugees Pour into Croatia."

110. "Croatia Average Net Monthly Wages," http://www.tradingeconomics. com/croatia/wages.

111. "Historical Converter," http://fxtop.com/en/currency-converter-past.php? A=1&C1=USD&C2=HRK&DD=01&MM=01&YYYY=1992&B=1&P=&I =1&btnOK=Go%21.

112. Mennonite Central Committee, *Workbook* (1992), 77.

113. "Sidebar: MCC continues to respond to need in former Yugoslavia," MCC News Service, April 30, 1993.

114. Mennonite Central Committee, *Workbook* (1993), 64.

115. Groff, "Word and Deed," 7.

116. "About," http://www.breadoflife.org.rs/en/about.php.

117. "Foreign Partners," http://www.breadoflife.org.rs/en/strani-partneri.php.

118. "Serbs Send Thanks to Meat Canners," *MCC News Service*, January 7, 1994.

119. "MCC to Send Additional Emergency Relief to Central Bosnia," *MCC News Service*, May 6, 1994.

120. Mennonite Central Committee, *Workbook* (1994), "MCC Food assistance in FY," 106.

121. Due to space, I cannot report all that Bread of Life and similar organizations have done. I wanted to focus on the period we lived there in Novi Sad, Serbia, and those organizations I knew of. For further reading about the role of Bread of Life after the NATO bombing see: Toalston, "Refugee ministry in Belgrade"; and Perry, "Needs multiplying, Resources Scarce."

122. Groff, "Word and Deed," 7.

123. Based on a conversation with Mark Jantzen on June 22, 2017.

124. Based on a conversation with Mark Jantzen on June 22, 2017.

125. "The Dutch say a 'devastating no' to EU Constitution." *The Guardian*, June 2, 2005, https://www.theguardian.com/world/2005/jun/02/eu.politics.

126. "How the EU Pushed France to Reforms of Labour Law," Corporate Europe Observatory, June 27 2016, https://corporateeurope.org/en/eu -crisis/2016/06/how-eu-pushed-france-reforms-labour-law.

127. Squires et al., "Macedonia Closes Its Border."

128. Rankin and Smith, "Immigrants in Greece Face Winter Crisis."

129. Hjelmgaard, "Trump Isn't the Only One Who Wants to Build a Wall."

130. Revill and Kasolowsky, "Austria Far-Right Leader Ramps Up Anti-immigration Rhetoric."

131. "Turkey Lashes Out at EU over Refugee Deal Ahead of Merkel Visit," *Deutsche Welle*, January 23 2020, https://www.dw.com/en/turkey-lashes-out-at-eu-over-refugee-deal-ahead-of-merkel-visit/a-52116005.

132. "Dutch Are Sending Yezidi Refugees back to Camps in Iraq: Asylum Lawyers," *DutchNews.NL*, April 28, 2019, https://www.dutchnews.nl/news/2019/04/dutch-are-sending-yezidi-refugees-back-to-camps-in-iraq-asylum-lawyers.

133. "Irregular Migration and Return," http://ec.europa.eu/dgs/home-affairs/what-we-do/policies/irregular-migration-return-policy/index_en.htm.

134. See "Table 2.1 Evolution of asylum seeker inflows in selected EU Member States" and the column "2016 first time asylum applicants" on page 12 of "An Economic Take on the Refugee Crisis: A Macroeconomic Assessment for the EU," https://ec.europa.eu/info/sites/info/files/file_import/ip033_en_2.pdf.

135. "IOM Resettlement 2018," https://publications.iom.int/system/files/pdf/resettlement_2018.pdf, 10.

136. "Global Trends in Forced Displacement 2018," 3, 7, https://www.unhcr.org/statistics/unhcrstats/5d08d7ee7/unhcr-global-trends-2018.html?query=global%20trends%202018%20pdf.

137. Ripper, "Thomas de Maizière"; and in English, Ripper, "Germany Wants Camps to Sort Through Migrants."

138. "Wir müssen unterscheiden zwischen denen, die wirklich schutzbedürftig sind, und denen, die keinen Schutz brauchen, die müssen ein faires Verfahren bekommen, aber dann unser Land verlassen" ["We must distinguish between those who are truly in need of protection, and those who do not need any protection, these must get a fair trial, but then they must leave our country." —PAG translation] (Ripper, "Thomas de Maizière").

139. Ripper, "Thomas de Maizière."

140. "Migration Data in Europe," https://migrationdataportal.org/regional-data-overview/europe.

141. Neil G. Ruiz in "The Geography of Foreign Students in U.S. Higher Education: Origins and Destinations" says up to 45%. However, this is surely not entirely true, as this is just those who remain in the area in which they studied and doesn't give the entire picture.

142. Cheung, "Half of Chinese Students at Elite US Colleges Don't Want to Return." Though, the title says it all, the article reports: "According to a report by the Chinese Academy of Social Sciences, there were more than a million Chinese students studying abroad between 1978 and 2006 and 70% failed to return to China after graduation."

143. "Common European Asylum System," http://ec.europa.eu/dgs/home -affairs/what-we-do/policies/asylum/index_en.htm.

144. "The EU and the Refugee Crisis July 2016," http://publications.europa.eu/ webpub/com/factsheets/refugee-crisis/en.

145. "Legal Migration and Integration," http://ec.europa.eu/dgs/home-affairs/ what-we-do/policies/legal-migration/index_en.htm.

146. "The United States Refugee Admissions Program (USRAP) Consultation and Worldwide Processing Priorities," https://www.uscis.gov/humanitarian/refugees-asylum/refugees/united-states-refugee-admissions-program-usrap-consultation-worldwide-processing-priorities.

147. "The International Red Cross and Red Crescent Movement," https://www. icrc.org/en/who-we-are/movement.

148. "The United States Refugee Admissions Program (USRAP) Consultation and Worldwide Processing Priorities," https://www.uscis.gov/humanitarian/refugees-asylum/refugees/united-states-refugee-admissions-program-usrap-consultation-worldwide-processing-priorities.

149. Brody, "Persecuted Christians Given Priority as Refugees."

150. "The United States Refugee Admissions Program (USRAP) Consultation and Worldwide Processing Priorities," https://www.uscis.gov/humanitarian/refugees-asylum/refugees/united-states-refugee-admissions-program-usrap-consultation-worldwide-processing-priorities.

151. "The United States Refugee Admissions Program (USRAP) Consultation and Worldwide Processing Priorities," https://www.uscis.gov/humanitarian/refugees-asylum/refugees/united-states-refugee-admissions-program-usrap-consultation-worldwide-processing-priorities.

152. "Refugee Admissions," http://www.state.gov/j/prm/ra/admissions.

153. "Application and Case Processing," https://www.state.gov/refugee-admissions
     /application-and-case-processing.

154. "United States Refugee Admissions Program (USRAP)," https://www.uscis.
     gov/sites/default/files/document/charts/USRAP_FlowChart.pdf.

155. "U.S. Refugee Admissions Program," archived content, https://2009-2017.
     state.gov/j/prm/ra/admissions/index.htm. See also "United States Refugee
     Admissions Program (USRAP)," https://www.uscis.gov/sites/default/files/
     document/charts/USRAP_FlowChart.pdf.

156. "U.S. Refugee Admissions Program," archived content, https://2009-2017.
     state.gov/j/prm/ra/admissions/index.htm. See also "United States Refugee
     Admissions Program (USRAP)," https://www.uscis.gov/sites/default/files/
     document/charts/USRAP_FlowChart.pdf.

157. "U.S. Refugee Admissions Program," archived content, https://2009-2017.
     state.gov/j/prm/ra/admissions/index.htm. See also "United States Refugee
     Admissions Program (USRAP)," https://www.uscis.gov/sites/default/files/
     document/charts/USRAP_FlowChart.pdf.

158. Though this material was gathered from earlier archived State Depart-
     ment materials the essential steps are still quite similar. "Application
     and Case Processing," sec. "U.S. Refugee Admissions Program: Overseas
     Application and Case Processing," https://www.state.gov/refugee-ad-
     missions/application-and-case-processing/ as well as https://2009-2017.
     state.gov/j/prm/ra/admissions/index.htm. See also "United States Refu-
     gee Admissions Program (USRAP)," https://www.uscis.gov/sites/default/
     files/document/charts/USRAP_FlowChart.pdf.

159. Nowrasteh, "Terrorism and Immigration," 1.

160. "Asylum Policy," https://www.government.nl/topics/asylum-policy.

161. "Asylum Policy" https://www.government.nl/topics/asylum-policy/contents/
     refugees-in-the-netherlands.

162. "Asylum Policy" https://www.government.nl/topics/asylum-policy/contents/
     refugees-in-the-netherlands.

163. "Reception of Asylum Seekers in the Netherlands," https://www.govern-
     ment.nl/topics/asylum-policy/asylum-procedure/reception-asylumseeker.
     NB: This is an archived page. The diagram has changed due to changes in
     the number of refugees and government policy. However, it is representa-
     tive of the Government of the Netherlands' procedures in April of 2016.

164. "Asylum Procedure," https://www.government.nl/topics/asylum-policy/contents/asylum-procedure.

165. "Who were the Pilgrims?" http://www.leidenamericanpilgrimmuseum.org/Page31X.htm.

166. "Huguenot in Amsterdam," http://www.visitholland.nl/index.php/history/98-huguenot-in-amsterdam.

167. "Waalse kerk (Leiden)," https://nl.wikipedia.org/w/index.php?title=Waalse_kerk_(Leiden)&oldid=51088537.

168. "The Portuguese Synagogue," https://jck.nl/en/longread/portuguese-synagogue.

169. "Jewish Communities: Leiden," https://jck.nl/en/page/leiden.

170. "In the middle of the 1960s the Dutch economy boomed. The Dutch government decided to invite guest workers from Turkey and Morocco" ("History of Immigration in the Netherlands," http://www.ucl.ac.uk/dutchstudies/an/SP_LINKS_UCL_POPUP/SPs_english/multicultureel_gev_ENG/pages/geschiedenis_imm.html).

171. See art. 8 of the European Convention on Human Rights: "Article 8 of the European Convention on Human Rights," https://en.wikipedia.org/w/index.php?title=Article_8_of_the_European_Convention_on_Human_Rights&oldid=933820749.

172. http://www.icimleiden.nl.

173. http://www.alhijra.nl.

174. http://www.mimarsinanleiden.nl/nl/home.

175. "Theo van Gogh (film director)," https://en.wikipedia.org/w/index.php?title=Theo_van_Gogh_(film_director)&oldid=938066099.

176. "Islamitische koepelorganisaties en contactorganen," http://polderislam.nl/achtergronden/moslims-en-islamitische-instituties-in-nederland/islamitische-koepelorganisaties-en-contactorganen. See also http://cmoweb.nl.

177. "Verhaal: Leiden Noord," https://www.erfgoedleiden.nl/collecties/uw-verhalen/uw-verhalen/leiden/verhaal/id/521.

178. "Polder model," https://en.wikipedia.org/w/index.php?title=Polder_model&oldid=873753573.

179. "Tunnel af in zomer," http://www.dichtbij.nl/groot-leiden/regionaal-nieuws/artikel/1936456/tunnel-af-in-zomer.aspx.

180. "WOP Noord: Meerjaren Uitvoeringsprogramma 2011 t /m 2018," http://leiden-noord.nl/wp-content/uploads/2019/03/29466-WOP-Noord-Meer-jaren-internet-2.pdf.

181. http://www.icimleiden.nl.

182. "Marekerk," https://en.wikipedia.org/wiki/Marekerk.

183. "Marekerk," https://www.visitleiden.nl/en/ontdek-leiden/leiden-highlights/monumenten/marekerk-2.

184. I thank my good friend, Mr. Fredrik Knoeff, for his invaluable help and correction of this section. I freely acknowledge my use of his suggestions, even to the point of using his very words. Fredrik studied Law at Leiden University. If I have misquoted or misconstrued anything he has communicated to me, I take the blame for any and all mistakes.

185. "Belgium Convicts Verviers Cell of Forming Terror Organization," https://www.dw.com/en/belgium-convicts-verviers-cell-of-forming-terror-organization/a-19377978-0.

186. "Belgium's Independence (1830–...)," https://www.belgium.be/en/about_belgium/country/history/belgium_from_1830.

187. *Jobs for Immigrants*, 47–49.

188. This story was recounted to me personally by a close Flemish friend sometime in 2016.

189. Martiniello, "Belgium's Immigration Policy."

190. "Asylum and Migration," http://diplomatie.belgium.be/en/policy/policy_areas/striving_for_global_solidarity/asylum_and_migration.

191. "Asylum and Migration," http://diplomatie.belgium.be/en/policy/policy_areas/striving_for_global_solidarity/asylum_and_migration.

192. "Asylum and Migration," http://diplomatie.belgium.be/en/policy/policy_areas/striving_for_global_solidarity/asylum_and_migration.

193. "Asylum," https://diplomatie.belgium.be/en/policy/policy_areas/striving_for_global_solidarity/asylum_and_migration/asylum.

194. "Asylum and Migration," http://diplomatie.belgium.be/en/policy/policy_areas/striving_for_global_solidarity/asylum_and_migration.

195. "Asylum and Migration," http://diplomatie.belgium.be/en/policy/policy_areas/striving_for_global_solidarity/asylum_and_migration.

196. "Asylum and Migration," http://diplomatie.belgium.be/en/policy/policy _areas/striving_for_global_solidarity/asylum_and_migration.

197. "Migration," http://diplomatie.belgium.be/en/policy/policy_areas/striving _for_global_solidarity/asylum_and_migration/migration.

198. "Migration," http://diplomatie.belgium.be/en/policy/policy_areas/striving _for_global_solidarity/asylum_and_migration/migration.

199. "Flanders: Huge leap for Vlaams Belang, N-VA Biggest Party," https://www. thebulletin.be/flanders-huge-leap-vlaams-belang-n-va-biggest-party.

200. Blenkinsop, "Flemish Far Right Gains."

201. From correspondence with a Belgian friend, 2016.

202. Reyntjens, "Agent boeide me."

203. "History," https://www.kuleuven.be/english/about-kuleuven/history.

204. See for instance their Master of European Studies, https://onderwijsaan- bod.kuleuven.be/opleidingen/e/CQ_50310754.htm.

205. "KU LEUVEN—Master and Postgraduate Programmes on Europe," http:// www.kuleuven.be/english/education/europe.

206. "Brussels Eaid: Suspect Killed in Anti-terror Operation," https://www.bbc. com/news/world-europe-35809974.

207. Smith, "How Belgium Survived 20 Months Without a Government."

208. Immanuel Kant, *Groundwork*, trans. Jonathan Bennett, 34. Or see Kant, *Groundwork*, ed. and trans. by Allen W. Wood, 37: "Act only in accordance with that maxim through which you can at the same time will that it be- come a universal law."

209. "Religion," http://www.yezidisinternational.org/abouttheyezidipeople/ religion.

210. "Iblis," http://corpus.quran.com/concept.jsp?id=iblis.

211. Campo, *Encyclopedia of Islam*. See on the Muslim view of Iblis or Saitan (Satan), 43, 603.

212. Morris, "Iraqi Yazidis Stranded on Isolated Mountaintop."

213. "Illinois Offers Its Regrets to Mormons," https://www.latimes.com/ar- chives/la-xpm-2004-apr-08-na-mormons8-story.html.

214. "Figures at a Glance," http://www.unhcr.org/pages/49c3646c11.html. "Internally Displaced People," https://www.unhcr.org/internally-displaced-people.html?query=internally%20displaced%20people.

215. Aguilar and Mahecic, "Restrictions on Humanitarian Work."

216. "Russia Offers Ukrainian Refugees Chance for 'New Life,'" http://m.na-harnet.com/stories/en/144046-russia-offers-ukrainian-refugees-chance-for-new-life. Stewart, "Families Flee the Bloodshed." "В Новосибирске детям беженцев с Украины отказали в бесплатном питании," https://regnum.ru/news/society/2178752.html. Khramov, "Как живут беженцы в Новосибирске."

217. Weir, "Ukrainian Refugees in Russia."

218. Simmons, "Ukrainian Refugees on Edge."

219. Dobbs, "Ukraine Conflict Uproots Hundreds of Thousands."

220. "IDPs stay within their own country and remain under the protection of its government, even if that government is the reason for their displacement. They often move to areas where it is difficult for us to deliver humanitarian assistance and as a result, these people are among the most vulnerable in the world" ("Internally Displaced People," http://www.unhcr.org/internally-displaced-people.html). "Although UNHCR's original mandate does not specifically cover IDPs, we have been using our expertise to protect and assist them for years" (https://www.unhcr.org/ceu/80-enwho-we-helpinternally-displaced-people-html.html).

221. On the issue of illegal immigrants to the US see Carroll R., *Christians at the Border*.

222. Ripper, "Thomas de Maziere." Also available in English, Ripper, "Germany Wants Camps to Sort Through Migrants."

223. Ensor, "Opposition Aleppo's Last Residents Cower."

224. Ruiz, "Geography of Foreign Students." Cheung, "Chinese Students at Elite US Colleges."

225. According to Nenad Tunguz, our Tyndale Theological Seminary, Badhoevedorp, NL, Vice President of Operations and Alumni Liaison.

226. Stott, "The Great Commission."

227. Jansen, "After Lives of the Yugoslav Red Passport."

228. Lowen, et al., "Europe's Forgotten Crisis."

229. Wildes, *William Penn*.

230. "Centre for the Study of Augustine, Augustinianism and Jansenism," https://theo.kuleuven.be/en/research/centres/centr_augustinianism; and "Centre for Liberation Theologies," https://theo.kuleuven.be/en/research/centres/centr_lib.

231. McGrath, *Heidegger*, 10.

232. See McDermott, *World Religions*, ch. 7 "Islam."

233. As told to me by the said Tyndale alumnus.

234. "Militia of Montana," https://en.wikipedia.org/wiki/Militia_of_Montana.

235. See Leaman, *Islamic Philosophy*.

236. "Surah 9 is a command to disavow all treaties with polytheists and to subjugate Jews and Christians (9.29) so that Islam may 'prevail over all religions' (9.33). It is fair to wonder whether any non-Muslims in the world are immune from being attacked, subdued or assimilated under this command. Muslims must fight, according to this final chapter of the Quran, and if they do not, then their faith is called into question and they are counted among the hypocrites (9.44–45). If they do fight, they are promised one of two rewards, either spoils of war or heaven through martyrdom. Allah has made a bargain with the *mujahid* who obeys: Kill or be killed in battle, and paradise awaits (9.111)" (Qureshi, "Quran's Deadly Role").

237 Stille, "New Theories of the Koran."

238. Gaynor, "Something Old Is New Again."

239. Fuoco, "50th Year for Nationality Days."

240. Godbee, "Seabees Rebuild History on NASNI."

241. Beyer, "Edmund Husserl."

242. "Teresa Benedict of the Cross Edith Stein (1891–1942): nun, Discalced Carmelite, martyr," http://www.vatican.va/news_services/liturgy/saints/ns_lit_doc_19981011_edith_stein_en.html.

243. Campbell, *Light for the Night in Europe*, 276–278.

244. Kane, *Life and Work on the Mission Field*.

245. The bust was on the grounds of the St. Sava Monastery in Libertyville, Illinois, http://www.stsavamonastery.org.

246. Dragoljub Mihailović was the general of the Royal Army of the Kingdom of the Serbs, Croats and Slovenes during World War II. When western support was withdrawn and Tito supported, Mihailović was branded a traitor. Normally I would not like to use Wikipedia, but the article on Mihailović is expensive and scholarly. "Draža Mihailović," https://en.wikipedia.org/w/index.php?title=Dra%C5%BEa_Mihailovi%C4%87&oldid=939670413.

247. Low, "Marko Kraljević."

248. Even this English translator notes in his introduction: "The view that Marko was guilty of treachery in the deceit he practised on the Moorish damsel is out of place here. It was impossible to be treacherous to an enemy" (Low, "Marko Kraljević," xxx). Notice that he doesn't say that Marko didn't deceive the girl, only that one may lie to an enemy without being considered to have done something "treacherous." This is why Serbs would say that he "*nadmudrio*," outwitted the girl. Lying to an enemy is an acceptable tactic.

249. Bonner, "Serbs of Bosnia Accept Peace Agreement."

250. I cannot find a source for this idea, except that it was told to me by the student mentioned who was a Serb. Her family was originally from Lika a region in Croatia. As with her Croatian uncle and Serbian aunt many people had intermarried.

251. Rosenberg, "Refugee Status," 422, 424.

252. "Thus, in the 1970s, of almost 250,000 emigrants, 150,000 went to Israel and 64,000 to the United States. In contrast, in the 1980s, of the 117,000 emigrants, 29,000 went to Israel and 79,000 to the United States" (Rosenberg, "Refugee Status," 425).

253. Woehrel, "Kosovo: Historical Background."

254. Kuranji and Kuranji, *"New Life" in Serbia.*

255. "Ukraine," http://www.internal-displacement.org/countries/ukraine.

256. "Ukraine," http://ec.europa.eu/echo/files/aid/countries/factsheets/ukraine_en.pdf.

257. Franka, "Aftermath," 155.

258. Sklabinská, "Slovaks in Serbia."

259. Franka, "Aftermath," 155.

260. Franka, "Aftermath," 155. During this time Franka received help from Christian Aid Ministries, International, of Berlin, OH, among other groups. See https://christianaidministries.org.

261. Franka, "Aftermath," 156.

262. Franka, "Aftermath," 159.

263. My recollection of the exchange.

264. Daniel and Vera Kuranji worked with many organizations: Eurovangelism (UK and Canada), C&MA (Canada), Oak Hall (UK), Samaritans Purse (UK), TEAR FUND (UK). Daniel says: "The agencies came from time to time and distributed aid with us, though we always shared the Gospel of Jesus with the refugees, who came to collect aid. We helped many refugees up until 1999, but after this we continued to receive a lot of aid from Samaritans Purse (Canada and the US). We did not make any distinctions among the refugees, but helped everyone. This lasted until 2003." From personal e-mail from Daniel Kuranji to the author, September 29, 2016.

265. Kuranji and Kuranji, "New Life" in Serbia, ch. 7 "War Refugees."

266. Kuranji and Kuranji, "New Life" in Serbia, ch. 9 "Dario's Story."

267. See Kuranji and Kuranji, "New Life" in Serbia, ch. 8 "Željko's Story," to read the story of her husband, whom she married a bit later, but who had a similar experience.

268. As reported by Bill Steele to me in an e-mail on June 29, 2016. Some references can be found at the following site of the IMB of the Southern Baptists: Bridges, "Yugoslav Baptists Feeding Refugees," and Creswell, "Southern Baptists Feeding Refugees."

269. William Steele, e-mail to the author, June 29, 2016.

270. Ruben, "Enemy of Our Enemy."

271. Zhao, "Immigration to the United States."

272. Su, "Yazidis Languish on Sinjar Mountaintop." If Aljazeera reference is not wise, see Chulov, "40,000 Iraqis Stranded on Mountain."

273. "Following a visit in January 2013, the UN Working Group on Arbitrary Detention stressed that the detention of non-citizens for up to 18 months, in conditions that are sometimes even worse than in regular prisons, 'could be considered as a punishment imposed on a person who has not committed any crime. This appears to be a serious violation of the principle of proportionality which may render the deprivation of liberty arbitrary'" ("Greece Immigration Detention Profile January 2018," 8, https://www.globaldetentionproject.org/wp-content/uploads/2018/01/GDP-Immigration-Detention-Report-Greece-2018.pdf).

274. Oikonomou, "Borderlines of Despair."

275. van Liempt and Zoomers, "Assessment of the EU-Turkey Refugee Deal."

276. Corrao, "EU-Turkey Statement and Action Plan."

277. "Greece Immigration Detention Profile January 2018," 2, https://www.glo-baldetentionproject.org/wp-content/uploads/2019/08/GDP-Immigration-Detention-Report-Greece-2018.pdf.

278. "The European Union Policy Framework: 'Hotspots,'" https://www.asylu-mineurope.org/reports/country/greece/asylum-procedure/access-proce-dure-and-registration/reception-and. Between October 2015 and March 2016, Greece set up five Reception and Identification Centres (RICs) on the Aegean Islands: in Lesvos (Moria) with a capacity of 1,500. Oikonomou, "Borderlines of Despair."

279. "It is not the first time that riots have shaken the Moria camp, where, until last week, some 7,300 people were residing in a facility designed to host a maximum of 3,000" (Georgiopoulou, "Plans for More Camps on Lesvos").

280. Ellis, "Koumoutsakos to Kathimerini."

281. "Greece Immigration Detention Profile January 2018," 7, https://www.glo-baldetentionproject.org/wp-content/uploads/2019/08/GDP-Immigration-Detention-Report-Greece-2018.pdf. "It can take as long as two years before the asylum seekers are either sent home or move on" (Kingsley, "Better to Drown").

282. "'Before, I thought that Greece would be one of the best places to live,' Mr. Ashrafi said. 'Now I feel it would have been better to drown while crossing the sea'" (Kingsley, "Better to Drown").

283. "EuroRelief exists to show compassion to the suffering in Greece and in the surrounding regions" (https://eurorelief.net/ and https://eurorelief.net/serve/).

284. "It is not the first time that riots have shaken the Moria camp, where, until last week, some 7,300 people were residing in a facility designed to host a maximum of 3,000" (Georgiopoulou, "Plans for More Camps on Lesvos").

285. Miller, "Behind the Statistics of Lesvos."

286. BBC.com "Moria Migrants: Fire destroys Greek camp leaving 13,000 without shelter." September 9, 2020. https://www.bbc.com/news/world-europe-54082201.

287. Tsiliopoulos, "Fires and Rioting Break Out."

288. Corrao, "EU-Turkey Statement and Action Plan," 1, and Kingsley, "Epidemic of Misery."

289. Güzel, "July 15 Coup Dented EU Reputation."

290. *Book of Common Prayer*, 826.

291. "Asylum Seekers Clash with Police in Moria Frustrated about Living Conditions and Asylum Delays," https://www.keeptalkinggreece. com/2017/07/18/asylum-seekers-moria-lesvos-protest.

292. The great German philosopher Immanuel Kant believed that this rule could be distilled from within his realm of practical reason. He called it "the categorical imperative." He gave several versions of it, but one is: "Do only that which can be made universal law." Despite his autonomous basis for this rule, he still saw that it was the basis for human ethical behavior and a proof of God's existence, at least in so far as it necessitated God as a "postulate of practical reason"; i.e., God must be the lawgiver and final judge. Kant, *Groundwork*, trans. Jonathan Bennett, 24.

293. Used by permission.

294. For examples of these sorts of stories see Kuranji and Kuranji, *"New Life" in Serbia*.

295. "Remembering THE RIGHTEOUS GENTILES."

296. See Tucker, *From Jerusalem to Irian Jaya*, 314–18 [163–66 in the Russian ed.].

Bibliography

Abutaleb, Yasmeen. "Leaders of Mosques Where California Shooter Prayed Say Rampage Betrayed Islam." *Reuters*, September 4, 2015. http://www.reuters.com/article/us-california-shooting-farook-mosque-ins-idUSKBN0TN05R20151204#pq1mpJdjfDql8zVx.97.

Abutaleb, Yasmeen, and Lisa Baertlein. "U.S. Authorities Look for Militant Links to Shooters in California Mass Slaying." *Reuters*, December 4, 2015. http://www.reuters.com/article/us-california-shooting-idUSKBN0TL2F120151204.

Aguilar, Sonia, and Andrej Mahecic. "UNHCR Concerned about New Restrictions on Humanitarian Work in Somalia." UNCHR.org, November 1, 2011. http://www.unhcr.org/news/latest/2011/11/4ed4fdab6/unhcr-concerned-new-restrictions-humanitarian-work-somalia.html.

Aquinas, Thomas. *Summa Theologiae*. https://www.newadvent.org/summa/1044.htm.

Augustine. *Tractates on the Gospel of John*. Translated by John Gibb. From Nicene and Post-Nicene Fathers, First Series 7, edited by Philip Schaff. Buffalo, NY: Christian Literature Publishing Co., 1888. Revised and edited for New Advent by Kevin Knight. http://www.newadvent.org/fathers/1701026.htm.

Bender, Harold S., and Elmer Neufeld. "Mennonite Central Committee (International)." Global Anabaptist Mennonite Encyclopedia Online. https://gameo.org/index.php?title=Mennonite_Central_Committee_(International)&oldid=145869.

Benjeddi, Hanaâ, et al. "Dutch Doctors Shocked by the Situation in Moria Refugee Camp: Physical and Mental Health under Great Pressure." https://bootvluchteling.nl/en/doctors-shocked.

Bergo, Bettina. "Emmanuel Levinas." Stanford Encyclopedia of Philosophy Archive (Summer 2015 Ed.). https://plato.stanford.edu/archives/sum2015/entries/levinas.

Beyer, Christian. "Edmund Husserl." Stanford Encyclopedia of Philosophy Archive (Summer 2015 Ed.). https://plato.stanford.edu/archives/sum2018/entries/husserl.

Blenkinsop, Philip. "Flemish Far Right Gains in Belgian 'Super Sunday' Elections." *Reuters*, May 26, 2019. https://www.reuters.com/article/us-belgium-election/flemish-far-right-gains-in-belgian-super-sunday-elections-idUSKCN1SW0K0.

Bonner, Raymond. "In Reversal Serbs of Bosnia Accept Peace Agreement." *New York Times*, November 24, 1995. https://www.nytimes.com/1995/11/24/world/in-reversal-serbs-of-bosnia-accept-peace-agreement.html.

The Book of Common Prayer. The Episcopal Church USA. New York: Church Hymnal Corporation, 2007. https://en.wikisource.org/wiki/Page:Book_of_common_prayer_(TEC,_1979).pdf/826.

Bridges, Erich. "Yugoslav Baptists Feeding Refugees." *Baptist Press*, September 30, 1992, 1–2. http://media.sbhla.org.s3.amazonaws.com/7259,30-Sep-1992.pdf.

Brody, David. "Brody File Exclusive: President Trump Says Persecuted Christians Will Be Given Priority as Refugees." *CBN News*, January 27, 2017. https://www1.cbn.com/thebrodyfile/archive/2017/01/27/brody-file-exclusive-president-trump-says-persecuted-christians-will-be-given-priority-as-refugees.

Brown, Stephen Rex. "Bungled Background Checks on Iraqi Terrorists Screw Over Would-Be Refugees Who Helped American Troops." *NY Daily News*, November 20, 2013. http://www.nydailynews.com/news/national/bungled-background-checks-iraqi-terrorists-screw-would-be-refugees-helped-american-troops-report-article-1.1523305.

Campbell, Robert J. *Light for the Night in Europe: Reflections on a Lifetime of Ministry.* N.P., 1999. https://archive.org/details/lightfornightineoocamp?q=light+for+the+night+in+Europe.

Campo, Juan E., ed. *Encyclopedia of Islam.* New York: Facts on File, 2009.

Carroll R., M. Daniel. *Christians at the Border: Immigration, the Church, and the Bible.* Grand Rapids: Baker, 2013.

Cheung, Alan C. K. "Half of Chinese Students at Elite US Colleges Don't Want to Return." *The Conversation*, May 29, 2014. http://theconversation.com/half-of-chinese-students-at-elite-us-colleges-dont-want-to-return-26548.

Chulov, Martin. "40,000 Iraqis Stranded on Mountain as Isis Jihadists Threaten Death." *The Guardian*, August 7, 2014. https://www.theguardian.com/world/2014/aug/07/40000-iraqis-stranded-mountain-isis-death-threat.

Cohen, Roger. "Haider the Rightist Is Firing Up Vienna's Election with Slurs." *New York Times*, March 12, 2001. https://www.nytimes.com/2001/03/12/world/haider-the-rightist-is-firing-up-vienna-s-election-with-slurs.html.

Connor, Philip, and Jens Manuel Krogstad. "U.S. On Track to Reach Obama Administration's Goal of Resettling 110,000 Refugees This Year." PewResearch.org, January 20, 2017. http://www.pewresearch.org/fact-tank/2017/01/20/u-s-on-track-to-reach-obama-administrations-goal-of-resettling-110000-refugees-this-year.

Corrao, Ignazio. "EU-Turkey Statement and Action Plan." http://www.europarl.europa.eu/legislative-train/api/stages/report/current/theme/towards-a-new-policy-on-migration/file/eu-turkey-statement-action-plan.

Creswell, Mike. "Southern Baptists Feeding Refugees, but Local Baptists the Real Heroes." *Baptist Press*, December 4, 1992, 3–5. http://media.sbhla.org.s3.amazonaws.com/7301,04-Dec-1992.PDF.

Daum, Menachem, and Oren Rudavsky, dir. *Hiding and Seeking: Faith and Tolerance after the Holocaust.* First Run Features, 2004.

Davis, Colin. *Levinas: An Introduction.* South Bend, IN: University of Notre Dame Press, 2015.

Desmond, William. *Being and the Between.* Albany, NY: State University of New York Press, 1995.

Dobbs, Leo R. "Ukraine Conflict Uproots Hundreds of Thousands." UNHCR, December 5, 2014. http://www.unhcr.org/news/latest/2014/12/548190aa9/ukraine-conflict-uproots-hundreds-thousands.html.

Dower, Nigel. *The Ethics of War and Peace*. Cambridge, UK: Polity, 2009.

Ellis, Tom. "Koumoutsakos to Kathimerini: Worrying Increase of Migrant Flows in the Aegean." August 11, 2019. http://www.ekathimerini.com/243485/article/ekathimerini/comment/koumoutsakos-to-kathimerini-worrying-increase-of-migrant-flows-in-the-aegean.

Ensor, Josie. "Opposition Aleppo's Last Residents Cower in Bombed-Out Buildings as They Wait for Their Fate." *The Telegraph*, December 8, 2016. https://www.telegraph.co.uk/news/2016/12/08/opposition-aleppos-last-residents-cower-bombed-out-buildings.

Farley, Robert. "9/11 Hijackers and Student Visas." FactCheck.org, May 10, 2013. https://www.factcheck.org/2013/05/911-hijackers-and-student-visas.

Feinberg, John S., and Paul D. Feinberg. *Ethics for a Brave New World*. 2nd ed., updated and expanded. Kindle ed. Wheaton: Crossway, 1993.

Franka, Ondrej. "The Aftermath of Ethnic Cleansing: How the Church Can Make a Difference." In *Globalization and Its Effects on Urban Ministry in the 21st Century: A Festschrift in Honor of the Life and Ministry of Dr. Manuel Ortiz*, edited by Susan S. Baker, 147–62. Pasadena, CA: William Carey Library, 2009.

Fuoco, Linda Wilson. "Ambridge Marks 50th Year for Nationality Days," Pittsburgh Post-Gazette, 23 July 2000. http://www.post-gazette.com/local/west/2015/05/08/Ambridge-marks-50th-year-for-Nationality-Days/stories/201505080047.

Gaynor, Pamela. "Something Old Is New Again for American Bridge." *Pittsburgh Post-Gazette*, July 23, 2000. http://old.post-gazette.com/businessnews/20000723ambridge2.asp.

Georgiopoulou, Tania. "Plans for More Camps on Lesvos after Riots." Ekathimerini.com May, 30, 2018. http://www.ekathimerini.com/229120/article/ekathimerini/news/plans-for-more-camps-on-lesvos-after-riots.

Godbee, Tim D. "Seabees Rebuild History on NASNI." *Seabees Magazine*. http://seabeemagazine.navylive.dodlive.mil/2015/02/11/seabees-rebuild-history-on-nasni.

Grier, Peter. "Supreme Court on Trump's Travel Ban: Why Its Tone Sounds a Bit Different." *Christian Science Monitor*, June 22, 2017. https://www.csmonitor.com/USA/Politics/2017/0627/Supreme-Court-on-Trump-s-travel-ban-Why-its-tone-sounds-a-bit-different.

Groff, Gwen. "Word and Deed: An Interview with Jasmina Tosic, Belgrade, Serbia." *MCC Peace Office Newsletter* 26.2 (1996) 7–8.

Güzel, Enes. "OPINION—The July 15 Coup Has Dented the EU Reputation." AA.com, July 17, 2019. https://www.aa.com.tr/en/analysis/opinion-the-july-15-coup-has-dented-the-eu-reputation/1534105.

Hartzler, J. S., and Daniel Kauffman. *Mennonite Church History*. Scottsdale, PA: Mennonite Book & Tract Society, 1905.

Heller, Sam. "Rightsizing the Transnational Jihadist Threat." International Crisis Group, December 12, 2018. https://www.crisisgroup.org/global/rightsizing-transnational-jihadist-threat

Hjelmgaard, Kim. "Trump Isn't the Only One Who Wants to Build a Wall: These European Nations Already Did." *USA Today*, May 24, 2018. https://eu.usatoday.com/story/news/world/2018/05/24/donald-trump-europe-border-walls-migrants/532572002.

Höbelt, Lothar. *Defiant Populist: Jörg Haider and the Politics of Austria*. West Lafeyette, Indiana: Purdue University Press, 2003. Accessed via Google Books. https://books.google.nl/books?id=qrsgaVfsUKAC&printsec=frontcover&dq-=Defiant+Populist:+Jörg+Haider+and+the+Politics+of+Austria&hl-=nl&sa=X&ved=0ahUKEwib9PbJsLDnAhVObVAKHa9eA94Q6AEILjAA#v-=onepage&q=Defiant%20Populist%3A%20Jörg%20Haider%20and%20the%20Politics%20of%20Austria&f=false.

Huda. "The World's Muslim Population: Statistics and Key Facts." LearnReligions.com, October 24, 2018. https://www.learnreligions.com/worlds-muslim-population-2004480.

Hurd, Hilary, and Yishai Schwartz. "The Supreme Court Travel Ban Ruling: A Summary." *Lawfare*, June 26, 2018, https://www.lawfareblog.com/supreme-court-travel-ban-ruling-summary.

Jansen, Stef. "The After Lives of the Yugoslav Red Passport." *Bturn*, June 14, 2012. http://bturn.com/8704/yugoslav-red-passport-afterlives.

Jobs for Immigrants: Labour Market Integration in Belgium, France, the Netherlands and Portugal. Vol. 2. OECD Publishing, 2008. https://www.google.nl/books/edition/_/kl7fj2r8xsQC?hl=en&gbpv=1.

Jones, Seth, et al. "The Evolution of the Salafi-Jihadist Threat: Current and Future Challenges from the Islamic State, Al-Qaeda, and Other Groups." CSIS, November 20, 2018. https://www.csis.org/analysis/evolution-salafi-jihadist-threat.

Kane, J. Herbert *Life and Work on the Mission Field*. Grand Rapids: Baker, 1980.

Kant, Immanuel. *Groundwork for the Metaphysic of Morals*. Edited and translated by Allen W. Wood. New Haven: Yale University Press, 2002.

———. *Groundwork for the Metaphysic of Morals*. Translated by Jonathan Bennett. Self-published, 2010–2015; last revision 2008. http://www.earlymoderntexts.com/assets/pdfs/kant1785.pdf.

Khramov, Vsevolod. "Как живут беженцы в Новосибирске: устали ждать оформления." September 16, 2014. http://www.nsk.aif.ru/society/1338930.

Kingsley, Patrick. "'Better to Drown': A Greek Refugee Camp's Epidemic of Misery." *New York Times*, October 2, 2018. https://www.nytimes.com/2018/10/02/world/europe/greece-lesbos-moria-refugees.html.

Krehbiel, H. P. *The History of the General Conference of Mennonites of North America*. St. Louis, MO: A. Wiebusch & Son, 1898.

Kruse, Colin G. *John: An Introduction and Commentary*. Tyndale Commentary Series. Olive Tree version. Downers Grove: InterVarsity, 2017.

Kuranji, Vera, and Daniel Kuranji. *"New Life" in Serbia . . . The Novi Sad Christian Fellowship Story*. Rev. ed. Novi Sad, Serbia: N.P., 2011.

Lacan, Jacques. *Four Fundamental Concepts of Psychoanalysis*. New York: W.W. Norton & Co., 1981.

Leaman, Oliver. *Islamic Philosophy: An Introduction*. London: Polity, 2009.

Low, David H., trans. "Marko Kraljević and the Daughter of the Moorish King." In *The Ballads of Marko Kraljević*, 104–6. Cambridge: Cambridge University Press, 1922. https://ia800202.us.archive.org/32/items/balladsofmarkokroolowduoft/balladsofmarkokroolowduoft.pdf.

Lowen, Mark, et al. "Europe's Forgotten Crisis." *BBC News Turkey*, July 23, 2017. https://vimeo.com/226661092.

MacKinnon, Ian. "Burmese Regime Blocked International Aid to Cyclone Victims, Report Says." *The Guardian*, February 27, 2009. http://www.theguardian.com/world/2009/feb/27/regime-blocked-aid-to-burma-cyclone-victims.

Martiniello, Marco. "Belgium's Immigration Policy." *International Migration Review* 37.1 (2003) 225–32. https://doi.org/10.1111%2Fj.1747-7379.2003.tb00135.x.

Mayntz, Gregor, and Eva Quadbeck. "Erst 30.000 Flüchtlinge haben einen Job." *Rheinisch Post*, July 11, 2016. http://www.rp-online.de/politik/deutschland/interview-mit-bamf-praesident-weise-erst-30000-fluechtlinge-haben-einen-job-aid-1.6111184.

McDermott, Gerald R. *World Religions: An Indispensable Introduction.* Nashville: Thomas Nelson, 2011.

McGrath, S. J. *Heidegger: A (Very) Critical Introduction.* Grand Rapids: Eerdmans, 2008.

Meek, James Gordon, et al. "US May Have Let 'Dozens' of Terrorists into Country as Refugees." *ABC News*, November 20, 2013. http://abcnews.go.com/Blotter/al-qaeda-kentucky-us-dozens-terrorists-country-refugees/story?id=20931131

Meijer, Bart H. "Highest Dutch Court Orders Government to Fund New Islamic School." *Reuters*, July 26, 2017. https://www.reuters.com/article/us-netherlands-islam-schools/highest-dutch-court-orders-government-to-fund-new-islamic-school-idUSKBN1AB1Y9?il=0.

Mennonite Central Committee. *Workbook Containing Reports and Statistics for 1991 Presented to the Mennonite Central Committee.* Akron, PA: Mennonite Central Committee, 1991.

———. *Workbook Containing Reports and Statistics for 1992 Presented to the Mennonite Central Committee.* Akron, PA: Mennonite Central Committee, 1992.

———. *Workbook Containing Reports and Statistics for 1993 Presented to the Mennonite Central Committee.* Akron, PA: Mennonite Central Committee, 1993.

———. *Workbook Containing Reports and Statistics for 1994 Presented to the Mennonite Central Committee.* Akron, PA: Mennonite Central Committee, 1994.

Merleau-Ponty, Maurice. *The Primacy of Perception.* Edited by James M. Edie. Evanston, IL: Northwestern University Press, 1964.

Miller, Emma. "Behind the Statistics of Lesvos." November 5, 2018. https://www.gemission.org/pray-articles/behind-the-statistics-of-lesvos?A=SearchResult&SearchID=9789879&ObjectID=16661347&ObjectType=35.

Misra, Tanvi. "What's It Like to Run an After-School Program for Refugee Children?" CityLab.com, December 2, 2015. http://www.citylab.com/navigator/2015/12/whats-it-like-to-run-an-after-school-program-for-refugee-kids/418149.

Morris, Loveday. "Iraqi Yazidis Stranded on Isolated Mountaintop Begin to Die of Thirst." *Washington Post*, August 5, 2014. https://www.washingtonpost.com/world/iraqi-yazidis-stranded-on-isolated-mountaintop-begin-to-die-of-thirst/2014/08/05/57cca985-3396-41bd-8163-7a52e5e72064_story.html?utm_term=.18fd21629bb3.

Mujahid, Abdul Malik. "Islam's Manifesto of Universal Brotherhood of Human Beings." *Sound Vision*, accessed 27 July 2019, https://www.soundvision.com/article/islams-manifesto-of-universal-brotherhood-of-human-beings.

North Way Christian Community, "Part 2 - Obadiah - Pastor Scott Stevens," Video of sermon given on July 9/10, 2016. https://www.youtube.com/watch?v=Zu-SSxLM4MA.

Nowrasteh, Alex. "Terrorism and Immigration: A Risk Analysis." CATO Institute, *Policy Analysis* 798 (2016) 1–26. https://www.cato.org/sites/cato.org/files/pubs/pdf/pa798_2.pdf.

———. "Terrorists by Immigration Status and Nationality: A Risk Analysis, 1975–2017." *Policy Analysis* 866 (2019) 1–67. https://object.cato.org/sites/cato.org/files/pubs/pdf/pa_866_edit.pdf.

Oikonomou, Spyros-Vlad. "Borderlines of Despair: First-Line Reception of Asylum Seekers at the Greek Borders." May 25, 2018. https://www.gcr.gr/media/k2/attachments/SCIZReportZfinalZPDF.pdf.

Paul, Deanna, and Avi Selk. "How the Supreme Court Struck Down a WWII-Era Travesty When It Upheld Trump's Travel Ban." *Washington Post*, June 27, 2018. https://www.washingtonpost.com/news/retropolis/wp/2018/06/27/they-traded-one-injustice-for-another-how-the-supreme-court-struck-down-a-wwii-era-travesty-when-it-upheld-trumps-travel-ban/?utm_term=.14dc8c3f8e3c.

Penne, Horst, and Foth, Peter J. "West Prussia." Global Anabaptist Mennonite Encyclopedia Online. https://gameo.org/index.php?title=West_Prussia&oldid=146338.

Perry, Tobin. "Needs Multiplying, Resources Scarce, Ministry Leader in Serbia Reports." *BaptistPress*, December 15, 2000. http://www.bpnews.net/7041/needs-multiplying-resources-scarce-ministry-leader-in-serbia-reports.

Qureshi, Nabeel. "The Quran's Deadly Role in Inspiring Belgian Slaughter: Column." *USA Today*, March 22, 2016. http://www.usatoday.com/story/opinion/2016/03/22/radicalization-isil-islam-sacred-texts-literal-interpretation-column/81808560/

Rankin, Jennifer, and Helena Smith. "Immigrants in Greece Face Winter Crisis after Public Sector Cuts." *The Guardian*, November 27, 2018. https://www.theguardian.com/world/2018/nov/27/immigrants-greece-winter-crisis-public-sector-cuts-un-envoy.

"Remembering THE RIGHTEOUS GENTILES." Mission of St. Clare: Online Daily Office, Episcopal Book of Common Prayer. Facebook, July 16, 2015. https://www.facebook.com/DailyOffice/posts/958352674207807.

Revill, John, and Raissa Kasolowsky. "Austria Far-Right Leader Ramps Up Anti-immigration Rhetoric before European Elections." *Reuters*, May 5, 2019. https://www.reuters.com/article/us-austria-immigration/austria-far-right-leader-ramps-up-anti-immigration-rhetoric-before-european-elections-idUSKCN1SB0C2.

Reyntjens, Sam. "Agent boeide me en probeerde mijn oog uit te trekken." *Gazet van Antwerpen*, June 10, 2016. http://www.gva.be/cnt/dmf20160611_02334544/agent-boeide-me-en-probeerde-mijn-oog-uit-te-trekken.

Ripper, Kirsten. "Germany Wants Camps in Italy, Greece, Turkey to Sort Through Migrants Seeking Asylum." *EuroNews*, August 28, 2015. https://www.euronews.com/2015/08/28/germany-wants-camps-in-italy-greece-turkey-to-sort-through-migrants-seeking.

———. "Thomas de Maizière fordert EU-Auffanglager für Flüchtlinge in der Türkei." *EuroNews*, August 25, 2015. http://de.euronews.com/2015/08/28/thomas-de-maiziere-im-euronews-interview-junge-menschen-aus-dem-kosovo-koennen.

Rosenberg, Victor. "Refugee Status for Soviet Jewish Immigrants to the United States." *Touro Law Review* 19.2 (2015) 419–50. http://digitalcommons.tourolaw.edu/lawreview/vol19/iss2/22.

Ruben, Elizabeth. "Enemy of Our Enemy." *New York Times*, September 14, 1997. https://www.nytimes.com/1997/09/14/magazine/the-enemy-of-our-enemy.html.

Ruiz, Neil G. "The Geography of Foreign Students in U.S. Higher Education: Origins and Destinations." August 2014. https://www.brookings.edu/wp-content/uploads/2014/08/Foreign_Students_Final.pdf.

Rush, Nayla. "'Private' Refugee Resettlement Agencies Mostly Funded by the Government." Center for Immigration Studies, August 10, 2018. https://cis.org/Rush/Private-Refugee-Resettlement-Agencies-Mostly-Funded-Government.

Sartre, Jean-Paul. *Being and Nothingness: An Essay on Phenomenological Ontology.* Translated by Hazel E. Barnes. London: Routledge, 1958.

Shenk, N. Gerald. "Is This the End? Former MCC Yugoslavia Worker Reflects on Visit There." *MCC News Service*, July 12, 1991.

———. "Protestants Reclaim Cultural Heritage in Yugoslavia," *MCC News Service*, November 20, 1987.

Silverstein, Jason. "Trump's New Travel Ban Cites Foiled Oregon Bomb Plot, Doesn't Mention That Refugees Helped Stop It." *NY Daily News*, March 8, 2017. http://www.nydailynews.com/news/politics/new-trump-travel-ban-cites-attack-refugees-helped-stop-article-1.2992163.

Simmons, Ann M. "Ukrainian Refugees on Edge as They Flood into Russia." *LA Times*, September 14, 2014. http://www.latimes.com/world/europe/la-fg-ukraine-refugees-20140913-story.html.

Sklabinská, Milina. "Slovaks in Serbia." Translated by Ondrej Miháľ. http://www.slovackizavod.org.rs/en/kultura-i-sira-javnost/12949.

Smith, Raymond A. "How Belgium Survived 20 Months Without a Government." *The Washington Monthly*, October 9, 2013. http://washingtonmonthly.com/2013/10/09/how-belgium-survived-20-months-without-a-government.

Spencer, Herbert. *The Principles of Ethics.* New York: Appleton, 1896.

Squires, Nick, et al. "Macedonia Closes Its Border 'Completely' to Migrants." *The Telegraph*, March 9, 2016. https://www.telegraph.co.uk/news/worldnews/europe/macedonia/12188826/Macedonia-closes-its-border-completely-to-migrants.html.

Stella, Rachel. "Pennsylvania Church Welcomes Syrian Refugee Family." *Mennonite World Review,* November 30, 2015. http://mennoworld.org/2015/11/30/news/pennsylvania-church-welcomes-syrian-refugee-family.

Stewart, Will. "Families Flee the Bloodshed Ukrainian Refugees Are Sent to Siberia to Begin New Life." *MailOnline*, August 25, 2014. http://www.dailymail.co.uk/news/article-2733835/Tensions-rise-Ukraine-Russia-accused-secretly-sending-tanks-border-Moscow-plans-second-aid-convoy.html#ixzz4pY2itoY3.

Stille, Alexander. "Scholars Are Quietly Offering New Theories of the Koran." *New York Times*, March 2, 2002. http://www.nytimes.com/2002/03/02/arts/scholars-are-quietly-offering-new-theories-of-the-koran.html?pagewanted=all&_r=0.

Stott, John R. W. *Christian Mission in the Modern World.* Downers Grove: InterVarsity, 1975.

———. "The Great Commission." http://www.sermonindex.net/modules/mydownloads/singlefile.php?lid=11652&commentView=itemComments.

Su, Alice. "Yazidis Languish on Sinjar Mountaintop 'with Almost No Help.'" AlJazeera, October 24, 2014. http://america.aljazeera.com/articles/2014/10/24/forgotten-yazidissinjarmountaintop.html.

Takei, George. "George Takei: They Interned My Family. Don't Let Them Do It to Muslims." *Washington Post*, November 18, 2016. https://www.washingtonpost.com/posteverything/wp/2016/11/18/george-takei-they-interned-my-family-dont-let-them-do-it-to-muslims/?utm_term=.f6e987ebd40e.

Toalston, Art. "Refugee Ministry in Belgrade Serbia Declares, 'WE ARE STILL HERE!'" *BaptistPress*, August 6, 1999. http://www.bpnews.net/354/refugee-ministry-in-belgrade-serbia-declares-8216we-are.

Trump, Donald J. "Executive Order Protecting the Nation from Foreign Terrorist Entry into the United States." Order 13769, January 27, 2017. https://www.whitehouse. gov/the-press-office/2017/01/27/executive-order-protecting-nation-foreign-terrorist-entry-united-states.

———. "Executive Order Protecting the Nation from Foreign Terrorist Entry into the United States." Order 13780, March 6, 2017. https://www.whitehouse.gov/presidential-actions/executive-order-protecting-nation-foreign-terrorist-entry-united-states-2.

———. "Presidential Proclamation Enhancing Vetting Capabilities and Processes for Detecting Attempted Entry into the United States by Terrorists or Other Public-Safety Threats." Proclamation 9645, September 24, 2017. https://www.whitehouse. gov/presidential-actions/presidential-proclamation-enhancing-vetting-capabilities-processes-detecting-attempted-entry-united-states-terrorists-public-safety-threats.

Tsiliopoulos, E. "Fires and Rioting Break Out in Moria Hotspot on Lesvos." *New Greek TV*, July 11, 2017. http://www.newgreektv.com/news-in-english-for-greeks/greece/item/22952-fires-and-rioting-break-out-in-moria-hotspot-on-lesvos.

Tucker, Ruth. *From Jerusalem to Irian Jaya: A Biographical History of Christian Missions.* Grand Rapids: Zondervan, 1983, 2004.

Unruh, Benjamin H. "Dutch Backgrounds of Mennonite Migration of the 16th Century to Prussia." *Mennonite Quarterly Review* 10 (1936) 173–81.

van der Zijpp, Nanne, and C. F. Brüsewitz. "Netherlands." Global Anabaptist Mennonite Encyclopedia Online. https://gameo.org/index.php?title=Netherlands&oldid=161261.

van Liempt, Ilse, and Annelies Zoomers. "Evidence-Based Assessment of the EU-Turkey Refugee Deal." https://www.uu.nl/en/research/human-geography-and-planning/evidence-based-assessment-of-the-eu-turkey-refugee-deal.

Volf, Miroslav. *Exclusion and Embrace: A Theological Exploration of Identity, Otherness, and Reconciliation.* Nashville: Abingdon, 1996.

Walker, Neha. "A World Indifferent to Refugees." CPD Blog, May 13, 2016. https://www.uscpublicdiplomacy.org/blog/world-indifferent-refugees.

Weir, Fred. "Ukrainian Refugees in Russia: Did Moscow Fumble a Valuable Resource?" *Christian Science Monitor*, December 1, 2015. https://www.csmonitor.com/World/Europe/2015/1201/Ukrainian-refugees-in-Russia-Did-Moscow-fumble-a-valuable-resource.

Westcott, Lucy. "American Muslim Organizations Condemn San Bernadino Shooting." Newsweek, December 3, 2015. http://europe.newsweek.com/american-muslim-organizations-condemn-san-bernardino-shooting-400727?rm=eu.

Wildes, Harry Emerson. *William Penn.* New York: Macmillan, 1974.

Will, Emily. "Refugees Pour into Croatia: MCC Plans Further Response." *MCC News Service*, August 21, 1992.

Woehrel, Steven. "Kosovo: Historical Background to the Current Conflict." CRS Report for Congress, June 3, 1999. https://fas.org/sgp/crs/row/RS20213.pdf.

Wong, Edward. "Sunni Arabs Driving Out Kurds in Northern Iraq." *New York Times*, May 30, 2007. http://www.nytimes.com/2007/05/30/world/africa/30iht-30mosul.5922963.html?_r=0.

Zhao, Xiaojian. "Immigration to the United States after 1945." July 2016. https://oxfordre.com/americanhistory/view/10.1093/acrefore/9780199329175.001.0001/acrefore-9780199329175-e-72#acrefore-9780199329175-e-72-note-45.